D0408506

THE MOST
FUN THING

ALSO BY KYLE BEACHY

The Slide

THE MOST FUN THING

Dispatches from a Skateboard Life

KYLE BEACHY

GRAND CENTRAL
PUBLISHING

NEW YORK   BOSTON

All or portions of the following have appeared in the following publications: "On Benches" in *Push Periodical*; "For Whom Is the Fun Thing Fun?" in *The Point*; "You're Not Me" and "A Chronicle of Doing It" in *The Classical*; "The Deep Seams" in *The Chicagoan*; "A Very Large Puzzle," "Making Up Legends in the Era of Zero-Budget Skateboarding," "Pretend We Haven't Grown," "A Most Mundane Perfection," "Clearing a Space for Meaning," "A Day with Chaz Ortiz," "A Serious Man: Mark Suciu's 'Verso'" in *Jenkem*; "Toward a Poetics of Skateboarding" in *The American Reader*; "Nearly" in *Fanzine*; "On Bitul Z'man" in *Urban Pamphleteer*; "Primitive Progressivism" in *Free Skateboard Magazine*; "Seven Small Bafflements" in *Portable Gray*.

For K, my friend who I married

CONTENTS

PART THREE

PART FOUR

I suppose, as a poet, among my fears can be counted the deep-seated uneasiness surrounding the possibility that one day it will be revealed that I consecrated my life to an imbecility.

—Mary Ruefle

You suck the slice, toss the rind, skate away.

—Anne Carson

On Benches

Begin with a bench, wooden and backless and tucked into a shadowy, quiet corner in the Modern wing of the Art Institute of Chicago. Before it, a towering window overlooks an expansive park known for its playful public art and metallic concert venue and a perimeter of historic buildings that seem to lean over the park like tourists, like fawning onlookers who have for some reason forgotten their pride. Anyway, I don't look out that window. When I come to the bench, I sit facing the other direction. There are visits when I skip the art entirely and come straight here to inhale the strange netherness of the space and watch the feet and shins of people climbing and descending through the pale slats of a floating stairway.

I have spent, you might say, much of my life looking at nothing. Before this bench, it was another bench in a park not far from my home. I'll try to describe how it happened: One afternoon, I headed out for a walk, and coming upon this bench was compelled to stop walking. Here it gets tricky. I can say that I felt or heard something shaking toward the edges of this place, that I sensed the bench was looking at me, a sort of two-way interrogation. So, I sat down as the bench would have me, with my back to this strip of the historic Emerald Necklace in Chicago, the city in a garden, my back to the ashes, beeches, and elms, the Kentucky coffee trees, catalpas, and tulip trees—everything green and living. Instead, I faced the undefined patch of asphalt before me, a crosshatch of unnamed and unaddressed pavement that belongs, I suppose, to Richmond Street, where it intersects the byway and boulevard and turns into a proper residential street to my left.

But here: not a street. Something else. With the museum bench this place shares a sense of...what? A kind of benevolent abyss? A peculiar virtue of non-ness? They have no place among a world that commands attention. They are weird and deliberate breaks in the city's system, small moments set aside like gifts. And somewhere at their core, in their chemistry or constitution, these two places owe my experience of them to the activity that has shaped much of my life. In this way, they recall another place I discovered by total accident seventeen years ago, just weeks after I moved to Chicago.

* * *

I have my wife to thank for my casual access to the art museum. I remember passing by the museum one fall afternoon while out for a walk between classes and sending a text that I would like a membership for Christmas. So, it was a gift, or sort of a gift, that three years on has become something of a tradition. Each year, I open a card that reminds me of the time I texted and asked for the membership, and I smile and lean to kiss or embrace her with thanks. One could wonder, if one's the type, where exactly to slot these memberships in terms of generosity—is it a gift, really, if it's specifically requested? Or is it more a matter of following instructions? And, furthermore, what of the gratitude conveyed by my smile and embrace when I know full well what the envelope contains? Are these lies? And if so, small ones? Or is this the biggest and most encompassing lie there is, the old one about two people living in love and harmony until they die?

In any case, it began with wanting a thing and knowing that the best way to get the thing was to ask for it directly. The alternative was, I guess, to convey my desires in an indirect way so that we might both participate in the romance of gifting—to have enough faith in both my performance of desire and my wife's interest in sensing that desire, reading it like a fisherman reads the sea. And then, poof—produce from all of this the perfect gift, given perfectly.

* * *

There's a line that I think of all the time. It comes from a novel that I love and that nobody else seems to even like, really. The line goes, "Why is it so hard to be serious, so easy to be too serious?"

I was thinking these words when I returned to that original nonplace several weeks ago. As the city's six elevated local train lines come into the Loop, two of them descend underground. Down here, riders of the Blue Line who are inclined to wander can, with little effort, discover stretches of platform where no trains stop—where nothing, in fact, starts or stops. Here, everything just continues on either side in a rattling blur of lights. The stretch that I know best lies between the Monroe and Jackson stations. Can I describe to you the promise I've been trained to see in this long stretch of nothing? As with the museum bench against that window, and the bench before the crosshatched square of asphalt, to occupy this stretch of antiplatform is to sense a contradiction, or perhaps something stolen—the feeling of a thing just beyond my reach.

* * *

A big challenge of marriage that nobody likes to talk about is how you will continue, always, to know yourself better than your spouse does. Your spouse, who likely knows you better than anyone else alive—at least, the *you* that you've become, who is similar to but not the same *you* that your oldest friends and family know—will still find new ways *not* to know you. Regularly. Daily, it feels. And these uncloseable fissures in understanding are disappointing. *How can they still not know?* What a terrible insult to the very principle that, by getting married, after much romance and consideration, the two of you agreed to buy into.

Standing in the middle of the platform—or nonplatform—you sense that you're not supposed to be there. It is not hidden, exactly. It's not fenced or blocked on either end, nor can it really be said to have an *end*. You come down the seventy-four steps from street level and…just keep walking—or rolling, if you're on a skateboard—until one station disappears and the next is there in the distance. Something is wrong, and yet I am more myself here than I was just ten, twelve steps ago. Do you know this feeling? The ground is perfectly smooth red concrete, water sealed and seamless but for a couple grates that make for perfect incidental gaps to scrape a tail or pop over. In fact, the whole place looks designed for filming. No—as if it's already being filmed and you've just happened to step or roll inside.

* * *

Marriage is an idea that is a law that is a speech act—the officiant pronounces, and as soon as it's pronounced, the thing becomes reality. You are what they say you are. Married. United. Bound. But somehow, also, still yourselves. You continue to be private, separate people who continue to grow and shift in totally different ways with little concern for symmetry or coordination. I love my wife profoundly and still, always, feel that I never quite have secure footing inside this agreement we've made. Why wouldn't I simply buy the membership myself? Why did I want so badly for it to come from her? What is behind these mundane contortions of generosity and gratitude and torqued communication? I have no idea, except to say the word itself, knowing the word does nothing to answer the question: *marriage*.

* * *

I can recall, as a child, staring up at the clean, languid vaults of the main terminal of St. Louis Lambert International Airport, and without pause or effort inverting the ceiling so it became a landscape of skateboarding dreams. What I'm describing goes beyond wanting to play where laws of decorum and physics insist that I cannot. Skateboarders will understand: there is a way of being that grows out of our time with the activity—something earned, learned, or lived that has yet, to my eyes, to be adequately explored.

I have been told that I take skateboarding too seriously. And, well, maybe. But there is a mystery at hand, and in it I hear the echoes of others. Of meaning and meaninglessness, of the stories we cannot help but tell and the times when stories are shaped all wrong. I speak only for myself, from these places that this life has trained me to find and occupy and take as small, strange comfort. These are the nonstations and nonplaces where the very concepts of beginning and ending are upended and made moot, where I can confront the fragile, contingent, and obvious—can confront, I suppose, myselves.

This is where the meaningless activity has brought me. Via a long sequence of questions about selfhood and performance, about watching and comprehending, I have come to think that the *style* skateboarders speak of might, in fact, be a tool for understanding what mankind used to call the *soul*. Standing on the nonplatform between two rushing trains, it all feels so incredibly clear. What if the soul exists not as some orb or interior essence, but rather as a process of release, on one side, and perception, on the other? Does that make sense to anyone but me? I have so far only really tried to explain this to my wife. *Soul*, I mean, as a system between actor and audience, the membrane across which one individual and another converse. Is this…too serious? Have I gone too far?

In our kitchen in the morning I will sing, and occasionally I will dance through our home like a fool. My wife will do the same, though her voice is lovely and her moves, unlike mine, are beautiful. We speak in codes and we speak directly, our stuttered conversation endless and ongoing. We cover the same familiar ground again and again. We watch each other and try to understand.

PART ONE

CHAPTER ONE

For Whom Is the Fun Thing Fun?

On a sunny afternoon in the middle of a global pandemic, I go out for a long, solitary walk through Blue Line Chicago. To live in a city is to find oneself constantly choosing among modes of transportation. For most of the seventeen years I've lived here, when I've walked it's been from my home to the train, from the train to my destination. But these are days of working from a shared in-home office, my wife's desk and my own facing each other so that our two offset monitors create a partition. In the evenings, we walk the neighborhood together like retirees. Alone, I construct full outings around slow, single tasks. I pass the bars and stores along Milwaukee Avenue, all shuttered and the parking spots empty. Today the sun is high and the sky very clear. I make it to the park and sit for a time with a book, watch some dogs, then decide to get to my errand.

I backtrack, peel off, and wind behind a row of storefronts—you can cross Chicago entirely through alleys if you like. This one is beneath the tracks. I press fingers into my ears to muffle the sound of an inbound train and stand before the open rear door of Uprise. I can see inside through a locked scissor gate, so I holler to my two friends working up front, Paul and G. After some discussion, G lets me in. We move through one of two inventory rooms, past shelves filled with row upon row of turquoise Nike SB boxes (the other room, behind the abutting storefront Uprise expanded into in 2016, is devoted entirely to red-and-cardboard-colored Vans stock). The front room, the show floor, has been turned into a shipping and receiving station full of outgoing orders, tape guns, and packing slips. The lights are off but the sun through the windows is plenty. Still, despite there being no customers, an old skateboard video is playing on the TV mounted up near the ceiling.

The shop is closed and I shouldn't be in here. But they're bored with this new mode of business and I've gone weeks without a fix, so we risk it, respecting one another's distance. I lean against the glass case of wheels and we catch up about Paul's art, G's side hustles, my writing. I do what I've always done in skate shops, moving along the racks of hanging clothes. I pick a thing and hold it, put it back, then lean over the glass case and examine the wheels. G asks about my wife, who likes G, likes pressing him on his life-style and vernacular and casual offhand comments. Then, G takes one of several phone calls that will come during the fifteen minutes I'll spend here, which are of two sorts: The first are inquiries into the upcoming Nike SB quickstrike drop on Friday, for which there is a raffle with *very rigid* entry guidelines. These calls have become standard for shops like Uprise, which serve as temporary holding cells for these footwear commodities that arrive with great hype, sell out immediately, and go straight to resale websites.

The second sort of call would seem tied to the current pandemic. Parents, you see, are growing desperate for new ways to entertain their children at home. So, G slowly and patiently explains what he'd otherwise hold, show, and compare side by side. A skateboard is built from a wooden deck, two trucks that serve as suspension, and four wheels, each of which spins upon two sets of ball bearings. A pack of bolts and nuts holds it all together, and a sheet of griptape is filed and razor cut to fit the board's shape.

"Boards are all about thirty-two inches long, unless you get a mini. How old is your kid?" I am tickled to hear G adopting professional patience. "They go from about seven and a half inches to eight and a half or nine, for a standard popsicle. Or we've got bigger shaped decks, like the old-school decks from the eighties? Yeah, like reissues."

Soon, I will leave carrying my own new deck and a sheet of grip rolled into a tube. At home, I'll tear away the cellophane and peel off the warning sticker: *Skate within your abilities. Injury or death may result from improper use. Wear safety gear. Follow traffic/ pedestrian safety rules.* I'll hear my wife on a work call in the office, unroll the grip and remove its paper to expose the adhesive, then lay and press it carefully onto the deck so that a sliver, a tiny slice, of the board's nose (its front) remains uncovered. This blip of revealed wood grain will mean that I won't have to think about which direction is forward. I cannot stress enough how important this last step is, ensuring a future occasion when I'll not have to think.

But for now, I linger a few minutes longer. The video up on the screen is an old one, not quite a classic but one I've watched four or five times. Would that I could pull a G here, and speak in clear, professional terms to communicate the ways these videos matter. Unlike music and sports, skateboarding has little use for live-action events attended by fans. Its media is the message—between magazines and these videos lives a culture that rejects official rules while resting upon a rich latticework of values, authored and archived by this same media. Precedent is established only to be challenged and warped by each successive new release. These videos are portals to worlds askew, and I can still recall the way my first exposure left me dizzy with possibilities for movement, for appearance and attitude—well, possibilities for being. As objects, the best of them are rich with tonal shifts and allusion and homage, working within and pushing against established forms like the most exciting works of art. And how *fun* they are to watch, how visceral at times, like little grenades of spectacle that explode with affect.

I've been lucky in these thirty-some years of skateboarding to have always had a good shop nearby, and Uprise is the best of them by far. I could list these shops in the order they matter, could sketch their layouts as sure as I could describe old familiar routes to school or family seating arrangements at the dinner table. Two days ago, I chipped my current board by throwing it against a wall during a minor, halfway-serious tantrum. It was stupid and childish, and I regretted it immediately, but not enough to keep skating on a chipped board. I am a forty-one-year-old man with a steady income for whom skateboarding continues to fill a necessary if difficult-to-name void. So, while I protest the discount G gives me at the register and make a show of wanting to support the business during this tough economy, I eventually relent. I accept his discount just as I accept the boxes of boards and other hardware, the shoes and apparel that have on occasion appeared on my door-step—*with absolute glee*. Because in truth, there is no other thing I know will bring me joy like having somehow earned my way into these small but divine returns.

* * *

In August 2011, I wrote an e-mail to the editors of a start-up online sports magazine called *The Classical*. I introduced myself as a professor of literature and creative writing with one novel published and a second in progress. If you want to know skate-boarding, I told them, look at a skater's elbows. Examine their shins.[1] It was a plea rooted in the authenticity to which my own scarred elbows and shins did attest. I wanted, I told them, to be their new skateboarding columnist.

As soon as I sent it, I felt ridiculous. I was no journalist. Anything I'd written about skateboarding had been either private, fictional draft work or a casual blog post. I had a brand-new, full-time,

---

1   In fact, I wrote, "his shins."

maternal family and then to Paris to visit the city of fame and renown. In Bristol and Bath, the two of us moved through homes and pubs with what felt to me like new authority and purpose. We were feted and looked at and loved by family members whose names my wife helped me with, because her memory is very good, while mine is shit, truly, shit.

In those early days of marriage, I'd occasionally catch myself looking at her with newfound gravity, as if the air around her had become more interested in her skin. We had been friends for eight years by then, lovers for four, but I do not exaggerate when I say that time and space were working differently about my wife's physical form, rendering her personhood newly familiar, or unfamiliar; I wasn't quite sure. Something invisible was different.

Anyway, under the Channel we went, to emerge in a city I'd visited twice before and she had never seen. Our rental was in Montmartre, a short walk from Gare du Nord. For four days we toured the city by foot and bus and boat. We wandered and had sex in a stranger's bed surrounded by a stranger's intimate things, and occasionally one of us would repeat the small private joke we were using as a kind of refrain to mark the time of our honeymoon. The joke was that, without warning and apropos of nothing, one of us, in a bad French accent, would go, "You know, Maupassant used to…" and then something about umbrellas or snails or whatever. Whether or not my wife found the joke half as funny as I did, she humored me convincingly. For this was early enough in marriage that we hadn't yet tired of convincing each other of that which we believed the other should by now know.

"It's the only place in Paris," writes Roland Barthes, speaking in the voice of Maupassant, "where I don't have to see it." *It* meaning the Eiffel Tower, where *Maupassant used to* eat lunch so he could escape having to see it. From the second-floor observation deck, we saw, more or less, what Barthes saw: the transformative power of altitude that "makes the city into a kind of nature." So, together we saw the city anew, and down the stairs we laughed, and on the ground laughed even more, wife and husband crossing the Seine on the Passerelle Debilly and strolling beneath a clearing sky along the Avenue de New York, approaching the Palais de Tokyo from the south, through a massive marble courtyard encircling an expansive central fountain with mellow, marble steps and reclining statues. At which point I had a strange experience that separated us totally.

It was a phenomenon I'd felt twice before. The first was in 1996 in San Francisco, moving down Market Street with my father, there to visit colleges. I remember moving quickly, watching the bricks of the sidewalk pass under my shoes and knowing where I was leading us but fearing he'd think it stupid, feeling this fear as a kind of pain and thinking, No, turn back. It's not here anyway, is it? But when I saw the palm trees I knew to look left and suddenly all fear was gone. It didn't matter if it was stupid, because we had arrived, and I was standing before Justin Herman Plaza, the world-famous Embarcadero, birthplace of modern street skating in the early 1990s, bursting open before my eyes. It happened again in 2003 in Philadelphia, this time with a handful of like-minded travelers who shared my aim, Center City smaller than any of us expected and the statue surprising all of us at once—LOVE— every ledge waxed, every planter laid there explicitly for us, to stop us just as they'd tried to stop everyone else. It was itself, and we were there.

In Paris, my wife carried on a few steps before realizing that I'd stopped, struck by the dream logic that had drawn me here without warning. I've written about this before and surely will again, because I know, looking over it, that I haven't gotten it right— might never get it totally right. If the world obvious is the one we see, then skateboarding works upon that world as a prism works upon white light, separating its parts. Though I had never been to the Palais de Tokyo courtyard, I had seen it more times than I could count. I knew the place by a different name, Le Dôme, from years of videos and photographs, history accrued in skate media and my mind and, if I were to pull it out, my phone. The place I knew was disoriented by this one in which we now stood, thrown awry by the anamnesis of an absent world that had formed in some strange geographical region of my mind.

So, is it dramatic, I ask, is it even necessarily metaphorical to say that at this moment I was occupying a place that my wife was not? That despite the bonds of proximity and a shiny, new, and lawfully ordained union, we were—and perhaps always would be—citizens of two different worlds?

* * *

There will be asides. There will be cracks and materials that gather into them. This book is drawn from essays, articles, and other miscellany written between 2010 and the middle of 2020. They are arranged more or less chronologically, because the iterative process by which I've worked, including my failures, is every bit as important as any conclusions I've reached.

Writing, it turns out, has saved me from writing. Still, there is a question that has been ringing through my head: For whom? The first answer is the truest, and it is: me. The performer and drama-turge Matthew Goulish has described being stopped along the road by a distraction: "The distraction grows into a fascination, and the fascination becomes a passion. Then, at last, the passion becomes your life's work." I set out to write a novel true to skateboarding's character, and the path of that struggle led me to wonder over that character, over and over again, which led me to wonder over my own.

For whom? The second answer is skateboarders, whose diet for much of our history has comprised story upon story that leave little room for questions. The principle medium of this project has been those full-length videos through which skateboard companies create brand identities. Recently, and again, the skateboarding industry has aimed to attract new skaters, recruiting them to a life-style sport that has begun marketing itself as a pro-social activity. I suppose I'd like us to be a little more conscious of these and other mythologies. It has been my working premise that skateboarding, like poetry, is structurally meaningless. Contained in or implied by this structural meaninglessness is a quality of non-narrativity that renders the signifier *skateboarding*—like the contiguous land parcel that became the United States of America—vulnerable. That without meaning is that which can be abused, manipulated, and leveraged toward any number of ends.

But not only skateboarders, I'd hope. There is too much of this time and this world contained within skateboarding for its interests to be unique to its practitioners. Skateboarding is among the greatest human developments, or discoveries, of the last century. The mere fact of its emergence, which is to say nothing of the circuitous path by which it's developed into its current global form, is as significant as any progress in music, language, or the visual arts. It is every bit as relevant to our moment as yoga, tarot, protest, fascism, or cooking. As relevant as any attempt, in fact, to sort through what it means to be a person who would like to live among and with other people. It is a practice of both faith and finite, hard reality, and its rightful place is among the humanities. In saying this, I mean that to know skateboarding is to know more completely the rigors, rewards, and negotiations of being human.

* * *

I was a better skateboarder when I was younger and jumped off stairs and onto handrails. But I was always a coward—always. I was a five-stair man on good days, maximum nine, ever, with marginal tech capabilities, but only when I was going slowly. Now I do not jump down anything I could not jump up. Now my body cries out in the night like a long-ignored rotten tooth. I bleed onto sheets from lower back abrasions at the precise sites of other, prior abrasions. My swellbows and sprained wrists require adjustments when I type or grade student work. In the mornings, I stretch both hands cautiously downward, with my fingers yearning for the floor like some anciently promised land. I reach upward for some imaginary peace hovering someplace behind and roughly above my head. It is a project of pops and creaks and fierce gusts of pained breath. I am not graceful.

How many of us, I wonder, are lucky enough or doomed enough to have a force such as this in our lives? A practice, I mean, or pursuit or activity, an entity, or really any kind of thing whatsoever that we fear and respect enough that we will not lie to it, or try to trick it, or approach it with anything short of total candor? A thing that we know can see through us, that will laugh at our folly without reserve, revealing sharp and yellow teeth, pointing a long finger with maniacal joy to mock our fealty? And will just as readily offer embrace for our persistence and reward us with a joy that has no cognate, that is its own unique end?

For me, the combination has produced an unlikely impulse. Forgive me for indulging this impulse at such length. This decade, my writing and my marriage and my life have not gone the ways they could have. But I have come to believe that what's hiding before us in plain sight—another form of the unseen is the too-seen—is rich enough, mysterious enough, to occupy ten years, or thirty-four years and counting, of my life.

And so, I begin again in the same place, which is a place of wonder. The passing curiosity that we pursue with language. It flees, of course, and we chase the fucker and wrestle it to the ground, then stand up an hour later, dirtied and bloody. What makes a thing special? What makes it dangerous? What is the nature of our play? There needn't be an answer. There needn't even be an argument. Sometimes to write is only to see how words respond to new company, and that is all.

For still, we are out here playing. We travel in packs, large and small, forever plural, some of us steering cars between spots while others walk or bike with boards balanced dumbly on handlebars.

In cities, we push through vacant nighttime streets. We push through crowded nighttime streets. We linger in front of buildings with clear views of security guards wearing their bland uniforms with a pride that's halfway convincing. Time, for now, derives totally from them. So we go quickly at the stair set or the fountain ledge until we see the guard shift behind their desk and start toward us with a mien of disapproval and one long finger wagging on behalf of the faceless bank or venture capital firm or whichever global finance group owns the tower, the courtyard, and the ways it's to be used.

If we are youthful, tomorrow we'll go out again. If we are aging, whenever our legs and our backs are up for it. Assuming we do not have to work. And the wife's blessing, of course, the husband's. The partner's blessing, or not. We're crossing suburban strip malls and scaling fences, and in the country, we amass inside the little rectangles that they toss our way, saying, Here you go, kids—now play nice. Hoofing across a cobblestone back alley through the rain and snow to find a garage door to heft open and reveal a cramped half-pipe inside.

And do you know the carpet outlet store, where the wheelchair ramp meets that rail with the hedge tidily trimmed? Every night, the manager will flip the door's sign to reveal the store's hours. Closed by six Monday through Friday. Saturdays ten until five. Closed every single Sunday, especially in the South.

CHAPTER TWO

You're Not Me: Nyjah Huston and Inflationary Spectacle

2011

Barely seventeen, Nyjah Huston was conventionally awkward. His shoulders drooped, his frame was narrow and noodly, and his shoes looked silly big. His forehead was brailled by faint acne and his facial features didn't seem yet to agree, quite. It was the late months of 2011. In video interviews he was uncomfortable, issuing smiles only halfway organic and blinks that lingered a little too long. He was a gentle boil of adolescent anxiety—you could just tell he was thinking about going back outside.

But this was also the most comfortable Nyjah Huston had seemed since his 2004 arrival as that tiny, impossibly skilled skateboard grommet with dreads dangling to midchest. Back then, he was as shy as any little boy, speaking blankly in 2006 of "blessings" he felt skating with pros he had "looked up to for so long" (at that point he was eleven). The child Nyjah was unsmiling and off enough to notice; concerned observers might have wondered what could cause such vacancy at such a young age. But, too, he was the millennium's first genuine skateboard wunderkind, so it was difficult to judge him against our normal human expectations. Mainly, we all wished he would go away.

And for several years, he seemed to. After three barely watchable video parts of the small, big-eyed child shaking his dreads and leaping down stairs, it was as if the people who'd manufactured him had decided to pull him from the shelves and tinker. Then, quite suddenly, Nyjah returned—both more and less awkward than before—to slaughter every contest he entered. Skate contest results, however, were then and remain today a bit like weather forecasts for a distant or imaginary land—it's cool that someone keeps track, but nobody truly cares. Nyjah winning did not violate anyone's sense of propriety; this was his purpose. Then, Nyjah's contest spree segued almost too neatly into his first professional video part, the theater in which skate opinion is crystalized and legends are born. Released with much hype on November 11, 2011, *Rise & Shine* is an extremely high-definition three-dollar iTunes download. It even has a plot summary:

Element presents "Rise & Shine"—The Nyjah Huston video, an iTunes exclusive starring Nyjah Huston. In 2011 Nyjah 3-peat'd at Street League, won X-Games gold, and became the Berrics Battle Commander. Now he's out now to prove his talents where they matter most; in the streets.

Except not the streets, exactly. Featuring not a single shot in an urban center, the film—one of just three notable examples from a short-lived industry experiment with for-purchase à la carte video parts (within months such videos would, like the vast majority of skateboard content since 2010, be distributed for free)—exudes a soundstage polish. Its credits list three directors and three producers, and Nyjah himself receives billing as an actor. In short, it was another difficult moment for anyone watching the way skateboard culture and industry were warping in young Nyjah's significant wake—difficult enough, in fact, to make some older skateboarders echo Jason Jessee's famous anti-joke: "I love skateboarding so much I want it to die."[1]

* * *

Two heads of notable dreadlocks disappeared from skateboarding in 2011. The other set belonged to a Brazilian named Adelmo Jr., whose braids reached his thighs before he was sent (on a dubious conviction) to state prison in Rio de Janeiro. Discussing the circumstances, he spoke with calm sincerity: "My locks are gone, but the roots are deep in my heart."

But how to think of dreads grown by a child too young to understand why? Whatever they might have meant to the boy, they were central to the character we watched on screen—skateboarding's effect is rooted in the aesthetic. We might consider that the very best that professional skateboarder and company owner Andrew Reynolds could say to capture the effortless magic of his employee Bryan Herman was that Herm "looks the coolest and looks the coolest doing it." Nyjah's haircut marked a shift, or an attempted shift, from pure aesthetic effect to narrative meaning. Over e-mail, *Big Brother* alumni and sudden ESPN correspondent Chris Nieratko explained to me that Nyjah had "finally grown into the tricks he's had all along and lost that little kid style that any child is plagued with." (That skateboarding coverage in 2011 had graduated from *Big Brother*—a hornier and much, much more stoned cousin of *Thrasher* from the 1990s—to ESPN presents a narrative too thorny to address here.) But Nyjah's story was more interesting than the standard coming-of-age, as Nieratko wrote to introduce his own interview with Nyjah:

He always seemed so sad. You know the look; it's the one we've seen on his face since we were first introduced to him.

---

1   In late 2011, one could still quote Jason Jessee without asterisk or personal conflict.

When he came to do a demo, I saw him constantly looking for approval from his father, almost completely afraid to speak. He was never permitted to stand by his teammates...I know what fear looks like and I know how hard it is to live under tyrannical rule...Not all abuse is physical.

So, it was a phenomenon common to sport—think Bollettieri, Capriati—but new to skateboarding. Coaching is one of the athletic norms that skateboarders explicitly aim to avoid by choosing the activity over organized sport. Though in Huston's case, *coach* wasn't the right term. Certain of us might have heard rumors: a stern, protective father who allowed Nyjah neither candy nor ice cream and was by all accounts the reason he got the boot from Element three years prior—which was softened by an open invitation back to the team if Nyjah somehow shed his dad. Then came Mr. Huston's failed start-up, I & I Skateboards, and a collection of video clips he wouldn't allow his son to use out of spite.

Now, here was Nyjah, back on Element with an eight-minute soliloquy beneath which Lil Wayne was hollering, "Fuck 'em, fuck 'em, fuck 'em, even if they celibate." All of that narrative background of a kid held financially and psychologically hostage cast Nyjah's unbelievable string of contest victories in a new, affirming light—he'd won over half a million dollars in 2011 alone—and positioned *Rise & Shine*'s stunt-based spectacle alongside a story with just enough traction to grab hold. Here, it seemed, was a video part worthy of its production credits and three-dollar cost of admission. Here was a triumph of agency.

* * *

If you are not a skateboarder, it is not unlikely that you've made at least one joke about skateboarding, and a fairly safe bet that the joke you've made has something to do with the names of skateboard tricks. It is true, admittedly, that a skater's vernacular combines known terms like *flip* with appropriated terms like *impossible* and *rock 'n' roll* to sometimes absurd ends—as do all sports. In *End Zone*, his football novel, Don DeLillo writes that "much of the appeal of sport derives from its dependence on elegant jibberish." While I may hear a kind of poetry in a play-by-play of Nyjah's tricks— nollie-backside-noseblunt, nollie-backside-heel-backside-lipslide— there's also a deadening effect of such technical talk, a reduction of the visceral to the flat statistic of a scorecard.[2]

Over the week of its release, in order to file my first assigned story as a skateboard journalist, I watched *Rise & Shine* upward of forty times. I did not then and do not now recommend doing such a thing, especially if you are a skateboarder. At the time, it was confounding just how brutal and alienating the video managed to be. Watching it now, knowing the way Nyjah's story has gone in the intervening decade, it is impossible to deny *Rise & Shine*'s standing as a document with profound ramifications in whatever history skateboarding was and is writing for itself.[3]

It opens with an argument. Despite the mountain of extant evidence against Nyjah Huston's standing as a fallible human being, consider this terrifying sack job on a rail somewhere foreign,

---

2   I am still not sure when or how best to translate skateboarding for the reader who hasn't spent their life immersed in this funny and ridiculous language. Huston's tricks, for one thing, just aren't super given to such an exercise—naming what he does requires a thread of terms, each of which is a dense bundle of signification to unpack. And I understand that for some of you, reading Part One of this book will feel a little trying, like you're traveling somewhere you've never been and have just stepped out of the airport and into the city. I do hope that you will press on. What is foreign and confusing now will be less so, soon.

3   I'm also going to suggest that you take a few minutes to watch *Rise & Shine*. I know! You're reading a book. But the video is short and, like all the videos discussed in this book, easy to find and free of charge. And I really do promise that they are fun to watch, this one especially. It reveals a human body doing bogglingly dangerous and impressive things that will surprise and delight and terrify you.

in Central or South America. The still-dreaded Nyjah absorbs full impact to his crotch and stays down, pained. Few are the skaters who've needed more than Nyjah to be humanized, and to be fair, the gambit works. Soon enough, the crowd is cheering the child king of arena skateboarding back to his feet, and yes, we want it, too, despite ourselves. We've come to see him perform, and in order to perform, first he's got to recover.

He does, of course. What follows is a full five minutes and fifty seconds of uninterrupted demolition of handrails, stairs, and very large gaps. In that time, Nyjah lands sixty-seven tricks, twenty-three of which earn a second viewing from another camera, often slow-motion for further appreciation. For nearly six minutes, we're pummeled at the rate of one trick every 3.9 seconds. For comparison, the similarly hammer-heavy Andrew Reynolds's part in *Stay Gold* feels healthy at four minutes and twenty seconds, with a trick rate of one every 4.3 seconds.

That I'd even compare Nyjah to a legend of skate culture like Reynolds speaks something to Nyjah's standing already at age seventeen. Anyway, do numbers matter to skateboarders? Jesus, no. In fact, just calculating them probably lost me some friends. But they do give a sense of the brutal pacing of Nyjah's part, which at moments overwhelms itself, achieving incomprehensibility. Few are the rails or gaps he skates that are smaller than ten stairs, and they come like boxcars on one of those endless Midwestern freight trains. The early videos were easy to laugh at, not least for the way he was falling down stairs even as he landed tricks—as in, there was no lift, just short legs and tiny feet going through the motions of what might look good from another skater. In *Rise & Shine*, his flip tricks are boosty, caught proper, stomped hard. While he's always been comfortable on rails, here Nyjah goes after them like a man owed money, locking into sitcom-length grinds or spinning 270 blindly with uncanny precision.

But as far as that most important "in the streets" copy is concerned? No. These are not populated urban centers, there is no weaving through traffic or fleeing from security. Nyjah's filming missions are selective and nocturnal. They are movie sets lit by floods run on generators that growl and smell of petroleum. He skates with trucks rigidly tight, keeping his lines straight and landings perfect. Anything less requires a quick tick-tack adjustment—a clunky, artless flourish and probable cause for editing that cuts landings as soon as his legs absorb the impact. Every time: feet wide, strategic, automatic. Soulless.

I do not believe this word is unfair or dismissive. Here is a number definitely worth weighing when considering this six-minute video: exactly twice in it do we see Nyjah push. To Nyjah, to push is a bother, an unfortunate labor he must exert between the obstacles where he performs his feats—this same push is, of course, the activity one does more than anything else while riding a skateboard. The same push behind one of skateboarding's most iconic images, our equivalent of the Michael Jordan silhouette, J. Grant Brittain's shot of Tod Swank in profile against a wall, pushing from left to right. The push being, in fact, something like a fingerprint—idiosyncratic and largely beyond our control, the mirror from which no skater can hide.

* * *

The dismay I feel while watching *Rise & Shine*, the essence of its threat to the activity of skateboarding, is not the way it greases narrative wheels to spin beneath Nyjah Huston's redemption story. Rather, it's the way the film goes about business in precisely the way its leading actor wins contest after contest—with ruthless cool and quiet ego, slaying with such insouciance that the activity itself is minimized. The rhetoric of *Rise & Shine*'s three falls, the last of which is visceral, an awful plummeting and bounce, is subsumed by the larger case made that there is nothing this young man cannot do. How interesting is the hero who *always* gets up? How meaningful the change that leads only to more and more success?

No, if Nyjah is to be meaningful it won't be by way of story. In fact, for any of this to mean anything, you yourself need to do something. Next time you climb a set of stairs, count them. When you find yourself at the top of a set of sixteen, or twelve, or even eight, stand at the top and turn, looking down to where you began the climb, the sidewalk or blacktop below, and imagine jumping. Consider two separate distances, height and length. Question whether you could make it. Imagine the impact. And the feeling this imagined leap brings: of doubt, fear, a totally sane preference to not find out? Try to muffle that voice whose task is to keep you unbroken. Duct tape its mouth and see its cheeks go red, arms waving to say no, no, no. Consider what it would mean to live without that voice, free from the evolutionary gift of hardwired fear. Imagine what kind of person could quiet this voice.

CHAPTER THREE

On Firsts

My first board was the wrong board, and I knew as much immediately, could feel my mistake eating away even as I crossed the parking lot between Island Water Sports and our silver Pontiac wagon. I remember the ride home, Mom driving and the board somewhere behind me. It was confusing. I knew that what I was supposed to feel if I was indeed a good person—gratitude—had very little space among whatever had come over me. We tend to speak wrongly of shame as a development of adolescence tethered to our changing bodies and evolving selves. In a photo from that summer of 1986 I am only eight, standing on this wrong board, a Vision Shredder, tail dragging so you can see its bland graphic and chunky black Vision Shredder wheels. It's night and the flash is close and uncompromising. I am illegally skinny with a pronounced scab on one knee, holding two burning sparklers and making a face like: God, I fucked up so bad; I should have gotten the Zorlac.

For months, I had been working my parents with my case for a real board. The plastic yellow one-piecer they'd picked up in the seventies, with its jelly-yellow wheels and steep, narrow tail, that lived in the garage and bent beneath even a boy's negligible weight? And was covered in chew marks from the dog? Not a real skateboard. Or that Valterra *Back to the Future* tie-in board from Target or Venture or KB Toys, which was wood, at least, but also pretty clearly a piece of garbage? Not real. As much as I'd like to find something of theoretical interest here, perhaps a nascent authenticity fetish, it was probably just envy. Other Kyle, my first best friend who lived up the street, had gotten—as he was always getting, constantly—something new and exciting and top-of-the-line.

But would I use it? countered my parents. Really, enough to justify a real board's real cost? When considering basketball and baseball and tennis? I was not a frivolous child, but I was a child, and they certainly would have understood how a family like Other Kyle's could lead to covetous behavior. His parents owned bottling and packaging factories and mine were educators, a professor of biology and a special-education speech pathologist. It was the mid-eighties, and skateboarding was a fad—a familiar one they'd lived through during the sixties, and maybe noticed in the seventies, but still a fad.

There's an old joke about "reading" skate magazines: this verb and its implied subject, skaters being not exactly known for our voracity. To read, for most of us, was to flip through, to absorb and marvel at the photos, feel the longing rising within. Skateboard writing has traditionally come in three forms: the photo caption, the scene or tour article, and the interview. This question about one's first board and its variants—first video, first spot, first issue of *Thrasher*—are longstanding interview staples. They're lazy questions, but you can see how they could potentially lead to a related and more interesting one: Why did you start? Or, even more interesting, why do you continue?

But they never did. We might trace this history of unasked questions back to the extremely effective mythmaking of C. R. Stecyk III, who in the late 1970s penned a series of articles about and interviews with the so-called Z-Boys of so-called Dogtown, Santa Monica, California. In the decades since, Stecyk has been quoted much more than read, the best pull quotes turning, over time, into a kind of bedrock skateboarding ethos. Scripture, after all, needn't be read by every worshipper—only those who deliver the sermons. The story is anti-authority and pro-progression, pushing limits as aggressively as one possibly can and suffering, *gladly*, whatever injuries are required.[1] Together with Glen E. Friedman's photographs, Stecyk's *Skateboarder* articles are the source text for the more recent cultural onslaught begun by Stacy Peralta's documentary, *Dogtown and Z-Boys* (2001). Since then, skate nostalgia has more or less simmered on a side burner, ready whenever Hollywood, Vans footwear, or pretty much any clothing, music, or visual designer needs to dip back in.

As far as Other Kyle and I were concerned, we were simply oblivious. Something shifted a little that day my mother and I stepped into Island Water Sports—I knew my Vision Shredder was wrong because it had come preassembled, and I *sensed* this was embarrassing. I'd keep feeling this way until, a couple years later, I got my hands on a Vision Gator with clear grip and pink G&S trucks with matching pink-and-blue Slimeball wheels. But for now, Kyle and I remained an isolated microculture. We knew nothing of attitude or values, nothing of culture. We were playing. We had pretended before—the yards of our neighborhood and the next one over were separated by patches of vines and maple trees, shallow ravines, walls of shrubs, and creeks; we were runners and

---

1   Under the loose framing of social anthropology, Stecyk's values did skew political—his first article opens in Barry Goldwater's Arizona estate—but only up to a specific and rather curious point, beyond which to politicize Dogtown and its iconography becomes a running joke about people who *just do not get it*. This point, at the risk of getting ahead of ourselves, is the image of a swastika. So, while one can applaud the way Stecyk charged skateboarding with significance beyond every other toy and hobby that has come and gone, even protected skateboarding from other attempts to narrativize it, one really must ask: At what cost?

leapers, man, Terabithians—but the game (Was it a game?) of skateboarding required brand-new mechanics even just to stand there upright.

One day, Kyle showed me that if you ride alongside the edge of an asphalt driveway, you can dip one of the wheels over the edge. This is how Kyle and I learned to grind: dipping a wheel into the grass and creating a sound we had never heard before. This was thirteen years after Dogtowners Tony "Mad Dog" Alva and Bob "the Bullet" Biniak began hitting the tiles of swimming pools and eking a wheel over the tile coping, the "off the lip" maneuver that would evolve into the modern grind. But we had no skate parks anywhere nearby—there wouldn't be a concrete skate park built within a hundred miles of us until 1999. We had no magazines, no videos, no older kids to stare at. It would be years before I landed my first kickflip. We didn't know anything.

Kyle eventually stopped riding a skateboard, as almost everyone does. He was the first of many I would watch quit. Anyway, by then it was 1989 and I'd settled into a crew of committed skaters with low-hanging bangs and access to driveway ramps. They wore T-shirts that announced their interests and shoes unmistakable in their clunk and condition.

And—Do you sense us winding back to convention?—they showed me my first official skate video, 1987's *The Search for Animal Chin*. First, in fact, of any textual object that I'd come to personally cherish, poring over the San Francisco section especially—the schoolyards and downhill driveway cuts and the wooden kicker ramp that they rolled into Golden Gate Park—roughly seven total minutes of the hour-long video. Play, rewind, play, the spools and reels suffering our studies, the VCR whining and clicking. Grab the board early, pull legs up behind you, straighten to land. Rewind and play it back.

The rest of the film follows the Bones Brigade, a group of "true believers" who search for Chin, who, even at age eleven, I must have recognized as a ham-fisted and exoticized personification of skateboarding's soul. Directed and produced by Stacy Peralta (production designer: C. R. Stecyk III), *Chin* was the first skate video to really narrativize the activity, framing it as an endless quest. There is a scrolling origin text about a fictional Won Ton "Animal" Chin, the world's first skater, who thrived ("He had fun") until "dark forces" sent him into hiding. My friends and I would quote its sketches like scholars sipping brandy by the fireside, but I never quite felt like my fervor was complete. It was silly by design, but still, the story was saying something about devotion, commitment, and purity. Even as I studied the film and was indoctrinated into its values, I did not give myself away to the quest. I continued to compete at tennis and basketball and baseball; I was not, in other words, a committed punk or counterculturalist. I did not *need* skateboarding, I'm saying. If it was an outlet in those days, I can't say for what. Nobody back then wanted to ask why.

I'm speaking broadly of a distant time, of course. It's difficult to overstate how poor a tool the calendar is for skateboard history, to convey how different the end of 1988 was from the beginning of 1990, how radical the shifts from any given moment of skate history to where we find ourselves now. Today's magazines are different, today's skaters different, *skater* now a word that has largely outgrown its connotative usefulness. Still, much of the activity we group under the banner *skateboarding* is reflection of the not-always-conscious kind. Skateboarding's past lives inside every new passing second of its present. And yet, the present is always so much brighter and louder, so much better defined.

Can I convey how incomprehensible and magical a kickflip seemed to us, in Missouri in the late 1980s? Probably not. I can, though, speak to a certain historic tribalism at play. We know of tattoos, now, and how that which once signified has lost meaning by way of becoming ubiquitous. The rubberized skate footwear of our premillenial years worked in the same way. The Airwalk 540 was a flagrant declaration, and later, though more subtly, the Etnies MC Rap, DC Syntax, the Axions, and early Lakais. Meeting someone, coming across a stranger in the mall, my eyes would fall to their shoes. Which I suppose is the best answer. Why did I continue? To be part of this thing. To be inside.

CHAPTER FOUR

A Chronicle of Doing It

2012

They've been calling us names for years. First, it was "extreme," which they sometimes spelled "X-treme," and we all slept soundly knowing there were people out there watching us and capable of uttering these words while keeping a straight face. Then, for a time, it was "action sports," which eventually became "lifestyle sports," which I guess still applies. It makes sense—they give themselves language to speak among themselves, knowing well that within each extreme or action or lifestyle sport there runs a private, native language among the doers that is comprised of terms and cadences and figures of speech that they, the sellers, cannot speak. Whenever they've tried, it has sounded stiff, stunted, hilarious. Or sad. In any case, it has exposed them for who they are, which is *not us*.

Who *we* are is a matter of some dispute, but one thing is sure: we are not them. However resistant we may be, or however resistant we want to appear, we can tell a parent or cop or corporation when we see one. Of these, corporations are the most capable of adapting strategies to suit the challenge. They've spent years handling us with extreme caution, poking at our language as if wearing rubber gloves. It's been amusing, but they're too smart not to learn; see, for example, the following post pulled from the Nike SB Facebook page in 2011:

> Nike SB flow killer Travis Erickson is steady holding it down on the real city streets, collecting more and more raw gems. Here's a concrete collection of random clips, with lots more on the way!

It is promotional copy, of course, but do you hear how well the glove strategy worked? What had for decades prior to 2011 been an obvious demarcation—In vs. Out, Us vs. Them, skateboard native vs. invading corporate interest—became blurred by R & D investments and a hypersensitive advertising team. Big data surely didn't hurt. Perhaps a highly evolved algorithm programmed to emulate skateboarding jargon? Or perhaps neither of these. Perhaps the strategy was less about the gloves as the hands that are paid to slip inside of them. Wouldn't it be simpler, if much more worrisome, if this were simply the natural language of an actual skateboarder serving as liaison between a $15 billion company and a youthful market share as fickle as it was coveted?

Whether such an ethical distinction contains a difference will depend almost entirely on your subscription to what's spoken of, both within and without skateboarding, as the "core" mentality. This is a kind of secular faith premised on there being something special, unique, and genuine about the activity and, by extension, the culture and industry that radiate out from it. Core is a nostalgic appeal to a pre-corporate epoch that shows preference, always, to independent and skater-owned businesses. This holistic preference filters downward to individual choices of gear, and fashion, and other outlets for consumptive expression. In his rambling, insightful 2011 interview with Quartersnacks, (then) non-Nike skater Jake Johnson about nailed it:

> The bottom line in skateboarding is that there was a message, whether we admitted it in the first few generations of skaters

or not, that came from a bunch of rebellious young kids being creative and ambitious, trying to show an unfiltered perspective on a trife society that was holding us back from being creative and ambitious.... The message had to do with breaking down societal standards, and destroying personal property.

Skateboarders, you see, have been Occupying since the beginning, playing through capitalist centers with open disregard for both law and financial order, crossing every possible line and trying all patience. Which is not to suggest that our destruction has gone unnoticed—that the products property owners attach to ledges and rails to make them unskateable are called "skate stoppers," like "roach be gone" or "rats away," conveys the verminous treatment we've earned by our practice. But we needn't resort to that old Us/Them bifurcation. Have a look at the ollie itself, an impact followed by friction. This motion, the bang of wooden tail and scrape of shoe against abrasive griptape, is repeated until it becomes instinctual, the basis for every grind and slide that erodes concrete ledges and dents metal rails.

And like all forms of destruction, these create opportunities. One's demand for replacement boards, wheels, and trucks runs directly proportionate to one's devotion and access to resources. When I am skating regularly these days, I'll go through a board every three or four weeks and shoes every five or six. Of course, I am an adult who receives a regular paycheck, and I no longer wish to screw around with razored tails or blown out insoles. But, then, I am also five feet nine and 155 pounds, and I no longer jump down stairs or skate nearly as often as I once did.

Fortunately, despite all its consumptive power, the skateboard marketplace has been largely immune to gadgetry and expensive technological disruption. With only minor exception, skate hard goods have been in a kind of cryo-sleep—unlike tennis rackets or skis, today's skateboards are essentially unchanged from those ten, even twenty years ago.

Footwear, however, evolves. As even the rattiest of kids can't duct-tape or Shoe Goo beyond a matter of months—plus given the emergence of skate culture as the 2010s' (and by some freakish deviation from historic pattern, 2020s' as well) go-to well for popular imagistic water bearers—the skate shoe market spins in a rare confluence of fashion and function that we might call a no-brainer. Or gold mine. Or what Mark Parker, Nike's former chief executive and president, did in fact call a "unique consumer segment…underserved in terms of product innovation" at a shareholder meeting in May 2011. At that point, action sports represented $390 million of Nike's business, up 120 percent since 2007, the fastest-growing category within the brand. The company aimed to double that figure by 2015. Among the moves toward that goal was the release of the first in its *Chronicles* video trilogy. The appropriate term for what Nike was doing was *strategy*, a word that would pass exactly never through the lips of those holding it down on the real city streets.

* * *

The quick version of the story goes like this: In 1996, Nike experienced what I imagine as an "Araby"-like epiphany regarding the sales potential inherent to a market premised on the destruction of footwear. Their first attempts at inroads, however, were failures both resounding and, for those of us wary of incorporation, *very* satisfying. While skaters and civilians of a certain age may recall the charming "What if we treated all athletes the way we treat skateboarders?" campaign from 1998, you probably don't remember the Choad, something like a custom orthopedic walking shoe stretched around an overfed badger. Skaters guffawed, the outsiders retreated, and we all kept skating DCs and Emericas.

In 2001, Nike returned with two either brilliant or brutal moves. First, they flexed their M&A muscle to acquire the start-up shoe brand Savier, keeping intact Savier's team and designs and patina of independence. Second, they introduced their first SB model, the Dunk: a low-cut and slightly modified version of the original Air Jordan high-tops, which had been an organic, accidental cult favorite among 1980s vert skaters for their high ankle support. The first SB model became, arguably, the start of what we now speak of as sneakerhead culture. The Dunk Low made a new class of passionate shoe collectors go drooly. After a year, Nike shuttered Savier and shanghaied its riders to the SB line, which they sold only to legitimate, or core, skate shops—no mall shops, no swimsuit or beach sport stores, no outlet malls. From that point forward, SB would keep the drool flowing via their strategy of "quickstrikes": hyperlimited, themed colorways that would draw overnight campers and lines around blocks, and often end up, after exponential eBay markup, in Japan. Thus did the corporate sprinkle the core with new species of customers otherwise uninterested in skateboarding. The benefits were mutual.

Midway through the aughts, in an effort to grow (their transitive verb, not mine) their share of the skate shoe market, Nike introduced their more affordable 6.0 line for wide distribution— that is, to stores that had nothing to do with skateboarding. Again, the strategy was dual—6.0 would serve new, beginning skaters who'd not yet been indoctrinated into philosophies of core and who, because they had eyeballs and were alive, recognized the Nike brand. The premium of the SB line, which was still accruing its own mythology, was only enhanced by comparison to its new little sibling.

Against all of this, there spoke a diffuse but vocal "Don't Do It" campaign that had been started by Steve "Birdo" Guisinger and his partner at Consolidated Skateboards, Leticia Ruano, during Nike's first 1998 sortie. In 2005, Birdo and Ruano established the Don't Do It Foundation to ensure there'd be no mistaking "Don't Do It" for a Consolidated Skateboards marketing campaign. The foundation sold T-shirts, gave away stickers and stencils, and maintained a presence at surf and skate events alike—eventually they would hire a pilot to fly a "Don't Do It" banner in the clear sky above the 2012 US Open of Surfing. When the pilot came in citing mechanical difficulties after just an hour and forty-five minutes of the five hours they'd bought, Birdo insisted Nike had gotten to the pilot.

Meanwhile, from the seed of the former Savier squad Nike began stacking a broad cache of diverse skater-endorsers by paying them at once very well—for skateboarders—and laughably compared to most any other pro athlete on a Nike shoe contract. Their team was a curatorial dream with a relatively limitless budget. In 2007, once sufficient hype had gathered, they released *Nothing But the Truth*, which to this day remains one of the empirically shittiest skateboard videos ever produced. Bloated, lethargic, and uncomfortably lacking any clear team identity, the video was a sudden reminder that all of this, the whole campaign, had been conducted from behind rubberized gloves. It was like waking up in the middle of a ball to realize, My god, that's right—we're the debutantes.

For many of us, the video's stumble was sickly pleasurable in the way of, say, the Yankees missing the playoffs. At this point, the "Don't Do It" campaign was reaching its most fevered pitch of media coverage with a collaborative shoe, the Drunk, released by Osiris with a banana where a swoosh might go. But by then, Nike had settled into the next phase of their strategy. They devoted tiny portions of their vast resources to sponsoring core events like Tampa's annual contests. They deepened relationships with shop owners, shop employees, and team riders—to celebrate the release of the P-Rod V, Nike flew select store owners to Barcelona and sent them out to film with assorted pros, and then treated them to a Raekwon concert. They poached industry-tested minds from skater-owned apparel and shoe companies, magazines, and elsewhere.

And, it should be said, they released footwear that even the staunchest opponent couldn't claim was anything short of superior from a performance standpoint, due to they're motherfucking Nike. In 2008, at age thirty, after delivering many anti-Nike lectures from my moral high ground, a lingering heel bruise broke me. When I slipped on my first pair of Blazer Lows, I was unsurprised and heartbroken at how much of an improvement I immediately felt in my aching feet.

* * *

With a title that's half-historical, half-promissory, *The SB Chronicles, Vol. 1* speaks from the assumption that skateboarding in 2012 was as much Nike's as anyone else's. From the skippable opening sequence, the video feels familiar. As it should—it's directed by the same Jason Hernandez whose heavy hands molded six trendsetting videos for the once-mighty *Transworld Skateboarding* magazine, though thankfully here he's abandoned the dramatic voice-over monologues.

In terms of tricks, *Chronicles* is packed. Youness Amrani's 5-0 to three flip[1] off a Youness-high ledge augured frightfully the era's tech-combo movement, but the backside noseblunt and kickflip manny that the young Belgian pops onto a handrail back smith[2] earns points for thoughtful homage to Messrs. Koston and Mariano, respectively. Stefan Janoski continues his gangling dominance of early pop outs from too-high rails, flopping languidly between regular and switch stance and rendering the unexceptional beautiful— his basic noseslide across the Spanish bench's top approaches the sublime. The multiple wallride slashers mix well with Daniel Shimizu's sidewalk blazing, and Lewis Marnell—one of the few

---

1   This is a grind balanced on the back truck followed by a terrifically ambitious dismount.

2   A backside noseblunt demands straight shoulders and a torqued lower half, and it usually ends with the skater's eyes going angry and their brow furrowed at the ground just before them. They're cool as hell. A manual (manny) is what we call a wheelie, though wheelie really is the better word. Popping into a back smith out of a wheelie requires a fairly radical shift of body weight, so if done wrong, it will convey an air of desperation and struggle.

who still skated Dunks in 2012 and who'd pass within a year due to complications with type 1 diabetes—earns his place among the halls of all-time greatest heelflippers. Given the speed of Marnell's final nollie three flip over the picnic table into the schoolyard ramp, his normal-size T-shirt and pants billowing, we forgive the Aussie for self-props.

Less forgivable, then and now, is Hernandez's camerawork, which zooms and pulls away with almost drunken force, unable to let the skating speak for itself. Ditto for the lifestyle segments he speckles throughout: we see Chet Childress brewing coffee on the beach, Clark Hassler acting a fool, Shimizu reading actual books, Marnell flicking his lighter to toughen his laces against wear, and Janoski wearing cardigans while hungover. These moments belie the title's confidence: How else to read them but as ham-fisted efforts to humanize these men, to convince us that, despite beefy contracts and first-class airfare, these are still skateboarders like you and me?

Except that in 2012, there was nobody left to convince. Ultimately, what's most interesting about *Chronicles* is how it throws light on the geologic change that had wrenched the skateboarding landscape during those five years between videos. If *Nothing But the Truth* rang pathetically for its overt longing to join a party, *Chronicles* was the host that kept refilling snack bowls, too aware of who's having a good time. The chorus of "Don't Do It" had gone silent, and we were all dancing, laughing, and grateful for the invitation to the party.

At the time, I wanted very much to learn from this, to use skateboarding as the petri dish for a fifteen-year study of triumphant corporate strategy. But the longer I stared, the more I realized that there was nothing left to learn. Recall: Nike aimed to double their stake in the action sports industry by 2015. This was about as newsworthy as a brick falling when dropped from a roof. So, it makes perfect sense that the next step of their strategy was to dissolve the 6.0 sub-brand and release 2012's fall line of pro model shoes—the

Janoski, Salazar, P-Rod, and Koston—for sale outside of core shops for the first time. Beyond a spattering of unique colorways and occasional quickstrikes for premier accounts, all of Nike SB would soon be united into one line for sale in mall shops, Foot Lockers, and the outlets the corporation would open across Asia. Nike 6.0, like Coke II before it, had served its temporary purpose.

If this seems cutthroat, or somehow in bad faith, it's because of skateboarding's fondness for making two rather stupid mistakes. The first is holding a corporation to the same standards we would a person, viewing Nike's "gift" of SB exclusivity as a mark of character. The regional sales reps were all tatted up, after all, and they went skating with us after meetings. The second is wanting always to believe that we are special. Nike's miscalculation in 1998 was thinking skaters desired equality. They struck back with the SB program, which pandered to both our exceptionalist self-images and our nostalgia for a time before Nike, back when we could wear Nikes on our *own* terms. They cast themselves as the opposition. How core is that?

The vacuum of unifying image that seemed a failure of *Nothing But the Truth* has over time morphed into something much greater: the transcendence of image. By 2012, there was no longer any "type" of skateboarder on whom Nikes looked out of place. It wasn't just their pro team, of course. The individual who wrote the aforementioned Facebook post (who I happen to know and admire, and who landed the job of digital communications for Nike after twenty-plus years working within skateboarding), together with every skater who works Nike sales and promotions and product development (who are paid well and enjoy hugely their time at Nike, because, who wouldn't?), form a kind of post-image army. To return to our earlier language, they are the leakless hazmat gloves the corporation has slipped over its hands to handle a creative, ambitious, and destructive consumer base.

Because one of the few things skateboarders believe in is skateboarders. And in 2012—and still today, frankly—none more than

Thrasher's 2011 Skater of the Year, Grant Taylor. From the opening sequence in which he trespasses into a dormant Six Flags amusement park to maniacally skate the giant Tornado funnel, Grant's closing section of *Chronicles, Vol. 1* is a testament to all that is good in skateboarding. No one more than he embodied the timeless claim of the video's title. We recognize Honolulu's Wallows ditch from 1987's *The Search for Animal Chin*, but never a kickflip like this. We gawk at a floating alley oop frontside air in a vertiginous deep end of but one of many chunky, gnarly swimming pools he handled like waders. Slayer provides the only soundtrack, and Jason Hernandez keeps it simple and full speed. The ollie over the enormous, gaping channel into the brick bank. The suicidal drop-in to the water treatment plant, or dam, or whatever it is, deadly and concrete. By the time of his backside 50-50 down the curved handrail, there is no conceivable argument to be made against him, against any of this.

In 2012, Grant Taylor was one of perhaps three skaters more recognizable by his shoe sponsor than board company. It was the same sponsor who weathered the PR nightmare of sweatshop injustice, elbowed themselves into golf and soccer, abandoned surfing and snowboarding, and might someday, though they have no reason to, manufacture their own skateboards. Because why not? The same sponsor whose strategy would in the decade to follow clear away the clutter of poorly and skater-run middling footwear companies, the inept and frail and upstart alike, acting as our free market's grand systematic broom. Whatever Nike's next step was, we understood that it would be, like Grant Taylor, bigger and faster. We would ignore the rubber gloves and hear the parrot's squawk as our own. Bigger, faster, bigger, bigger, bigger.

CHAPTER FIVE

On Direction

What percentage of skateboarding, I wonder, is talking about skateboarding? Half, probably. There is such rich joy to be found in these debates without stakes, these endless recollections that go nowhere, slowly. And if the impulse to write grows from the impulse to converse, one could reasonably suggest that writing about skateboarding is a natural extension of the activity, too. But skaters tend to have a cautious relationship with the written word. Our culture has produced an array of photographers and filmmakers and sculptors, so it's not a lack of work ethic or creative energy that's kept us from producing poets.

At some point in my early twenties, I decided I wanted to become a novelist. So, I worked very hard to become one. By necessity at first, and then by habit, I viewed most any non-novel writing as a threat to my primary purpose. For my second novel, it seemed obvious that I should write about skateboarding. It proved difficult. I hit a snag, as happens, and then another. By the third snag, which was substantial, I decided to send out an e-mail to friends in the name of research. It was four questions, a brief survey about a basic paradox or conundrum central to our practice: Is skateboarding inherently competitive, I asked, like diving or gymnastics? Is it possible for any of us to treat going skateboarding like going for a stroll in the countryside? Or does something within the activity, some internal characteristic, urge its practitioners toward improvement?

How sweet this all seems now, how endearingly naive to believe I could unspool this mystery so directly. I've mentioned that I was an athlete as a young person, an OK baseball player until I quit preseason workouts during my first year of college. I was also a competitive tennis player into my teens, when it became clear that I lacked the psycho-emotional fortitude to handle the game's total isolation and the funneled pressures thereof. Tennis, in fact, eviscerated me. But before it did, I found it thrilling, as I did boyhood soccer leagues, JV basketball, and Ping-Pong. And video games: Street Fighter, Mortal Kombat, Mario Kart. Caps. Pool. Darts. I have found great pleasure over the years winning whatever I could win. Losing, I have sometimes handled rather unwell. In tennis, this meant broken rackets and high-pitched outbursts I am happy to have forgotten. At some point, for example, my wife stopped playing gin rummy with me.

I am saying that it made a certain sense that I would treat writing as competition, viewing publishing as a scarce and precious resource. But skateboarding, especially after I turned thirty, had mostly remained immune. There may be threads of competition running through any session, either alone or with friends, but they come like shifts in the wind and are minor, fleeting. I think of what the surfer and skater from Malibu who called himself the Illusion had to say in 2011 on *Crail Couch*, an interview series that mixed Errol Morris with an endless loop of Belle and Sebastian's "I'm a Cuckoo." When asked if he ever plays team sports, the Illusion said the following:

> So, my whole theory, for like fifteen years, was no balls no nets, man. Like, any time anyone asked me to play tennis, like, nah, I don't do that. I don't do anything with a ball or a net. If it's got a ball or a net, man, that's just my cosmic sign not to mess with it, man.

People like to point to the early Zephyr Team as proof that competition is endemic to skateboarding (this, after all, is the rhetorical use value of establishing gods). In that half decade between crashing the 1975 Del Mar Nationals and the last of Stecyk's Dogtown articles, their crew did indeed compete as much with one another as with their gentler colleagues hailing from less mythical neighborhoods. Skateboarding's time line is pocked with such periods of concentrated progression—on vert ramps in the mid to late eighties, in streets and plazas in the early nineties, and through the handrail and stair-set escalations of the aughts. But the Illusion captures something truer about the way the broader world of skateboarding actually spins.

For a fairly simple activity, skateboarding's internal code of competition is more nuanced and complex and fluid than any single contest could possibly model. Because the Illusion is a burner from Malibu, he speaks of this nuance in terms of the cosmos. This cosmic side has led to some ironies over the years, like a photo I keep pinned to my bulletin board of a Nike 6.0 hoodie that says "Jocks Suck" across the chest. It is usually pretty clear who to call the *best* skater at any given session, or among a group of friends. But what looks like victory among pack dogs and, I suppose, salespeople and law students and most other worlds premised on rankings, is among skaters almost wholly irrelevant.

Oh, children will think differently about this. Each of us who's done the thing long enough has at some point believed in and even worked toward the dream of having our talents recognized as exceptional enough to merit sponsorship by a board company, or fantasized about a lifestyle supported by a shoe deal. Eventually, though, if we keep going, if we commit our lives to the practice, we will come to see how frictionlessly the scale slides, how even the slide is itself sliding. That the collective plural for a given brand's sponsored skaters remains "team" is as archaic and absurd as those stand-alone video "parts" lacking a whole. The best term for the nonhierarchical system around which skate performance is judged is one that I am 100 percent certain the Illusion, whatever he's doing now, has spoken of at least twice in the last hour. The term is *stoke*, and we might, for now, leave it at that.

Back to those snags. It was *stoke*, or some approximation thereof, that I couldn't translate into my writing. That *v* of *novelist* had needled into my old and ugly vein, that tennis player's lament. I'd begun to worry that I'd made perhaps the most foolish choice possible, committing to a life of isolated performance, or what felt at the time like performance, one novel down and the second expected. Suddenly, there was nothing I was doing that I was not doing wrong. It was not failure I felt but defeat. In merging my two pursuits I'd leaned so desirously far toward the one that I'd lost track of the other. I must have known what was happening when I sent that e-mail off to my friends. I wasn't conducting a survey, I was asking for a rope, or even just directions back from wherever I'd ended up. I was asking for a map.

CHAPTER SIX

The Deep Seams

2012

> The thing is that men have two different ways
> of creating and producing, and as yet these
> have not intersected: spontaneous vitality and
> abstraction. On the one hand, in pleasure and
> in play; on the other, in seriousness, patience
> and painful consciousness, in toil.
>
> —Henri Lefebvre

Join me in imagining a child. Let us see her, kindergarten aged, somewhere between five and seven years old, and let's imagine this child beneath a glowing afternoon sun during recess, playing with a group of classmates across a rubber-matted playground. They all run and climb and the structures shake and make noise and she could be a boy, too. That's fine.

It's sometime in the 1980s. The playground is built from metal and wood, the sort that is inconceivable by today's safety standards. There's a long sandbox running between the playground and the schoolyard's iron fence, and the girl or the boy is playing tag, or chase, or A-Team, or Voltron—the game isn't important—and running about. A host of overlapping fantasies swirl like pollen in the springtime air, they hurtle bad guys and crouch under bullets. Midway across the bouncing bridge, the child squeezes through the chains to drop onto what they've been thinking is a lava pit, frantic in escape, and once their feet get running again the child crashes square into their teacher who is completely out of place, all wrong, standing sentry-like on the playground with her arms crossed.

I can remember locking eyes with Mrs. Otten, seeing her watch me, and knowing that though she was physically nearby, the woman existed in a place far beyond the boundaries of my play. And I recall the terrible and brand-new sensation of thinking, Oh crap, I look stupid here, pretending like this, at which exact moment the fun of my game came to a sudden end.

The word *kindergarten* is a rather unsurprising near cognate of the German term for "children's garden." This pre-elementary year of school, the only grade before high school to get its own name, was the nineteenth-century idea of a man named Friedrich Wilhelm August Fröbel. His concept of "free work," or *freiarbeit*, relied on active games as both a basis of childish existence and a tool for learning and development. Which aligns nicely, I think, with a lingering notion of the garden as locus of knowledge that cannot be forgotten. But only for one year, kindergarten. And it could well be that fun, by definition, carries with it a promise of expiration.

In June 2011, I decided to drive to a city that represents, for me, the end of fun. I can explain both its representation and my desire to visit by pointing vaguely in the direction of a certain book, which is not a novel and definitely not a memoir, but is, everyone agrees, about boredom. Because I had recently published a novel, and because I had taught David Foster Wallace's work at the college level, I found myself in a position to review *The Pale King*. Writing that review, grappling with the man and his final, unfinished work, and by association all the work that came before it, did not accomplish what I'd hoped it might, whether we call the object of my hope *closure* or *peace* or any other variant that conveys a transition from an unwelcome stasis to *moving on*.

I also knew that Illinois's seventh-largest city was only a few hours from Chicago, where I live. Summer was sluggish to begin, and for far too long I'd been frozen. I needed to see how it was to play in Peoria.

> That thing is good : That thing is fun :: That is
> a good thing : That is a fun thing

Do you know the history of *fun*? It's a strange word, turns out. *Fun* began as a transitive verb, a thing done: fun meaning to cheat, or to hoax. And from this verb, as happens, came a noun, he or she who hoaxes, that would eventually produce *fun*'s more common contemporary use, the noun we speak with a dual meaning—that is, not only a diversion or amusement, a pleasure ("We had fun at the concert"), but also the source of that amusement, the object or event that leads to or causes pleasure ("The concert was fun"). This duality is a twentieth-century development described by Harvard linguist Dwight Bolinger as "the gradual emancipation of a form once securely barricaded behind the wall that separates nouns from adjectives." The result is exemplified by the analogy above, by which *It's so fun!* is a qualitative claim meaning, for all intents and purposes, *It's so good!* (How was the concert, I ask? Fun, they reply, and which I hear as: Good. A good concert.)

According to Bolinger, the path toward our modern equation of *fun* and *good* required a confluence of factors I will try to quickly outline here (you can maybe skip these two paragraphs if you're inclined). First, note the way that the addition of a *-y* suffix to our noun—a common tool for making an adjective out of a thing—produces *funny*, which narrows the word's meaning from broad pleasure toward humor specifically. Bolinger calls the noun *fun* "disadvantaged" from the start because *fun*, like *water* and *cutlery*, is a mass noun characterized by the fact that it would sound very strange to modify it with a numeral. Furthermore, *fun* is unique from other emotional abstractions that are amenable to an indefinite article; we can speak of *a pleasure*, *a joy*, or *an ecstasy*, but the noun *fun* never appears in the predicate with a determiner—your guests' company is not *a fun*. Finally, he includes *fun* in a select group of mass nouns that he says includes *madness*, *war*, *heaven*, and *torture*, in all of which, he says, we catch whiff of an "air of emotion and value judgment."

Over the course of the twentieth century, such connotations of judgment worked together to break down the traditional wall that divides noun and adjective. Consider the expressions: *Running is fun*, *A movie is fun*, or *Billy is fun*. "Obviously," Bolinger writes, "to identify actions, things, and persons with an abstraction is figurative language of a rather extreme kind. In normal discourse they may *yield* fun, but a predication that says they *are* fun strongly suggests hyperbole." And the distinction between hyperbole and neutral expression is a rather obvious one in practice: try substituting *waste* or *refuse* into the clause, *That speech was garbage*, and it simply does not work.

So, over time, *fun* crossed into common parlance as an adjective roughly equivalent to *good*. And here is where Wallace comes sprinting back into frame, an author who took upon himself the responsibility of reminding us that all fun isn't good. Or perhaps, rather, that no fun is *only* good. Candy, liquor, and treats taste delicious but lack nutrients. The same goes, he'd tell us over and over again, for types of entertainment that encase their empty calories within a shell of pure fun, maximizing revenues by indulging their viewers' basest desires. Like one of Barthes's *Mythologies*, Wallace's work confronted habitual American fun with the goal of exposing and working against this semantic equation of *fun* and *good*.

> The new beautiful freaks will teach us all how
> to play again.
>   —Richard Neville

Among those who are most invested in the activity, there is scant agreement about how skateboarding should be classified. Is it sport or hobby? Is it dance? Or is the ludic space seized by the activity, its ample "room for improvisation and unique personal style," most befitting, as longtime editor of *Slap* Mark Whiteley has argued, jazz?

The taxonomy has been and will likely remain a matter of much debate. Most of the time, I'm content thinking of skateboarding as a prize America awarded itself after World War II. Like the Hula-Hoop and yo-yo, the skateboard sneezed into popularity in the sixties and then, also like them, mostly disappeared as the decade came to a close. But not completely. In fact, it was during this window of retreat from the public view (obscurity during the early seventies marked the first of what would become a cyclic pattern of popular culture's embrace and rejection of skateboarding) that the real interesting developments begin. Because it survived. Those who did it were outcasts, yes, but banishment from the mainstream provided, as it will, a kind of permission for deeper transgression. They skated and they destroyed, assuming, during the down-time, the role of freaks and assholes. Then the eighties arrived, fluorescent and rad, and once more skateboards were cinematically and televisually *du juor* until the dawn of the nineties, at which point out went the money and down came the ramps, and quickly. Skateboarders, outcasts again, took to the streets and gutters anew, growing uglier and meaner, embracing the so-called underground (it was, after all, the nineties) and growing proudly resistant to any indication of the cycle's next uptick.

But capital finds a way. By the turn of the millennium, the nausea of watching this next uptick swell into a $2.5 billion industry was tempered only by the fun of seeing major corporations cautiously advance and retreat, uncertain whether the beast had truly been pacified. The nausea, though, can be debilitating. Suddenly, we had celebrity crossovers and MTV specials. We watched the death of unspoken traditions, values, and codes, and saw the rise of compet-itors with workout regimens and Olympic ambitions. Ambition, period, really.

> The diving would make a suitable literary
> symbol.
>
> —John Barth

Some context. The claim above falls in the middle of John Barth's "Lost in the Funhouse," a story that bears the considerable weight of Wallace's extremely complicated relationship with metafiction, a genre Barth helped spawn. In his story "Forever Overhead," Wallace's tack is straight appropriation. On the hero's thirteenth birthday, in the afternoon hours before the fun of a nighttime party, a second-person declarative narrator guides the boy's journey out of a public swimming pool, across the deck, then up onto the diving board.

It is, as Barth notes, the most convenient coming-of-age metaphor we could imagine: the board's precipice, the water below, a void—together, they shoulder the meaning of the irrevocable action to come, the boy's leap of faith into an unknown mode of adult life. More than this, though, the exposed board plays stage for one of Wallace's most common narrative projects, exploring the boy's relationship to himself. On this "first really public day," the boy finds himself prone to "a watching that spreads like hit water's rings." Suddenly up there, the seer finds for the first time that he is also *seen*. Thus does a borrowed and unambiguous literary symbol trigger the defining activity of Barthian metafiction: paralyzing self-awareness.

Zadie Smith's exegesis of *Brief Interviews with Hideous Men* is as erudite as we'd expect from a woman who recalls, at age thirteen, having to abandon "the idea that Keats had a monopoly on the lyrical." (What a fool Zadie Smith was at age twelve, with her blind devotion to Keats!) So, while I typically defer to Smith when it comes to matters literary, in this case, her reading of "Forever Overhead" strikes me as just about exactly wrong. "Examination does not result in paralysis," says Smith. "He still dives."

Except that no, he does not. In the immediate present tense of this normative second-person story, Barth's symbol remains unfulfilled. Yes, we are told that "the board will nod and you will go," but there is no going on the story's pages. We who are doubled—those of us reading the story who also cannot help but occupy the narrator's "you"—are denied the action of the story's implicit finale. We are left as Wallace often left readers, trapped inside a moment gravid with potential and lush immobility. Greg Carlisle, author of *Elegant Complexity: A Study of David Foster Wallace's "Infinite Jest,"* describes these moments as "chaotic stasis," a kind of battle between narrative tension and narrative sequence, immobile and unresolved.

For Carlisle, this is a tactic meant to resist traditional expectations of climax, a decentering of completion in favor of the moments that precede action. These chaotically static endings of stories and chapters serve as playgrounds for what, in Wallace's "morally passionate, passionately moral" writing, is a distinctive and almost paradigmatically Kantian deontology. *Deon* comes from the Greek word for duty—deontological moral philosophies focus on what is required, forbidden, and permitted. They do their heavy lifting during those gravid moments of choice that come prior to action, when a person—for example, an imaginary boy standing exposed on a public pool's high dive—considers what ought *to be done*. Aretaic theories, for the sake of comparison, explode the time frame of the moment into questions of what sort of person we ought *to be*.

In any case, in "Forever Overhead," the activity of the symbol (the diving board's purpose of providing altitude and spring so that one may not only choose to but in fact *dive*) is rendered moot. As is common for Wallace, consideration takes precedence over action.

> By the will, I mean nothing but the internal impression we feel and are conscious of, when we knowingly give rise to any new motion of our body, or perception of our mind.
>
> —David Hume

The first trailer park appeared once I merged from I-55 onto I-80 just outside of Joliet. To the north were tilled brown fields punctured by sprouts of corn barely tall enough to reach a wanderer's shin, and I recalled that out here clouds' shapes are doubled—the skyborne forms of childish imagination plus the shadows a city otherwise obscures, which in these open ranges of Illinois are granted both definition and movement.

I followed an inefficient route along the Illinois River, winding south and west. Here the hay bales were spiraled brown imperfections against great swaths of many-shaded green. Illinois Route 29 is a series of hairpin turns that straighten and open onto giant fields that rise into gentle slopes. Here beneath clouds moving like armies the corn had risen to knee height, and I passed Henry-Senachwine High School, "Home of the Mallards."

On the one occasion I met David Foster Wallace in person, I was private witness to at least two of the exceptionally quick-witted observations for which he was known. At that point I had not read his work, because I was neither a good reader nor any sort of writer. We were moving slowly through Frary Dining Hall on Pomona College's north campus. He was there for a campus interview, trial workshop, and small public reading for the Roy Edward Disney Professor of Creative Writing gig that he was offered and, to everyone's considerable surprise, accepted. I was nearby after we'd sort of hit it off due to a shared Midwestern thing, a born-in-Ithaca thing, and a double-major-in-English-and-philosophy thing.

Anyway, the first comment had to do with the sneeze guard at the salad bar. Then at the hot buffet, he pointed at an unlabeled meat dish.

"Sagehen," I said, feeling pretty sharp, our school mascot.

"Omnivore," he replied *immediately*. "Fiercely loyal. Known on the grouse circuit for their plumage. Real good dancers."

And if I may inflate the moment that followed: What a terrible excitement I felt, a most astringent mixture of desiring to be a way, seeing modeled a certain way of being right before my eyes—

a minor miracle of a comment, at once completely bullshit with respect to the fact of sagehens and glowing with a fiery core of total truth to the particular moment that was between us—and knowing with full certainty that I was not equipped to be the way he was. I physically shivered then, a tiny passing quake in terms of clock time, but which left me feeling frozen in a lingering way that I had never known before then, but do now, and by now most intimately.

Peoria is a river city approached by way of a cantilever bridge with trusses that make whipping sounds through rolled-down windows. Moving slowly and, admittedly, not without creep factor through downtown at 11:50 a.m. on a Tuesday left my expectations largely unviolated. I saw exiled smokers clustered fifteen legal feet away from building doorways, women wearing either long skirts or short pants, men in pleats with shirts tucked neatly and credentials swinging on lanyard necklaces or flapping from belt clips. Parking was affordable and ample, as were window signs for available office space. I saw unsurprising construction along the riverfront, mother-daughter pairs dressed in perfect echo, the elder's figure and posture a promise for what the younger would become, ungated railroad crossings, a Kelly Seed and Hardware, Mark Twain Hotel, and the kind of regular, unabashed obesity that seems neither selfish nor shameful, but rather evidence of a general and ambient acceptance of the joys and consequences of consumption. An orange-awninged Hooters offered unobstructed river views.

My immediate goal was Glen Oak Park, which basic online research told me housed the smaller of Peoria's two skate parks. The photos I'd found of Glen Oak were not promising, but promising wasn't the point. The point was activity: Come, engage, participate, and enjoy. Unfreeze. The point was fun. After my fifth lap around the park's one-way traffic loop, I was ready to accept that I was in the wrong place. As I saw myself pull alongside a police cruiser to request directions to a skate park, I felt the irony register as a round of mild interior applause that itself twined the muddled line between ironic and sincere.

> In the beginning, when you first start out trying to write fiction, the whole endeavor's about fun. You don't expect anybody else to read it. You're writing almost wholly to get yourself off.... And it works—and it's terrific fun.
>
> —David Foster Wallace

Wallace spoke more than once of hoping his readers might find the experience of reading *Infinite Jest* fun. To David Lipsky he explained, "The goal was to have something that was really pretty hard, but also to sort of be good enough, and fun enough, to make you be willing to do that." And to Laura Miller, "It's a weird book. It doesn't move the way normal books do. It's got a whole bunch of characters. I think it makes at least an in-good-faith attempt to be fun and riveting." In both of these cases, fun is a kind of enticement, the carrot he dangles before the laboring reader. The experience of moving through *Infinite Jest* can at times be fun, but never *just* fun. Never *only*.

The fun parts, the outlandish plot machinations and exaggerated characters and set pieces that can be uproarious, are offset by two prevailing messages the novel seems intent to convey. Both of these messages undermine, or at least complicate, the author's use of *fun* in the quotes above. The first is a matter of drug use, abuse, and addiction. Joelle hunkers into Molly's bathroom ready to "exit this vessel" by way of overdose: "She is now a little under two deliberate minutes from Too Much Fun for any one mortal to hope to endure." The idea is repeated, almost hammered: "Joelle is going to have Too Much Fun in here. It was beyond all else so much fun, at the start." The border between "fun" and "Too Much Fun" is one Wallace regularly spoke of as a uniquely American weakness—our inability to draw necessary lines.

The second theme involves tennis. Mark Bresnan's "The Work of Play in David Foster Wallace's *Infinite Jest*" convincingly paints Gerhardt Schtitt's philosophy, which percolates throughout the Enfield Tennis Academy, as an echo of mid-twentieth-century structuralist definitions of play like Johan Huizinga's *Homo Ludens* and Roger Caillois's *Man, Play and Games*. In these works, limited play provides the chance to escape the limits of the self, thereby achieving autonomy within a defined, restrictive space (see: the rectilinear space of a tennis court). But while there is indeed much activity in *Infinite Jest* that would seem to slot into common definitions of play, Bresnan is right to note that none provide their players anything close to escape. Hal's Tennis, Orin's football, and the E.T.A.'s annual game of Eschaton form a trio of playful activities that "translated into rigidly structured events that induce anxiety and paranoia rather than autonomy." Like recreational drug use, the novel's examples of play "might be represented as a playful liberation from the prevailing order"; *might*, but are instead "characterized as a profoundly banal, anxious, and isolating enterprise."

Any of these three adjectives would serve to describe *The Pale King*, a project that more or less abandons fun as a strategic authorial carrot. In Wallace's third novel, a reader hears detailed accounts of pages being turned one at a time. Clocks do not move forward. Watercooler breaks during work hinge on stories too mundane to repeat. A traffic jam is somehow less bearable for readers than the characters who suffer it. We are reminded to pay very close attention to often excruciating moments, and fun is nowhere to be found.

That he wrote the book from within the suffering of depression that would lead to his suicide, is not, I believe, where this conversation should stop. If we can agree that genuine play requires that one be not only active but *engagé*, committed to the play at hand, and if, following Wallace in *The Pale King*, we define boredom as a condition or state defined by a failure to engage—a casual, all-too-common disengagement from the particular or even general activity before us—then fun would stand, for all practical purposes, as boredom's opposite. As his biographer D. T. Max famously described it, Wallace's goal in *The Pale King* was to show readers "a way to insulate themselves from the toxic freneticism of American life." This alleged way, this so-called solution—a postmodern *Tao* that by design both is and cannot be fun—is at once the novel's alleged reward and its uncompromising, onerous demand.

But am I alone in wondering whether "insulation" from fun is actually what the rest of us need? Rereading *The Pale King* after my trip to Peoria, with the massive outpouring of critical and personal responses to the novel behind me, it seemed obvious to me that boredom could be avoided in any number of ways, including but not limited to, like, jumping off of a diving board.

> The four-wheeled device originally had something to do with milking cows. The Georgian soldiers had nicked it from an abandoned farm and, to stave off the boredom, they rode it up and down the road behind the battery where they were stationed.
>
> —Dave Carnie

Depending on where you live, the modern skate park serves one of two very different purposes. In rural and outer-suburban locations they are seen as a kind of gift, providing opportunities for movement not otherwise available. Within the explicit confines of the park, and especially as compared to the vast unpaved terrain of the region, the potential for play is theoretically limitless. The Peoria I saw from my car on the way to Becker Park was comprised of small homes and emergency loan brokers occupying what were formerly fast-food locations. Their parking lots were rough, gravelly, and veined with networks of weeds. When I got there, I found an EMT van parked at the park's far end, but otherwise, it was just me.

The Becker Park skate node was not, let's be clear, wanting for limits. Most definitely it was appropriately named: the node as defined was a strip of concrete I estimated at thirty by fifty feet, which is smaller than it sounds. This space was separate from the Becker Park skate trail that encircled the neighboring baseball diamond, basketball court, and picnic area and would function something like a NASCAR pit lane for skateboards, if skateboarders had any interest whatsoever in pushing around a looped trail. It all struck me as funny, in a way, and reminded me of something I had read almost a decade earlier by another very different Dave, who might be the most recognizable voice in skateboard writing.

Issue 102 of *Big Brother*, from November 2003, features the article "Why Modular Skateparks Are Evil," in which Dave Carnie takes a moral stance against companies who exploit the rising popularity of skate parks across the US by selling inferior prefabricated products to those who don't know any better. Such parks, curated from an à la carte menu from the back of a catalog, often end up like Becker Park in Peoria, arranged in ways that run directly counter to classical skateboarding impulses. In Peoria, the American Ramp Company provided a gentle quarter-pipe, a central pyramid structure with ledges running up and down two of its sides, and a four-foot embankment ramp. There is also what's known as a "fun box" and a low, short flat-rail, all crammed into 150 square feet of node.

After skating Becker Park for fifteen minutes, I was not convinced that it was evil, exactly, but I was quite damn bored—which gets at the second purpose skate parks can serve. If tennis is a sport defined by movement within limitations, skateboarding is about pushing back against them. Do you recall that aforementioned descent from fluorescent vert ramps to the gutter-hued and baggy-pantsed world of cyclical outcasts? Since 1990, the main limits we've pushed back against are limestone, marble, and concrete. Thus, skate parks in or near urban centers will be implemented as a kind of decoy, or cage. It's a strategy of quarantine. The problem is not that parks prohibit creativity per se, but that the silhouette of street skating they provide is a close enough approximation to dupe skaters out of the real thing.

So I cycled listlessly through a series of basic tricks I'd done a thousand times before coming here, pushing on nothing. Above me, the clouds had grown larger and more comfortable with one another. Later, once I was back in Chicago, one thing I did was explore American Ramp Company's website. On the "About" page, I found a link to "Jesus," which opened a page of text entirely about Him and what happens if we do and don't let Him into our lives. Mostly about when we don't: "That means no matter how bad your life is, you can be sure that eternity will be worse."

Another thing I did was pull a certain large book from my shelves. Here was Dave Carnie posing on the cover. He's wearing a golden spandex onesie, white sunglasses, a helmet, blue socks pulled up to midcalf, and a pair of pink Rollerblades. In bold, large orange letters is the book's simple and perfect title: *boob*. If you're wondering why it is in lowercase, it's so you can hold it upside down in the mirror and see the word *poop*.

> I don't want to sound like a cocksucker, but I
> don't get bored.
> —Dave Carnie

If the increasingly involuted, Gordian, and ultimately unfinishable narratives of late Wallace are indicative of the author's struggle to reconcile his multiple selves—public (David Foster Wallace), private (Dave), fictional ("Good Old Neon"), plural ("Big Red Son"), and virtually indecipherable (*The Pale King*)—then the singular and consistent ethos of Dave Carnie stands in stark opposition.

Over e-mail, he less admits than exults that his writing is "sloppy, and kind of crass, clumsy, and childish." The book *boob* covers fourteen years of his "Stories and Other Nonsense from *Big Brother Skateboarding Magazine*," which began as businessman/

megalomaniac/former freestyler Steve Rocco's solution to extant skate magazines refusing to run his frankly awful and sickeningly funny advertisements. This tension, too, grew from that same shift from the ethos of the "Big Three"—Powell-Peralta, Santa Cruz, and Vision—to the atomized and irreverent start-ups that emerged in the early 1990s. Carnie joined the staff soon after *BB*'s inception, but did not write his first article until Issue 16. His first real splash came the following month, with the sprawling "A Review of Religions." He begins with "Christianism":

> Couldn't have started with a more fucked up religion. The god that the Christians worship is a fucking DICK! When his children are bad, he tortures them forever! In fire! He drowns them in rivers of boiling shit! FOREVER! And for no reason!

While reading *boob* chronologically could theoretically provide a linear record of *Big Brother*, I've always found myself flipping to entries at random, trusting that they'll direct me elsewhere. When, for example, I see passing mention of "The Depends Party" I go searching through previous articles for the source (several men, a hotel room, adult diapers). A letter to the editor mentions "One Wipe Wonder," and I find the article wherein Carnie Nairs his anus.

There are precedents to the work—his style is part Céline, part Burroughs—but what distinguishes Carnie is the way his writing is grounded in the *Geist* of a single activity, one that has nothing to do with writing but is premised entirely on fun. As an archive of an undigitized magazine and hugely offensive log of one man's adventures, *boob* is indeed a relic. At times, especially in its early pages, it is a terrible thing to read. However, and without guessing what values calibrate Dave Carnie's moral compass, the more one reads of *boob*, the more one gleans a sense that much of the language—crass and childish and sometimes hateful—is performative, even spectacular in the situationists' sense. Whatever else *boob* does, it creates a large, cohesive space for the unrepentant abuse of rules, both legal and social. Decency is ignored and mocked. Nothing remains static for more than a sentence or two. Nothing, not a single word, resides anywhere remotely close to frozen.

> You're no longer writing just to get yourself off, which—since any kind of masturbation is lonely and hollow—is probably good.
>
> —David Foster Wallace

Near the end of his essay "The Nature of the Fun," Wallace speaks of breaking free from an apparent paradox wherein "the very thing that's always motivated you to write is now also what's motivating you to feed your writing to the wastebasket." Finally, he says, vanity and paralysis can be overcome by working "your way back to fun."

Even in my early years as a professor of creative writing, I had spoken this final step of Wallace's formulation more times than I could count. I've run the numbers, I tell my students, and writing good fiction is at least five times as hard as being a competent surgeon. We've all heard that quote about how it's easy, right? "All you do is sit down at a typewriter and bleed." But what's missing here, Ernest, is every occasion when the blood comes out wrong—wrong shape, wrong color. You see the blood and know it's not your own, and if it is yours, it's even worse, because now your own blood is wrong, and ugly, and so you hate it. You think it's the ugliest, most shameful blood ever to fall. It's disgusting, you're disgusting, so you rush to the kitchen for a sponge.

To be a writer, I say, is to roll your neck and breathe deep. To accept the blood's emergence for what it is, whatever its shape, watery or clotted, vivid or pale. To then work the blood. Add color and thicken it in places, then run away crying, then return hours later to bleed more blood, blood caused by the blood. To then play the blood. Throw yourself self-first into this shameful, awful blood and cover yourself in it, bathe in the blood and roll around and smear it across the page. Can't this, I ask them, be fun? Mustn't it?

What I do not tell the students is how much time I have spent frozen. How the very reason I decided to drive to Peoria was because it was not fun, writing. Not at all. That every time I spoke of its fun, with each new incoming group of MFA students I supported and critiqued and taught in ways I believed would facilitate their growth into, if not great artists, at least strong communicators, I was lying. There was imposter syndrome, which I knew well, and then there was this deliberate dishonesty I carried with me every time I walked into a classroom: I did not believe that writing could be fun.

Until, anyway, I rediscovered Dave Carnie. Here are some highlights from *boob*, arrived upon at random. On the hideousness of men: "Florida, you'll remember, is shaped like a penis. The shape of the state seems to have an effect on anyone within it. You know what happens when people start thinking with their dick? ... Its inhabitants appear to act with the reckless abandon of a man who has given the steering wheel of his being over to his cock." On authorial honesty: "The Bong Olympics was stupid. That first sentence should be the entire article, but I get paid by the word so I'm going to go into great detail about how stupid it was." On being, I suppose, full of shit: "I do know, however, that if you are taller than the president, you're not allowed to ride the buses in DC. Go Figure."

It was all so familiar, and not because I'd read many of these articles in their original published form. "I treat writing like skateboarding," Carnie has said. "There's no contest in skateboarding, and thus there's no practice. You're never preparing for 'the big game.' You make of it whatever you want. There's nothing to win." Curiously, though, I find Carnie's writing about skateboarding his weakest. The writing shines when it serves as direct medium for his character, which, again, is sometimes grotesque, but never split or conflicted, and certainly not paralyzed. It functions as a pure mimesis of skateboarding, capturing his and the activity's ethos both. Read *boob* and of one thing at least you will be certain: Dave Carnie finds masturbation neither lonely nor hollow.

> The true opponent, the enfolding boundary, is
> the player himself.
> —Gerhardt Schtitt, *Infinite Jest*

The sign at the Sommer Park North skate park, ten miles northwest of downtown Peoria, proclaims that, "Swearing, fighting, and bad attitudes will not be tolerated." Yet there I stood before an embarrassing artificial terrain that should not, by any stretch of necessity, exist. My attitude was currently quite bad.

"Fuck," I swore, and punched the sign.

Sommer Park surrounds a branching cul-de-sac of a new and upscale suburban neighborhood that, once I got back to my computer and saw it from above, looked to me exactly like a man bent at the waist, reaching for the floor with both hands outstretched, and hitting his head on a piano bench. The concrete of the skate park's ground and the angled terrain were the same flat beige, except for spots where surrounding mud had seeped and dried slightly browner. I climbed the quarter-pipe, which is the only modular addition to what is an otherwise poured concrete park. From there, I faced two hubbas running down a steep embankment, plus a long ledge with very little run-up or landing to my right. There's a low and awkward rail running from the path up above, over grass, and down into the park. It is a stupid, dumb rail and if I'm struggling to evoke this place it's because I was forgetting it even as I was standing there with my board on the quarter-pipe's edge, ready to drop into it. The ramp is positioned so that dropping in would send me straight into the steep embankment. If Sommer Park skate park were masturbation, it would be the sort done with an oyster shucker's protective mail glove. By this point in my excursion I was having a difficult time remaining unsad.

I may dream of how I once learned to walk.
But to what end? Now I can walk; no longer
can I learn to walk.

—Walter Benjamin

The thunder came from a distance. I left my car and began pushing along the same downtown streets I'd driven only hours earlier, which now seemed a different place entirely. The midday workers had all commuted home. Streetlights had come on but didn't yet make a difference. The streets were roughly paved and the sidewalks were only slightly less rough, and both had deep seams that you had to be aware of at all times. The big ones were the sort to ollie over or else do a quick lift of your front wheels, then semi-hop your weight off the back foot as the back wheels cross, otherwise your board will stop abruptly and you will fall. The sky was the early-night type that accented the clouds' blackness with what was gradually becoming its own.

I thought of her again on that night in Peoria, and have occasionally since—*The Pale King*'s Toni Ware, as fun a character as Wallace's late writing produced. Her attention is every bit as impressive as Drinion's or Fogle's. But unlike them, unlike all but a small handful of Wallace's characters (Michael Pemulis comes to mind), her focus is action: "The daughter had learned to trust actions and to read signs in details of which the run of children are innocent." And she is a complete character, the one we know perhaps most completely in the fractured, incomplete *The Pale King*, a real human with an "inner life rich and multivalent." Late in the novel, we find her both pre- and midaction, waiting for a phone call's order of copper piping to be filled, conspiring to mischief inside the "Tumor" of a convenience store. Her mayhem is morally ambiguous and a guilty pleasure. The operative word with Toni? *Affect*. The dozen bricks on her front seat are ready to be mailed and demand maximum return postage paid from marketing firms—an act I'm hesitant to call altogether bad. Like the booger she plants to get the Tumor's cashier into trouble, the bricks are a type of mayhem that might easily appear on the pages of *boob*.

A half hour later and the clouds had lost all definition. Somewhere nearby there were bullfrogs, mosquitoes, and the wind sweeping across the region like a hand across a tablecloth wrinkle. They do truly nod, all the plants' heads, while growing corn appears to genuflect.

Downtown Peoria at 6:30 p.m. is a city that presents as a gift of lines and shapes and surfaces. By the hill's bottom my feet were rattled numb. I walked a block, then climbed an adjacent street and felt my legs working, felt something larger begin working. I heard thunder again, sharper this time. I'd been driving, and staring, and thinking all day, even at those parks when I was skating. Now I was sweating. Now I was thawed. At the hilltop, I pushed and ollied and leaned and felt the mechanics of the board and mechanics of my body and there were angles everywhere, and I was indeed in there.

In *Infinite Jest*, Eschaton fails for a critical breakdown between game world and real world. Illicit play within the system shatters the ordered map, leading to chaos, injury, and serious narrative ramifications.

One theory has it that at the time of our beginning, God was simply bored.

The Pale King is not about *a way through boredom*, as the reviews and critiques of the novel, including the review I wrote before driving to Peoria, would have you believe. *Through* implies motion. However badly I and others like me might have wanted it, Wallace was never going to be our guide to any such movement.

To speak of any suicide is to presume. Here, causation resists codification; this is pain that does not translate. Suicide is the sub-linguistic province of one relationship only—the self's to itself. The danger of attempted empathy is a too-often premature belief that we have leapt over the wall of self when in fact all we've done is throw our own selves against that wall. Or, worse, sat back inside that self and thought very long and very hard about what could be on the wall's other side. One must actually leap.

I know more surely who I am when pushing along a city street, finding lines to pursue. On this night in Peoria, I managed to forget the dishonesty of my teaching, of calling myself a novelist, or critic, of all personae. When there was a sewer cap, I popped over it—my board's tail scraped and I lifted and when we landed on the cap's other side we were going faster than before. If you would like to know a skateboarder, study his elbows, examine her shins.

Our cities were built with functionality in mind, a process of closure. These three steps outside of a Chase Bank with their uses clearly defined—climbing and descent. It was indeed a challenge to this order when I spent five or ten minutes sessioning the second of these steps, which someone had waxed. It became a ledge. Grinding or sliding, per Derrida, is play that disrupts the system's boundaries. We can call it the reinterpretation of spaces of economic production. We can see the self as a small human body maneuvering among soaring architectural bodies. Self as a creator of *movement* above all else.

It is so much more honest to teach my students new ways to read, to train them to see reading as a creative act. Wallace's novel, or so-called novel of Peoria is like this, too. Learn to see and it's a city to move through. The book's lines are cracked, boundaries porous. If there's fun to be found inside, it is not in the story, the long and tortured scenes of discomfort and deliberate stasis of the narrative, but in treating his writing as terrain and playing through it. By pressing against its shapes and boundaries, being aware of its seams.

Back once more to that boy on the diving board, standing there at the end of Wallace's story, paralyzed by seeing and being seen. The boy could, for instance, jackknife, cannonball, front flip, belly flop, lift gracefully upward and unfold himself toward a peak, spreading then uniting hands and returning to slice into the pool's water. Or take one simple step and escape the cage of perception, and then one more to the edge, and a final step over and down, letting gravity take over and falling back into the water from which he emerged.

Pushing hard alongside a sidewalk for which I had no current use, I was not bored. The sound of wheels was tiny thunder over which a woman's voice yelled, "Do a kickflip!" Mark Besnan's triplicate account of play: unproductive, unpredictable, and even beautiful. And when I did fall, it was not the fault of rough pavement or sidewalk seam or any of the drivers moving through downtown. It was evidence of that classic, soft paradox of skateboarding by which injuries become more likely when you fall prey to a body's, or maybe a mind's, misguided instincts toward safety. Like the vast majority of all skateboarding failures, my fall that night was due to a commitment less than complete. So, they were watching. So, I was aware of them watching. This part is too basic to write down, but there was no cause for my failure other than: *fear*. Where, I wondered, did the sky go? Bits of street pebble were pressed into my forearm, and my elbow, which was already scarred to complete shit, had opened to reveal a dime-size swell of blood. I stood and walked slowly back up the hill. The blood wobbled a line down my arm until I lifted it and smeared the line with my other hand's thumb, starting in the middle and wiping upward to my palm. Then I bent to rub this bloodied thumb against the curb. And then the rain came.

CHAPTER SEVEN

On Bad Kickflips

I do not remember my first kickflip. Like a number of people, I took a break during the dark year of 1991, when skateboarding was at its absolute most hideous and confused. Skateboarding in 1991 was greasy of skin and stretched of body, a truly putrid crater of aesthetics. At question is whether my first kickflip came before this break or afterward. My friends from this time are some comfort in the matter, but no help.

If before, that would mean I did my kickflip on the shaped, wide-bodied boards of the eighties. Perhaps, for instance, on my friend Andrew's Ray Underhill board as my vague recollection would have it. He says it's possible, maybe in his driveway or on the flat bottom of his backyard half-pipe.

Certainly it did not come on my own Bryce Kanights gargoyle deck, the fattest and most cumbersome board I've ever ridden. Even once we had grasped the physics of our task—the standard mechanics of an ollie but with the front foot's slide tweaked into an outward and even downward, you know, *kick*—successfully flipping these old boards was a high-calorie endeavor. There was no finesse or grace. You'd jump and kick and try to land wherever the board would end up, and you would not believe how many times a half rotation meant landing on an overturned board. Over and over and over again, until you became certain that you were the one person whose feet were incapable of the task. Then, from out of the sky, a beam of heavenly grace or magic would conspire on one attempt to unite board, rotation, and jump into a single shared space-time that everyone who's experienced it, except for fucking me, will remember until their death.

If after 1991, that would mean my first kickflipped board was one of the narrower and more symmetrical new-school models that were, at the time, finding their form. These were pretty obviously easier to flip due to width. But there was also the growth of the board's nose into a shape and size equal to (and eventually bigger than) the tail's. As the board changed, the kicking motion settled into something more subtle, extending forward rather than outward or downward. On these decks, the toe flicked forward would collide with the rise of the nose so that the flip would rotate more flatly. In magazines, this led to photos of extended front legs with upturned toes and the soles of shoes made visible, the board's rear half rising to meet the skater's back foot, which had risen even higher by the familiar bent knees of a well-popped ollie. In video, it meant kickflips performed over objects that, in 1990, were inconceivable.[1]

One important piece of evidence: my kickflip is bad. For a committed skateboarder, to have a bad kickflip is akin, perhaps, to having an adult dog that recognizes but does not respond to its

---

[1]   The best of which in the long history of kickflips I am happy to name here. This would be Mike Carroll's 1993 (1992?) kickflip over the sideways trashcan on the blacktop of Raoul Wallenberg Traditional High School at minute 2:03 of FTC's *Finally* video, just as Posdnuos is rapping his "I've never played a sister by touching where her private parts reside" line from "I Am I Be," not unrelatedly one of the best songs in the history of music.

name. I will not describe the ends to which I've gone to try and "fix" my kickflip, and what small, irregular improvements I've seen. I get by. It is less likely for me to kickflip over something than, say, my friend Zack, whose kickflip is the most compact and regular I've ever seen; but again, I get by. I've even, at times, felt that mine are bad enough to serve as a kind of badge for we who learned or began learning on those fat and noseless relics.

My point is that there are such distinctions in skateboarding, these very small differences that we come over time to recognize in others and understand of ourselves. Some, like the kickflip, are mechanical comparisons between one body's methods and another's. Others are internal. To do a thing fearfully is not the same as to do it recklessly. Watch closely: There is commitment, and there is caution. There is, in fact, an entire spectrum of *how* that, at times, is important enough to take precedence over *what*. To see and recognize and understand these differences is indeed a kind of reading, a habit, a practice.

Some differences are in fact totally internal and private. Among them is a stark distinction between doing the thing and getting the thing on film. And while I am curious about younger skateboarders for whom recording and broadcasting are naturalized steps of existence, I cannot conceive that even they are immune to the difference of feeling in going out alone, unwatched, and without a camera. One way to describe this difference might be to think of one as *practicing* and the other as *performing*, but neither is quite right. More useful at this point to think in terms of means and ends. Skateboarding, a meaningless activity, is at its most meaningless and thereby most natural when it is treated as means alone, a pursuit of itself only, a means to a means.

Someone told me once, a writer who had once been a skater, that someone had once suggested to him to write like he was going out skateboarding, not going out filming. This remains the best and most difficult writing advice I've ever received. But what a life vest to have on hand, this reminder. What a thing to mutter under one's breath in times of despair. There are ways to do the same thing differently. And so, I decided to write for the first time as if I was going out skateboarding, and submitted to a magazine read only by skateboarders. And the truly wild thing is that it worked.

CHAPTER EIGHT

A Very Large Puzzle: On Andrew Reynolds

2012

Because many of us are assholes, and because our passion of choice lacks, thank God, any clear, established standards of value, even the briefest moments of agreement between skateboarders can feel like small miracles. And yet, try and you will be hard-pressed to find someone who genuinely claims that the frontside kickflip[1] belongs to anyone other than Andrew Reynolds.

It's easy to forget, though, that it was Mike Carroll's before it was his. Back then, it was a curb hopper for the streets of San Francisco, a thing to whip over knee-high brick walls. And today, there's no shortage of able practitioners of the form: Donnelly, Crockett, Gillette, Ploesser. The list is long and distinguished.

What makes the trick so indisputably Reynolds's is a matter of transition. In one glaring moment over one famous blue handrail—

---

1   It gets complicated when a skater's rolling backward (or *fakie*), but under standard conditions, to turn frontside is to open your shoulders and expose your chest to the direction of movement. Rotating backside means closing your shoulders and exposing your back, a movement that pairs naturally with the outward flick of a kickflip. A proper frontside flip, by comparison, requires an awkward combination of kicking out and reeling in, pushing and pulling.

a shot that Birdhouse's *The End* gave us three times—he transformed the frontside flip from a whipper to a booster, a floater, and a stomper. Months later, he was named *Thrasher*'s 1998 Skater of the Year.

If there's any real criticism of Reynolds to be found, it's that he's relied perhaps too heavily on the trick for which he's known, that each new video part finds him more or less copying or plagiarizing himself. And plagiarists, wrote the Chilean author Roberto Bolaño, "deserve to be hanged in the public square." But Bolaño also defined a true "classic" as someone who is "able to decode and reorder the canon." This feels more just: imagining each of Reynolds's frontside flips as a kind of homage to himself, a nod to his own younger knees and less disciplined head. Yes, this is better. Each new frontside flip stretches its moment of execution by pointing behind itself, alluding to all those many other Reynolds frontside flips that we recall, in Santa Monica or the one down the Hollywood High 16 or every other one, everywhere. Likewise does each contain a promise for all of the future frontside flips we know we will see, certain there are more to come.

Every conversation about Reynolds eventually becomes a conversation about time. He's balding now and he's lived hard and so we see age crowding around his eyes and forehead, but still, he's a country kid in his face, vaguely afflicted, a boy out at dusk in bare feet scuffling across a backwoods dirt road. The real changes we noticed weren't physical. We watched him watch the Cardiel footage and found ourselves in a kind of echo chamber of heroic worship, sensing that something important or at least meaningful was happening.

Because, for whatever reason, while certain aging pros began years ago to grate and stretch the limits of our faith, and others have fallen off completely, we still don't seem capable of getting enough Reynolds. We can dig a little and find a backlash, but it feels minor and defiant, contrary for the sake of being contrary.

* * *

In *The End*, we laughed at him drinking beers with a monkey and gawked at what he could do, this scrawny kid with a bowl cut. In motion, his spindly arms flailed without any design or strategy.

Then he began stacking Hollywood paper and falling over drunk with Baker, a board company crafted in his image just as Birdhouse had been built around Tony Hawk's. We cheered and laughed at the new skate celebrity and an economy that could support such cartoonish behavior. Was it funny that Reynolds was getting rich, specifically? Or was it funny that any skater was? We heard stories of fluids and powders and different-smelling smokes, watched them puke together, and wrestle, and continue, sort of miraculously, to produce.

At some point, we began hearing about him selling the big house with the private park in the backyard, giving away his Cadillac and *simplifying*, which we gathered, maybe wrongly, was due in part to his divorce. Done with the leather jacket, he turned to a backward baseball cap or cotton skully and T-shirts exclusively. For months it was that green shirt with *FLORIDA* in big block letters.

By then, we'd begun to see the completed transformation and recognize what we'd been watching all along—a theater of adolescence and painful transition. The reckless kid had become a model of control, endurance, and maintenance. He was carving Lance Mountain's pool and riding Spitfires, exhibiting a quiet dominance of his surroundings. On tour, he snuck in FaceTime chats with a daughter he obviously adored. His replacement addiction: Starbucks.

We in turn began to speak of his restraint, equanimity, and a particular kind of leadership. He approached Hawk about his son Riley before any transition was made between Birdhouse and Baker, because Reynolds the adult understood respect.

"I get paid the same as Braydon," he explained. "Dustin tried to ask for more money one time.... I had to tell him, like, everybody gets paid the same.... There's no favoritism."

He wasn't a saint, though. Neckface, street artist and Baker devotee, would say how he still heard stories, and that Reynolds "is weird in other ways now." There remained (remains) an institutional buffoonery to Baker, though it's also clear that their craziest days are behind them. With such ongoing fallibilities in mind, what we've seen of Reynolds sums into a kind of peace I want to call almost spiritual, though not necessarily religious. Having run through his supply of arrogance and adolescent hijinks, he's been left grateful in the way only adults can be.

The best word for this, I think, is *thoughtful*.

Because *can*, of course, does not mean *will*. And here is how Reynolds became even more meaningful to us: we viewed him, as we always had, in comparison to peers—Koston, Berra, Dyrdek, Howard, Thomas—who have each confronted the same unavoidable dilemma of skateboarding, and have responded differently. It is a crisis that you also, if you persist long enough at this most fun thing, will have to confront.

How does one live like an adult while engaging in an activity and lifestyle that are fundamentally childish?

* * *

Age. Aging. The old. Those among us who can feel ourselves crumbling. The bones and aches, the breakdown of tired bodies over years of abuse. The stairs, of course, all of the impacts, but also the rides home in cramped back seats, knees screaming. Hippers. Stitches in our chins and our lower backs scarred entirely. One Advil bottle after the next; Liqui-Gels for fast delivery. The stretching—the sheer annoyance of the daily routine. Reach for your toes. Lie back and lift one knee to your chest, then rotate and push the knee to the floor. Hear the pops of god-only-knows-what happening someplace inside.

Perpetual youthfulness isn't a dream unique to skateboarders, but it's little wonder why we especially fear growing old.

Except…there's a kind of secret that Reynolds and some others among us have learned. While it is true that becoming an adult is hard and bloody and tastes like someone else's spit in your mouth, actually *being* an adult is completely rad. The world begins to make a new kind of sense. Dreams are not destroyed so much as retrofitted by new perspectives. Reality itself is changed by eyes that grow more open.

In fact, once you are standing outside of it, childhood can begin to look a little bit like a prison, one filled with enough free time and super fun toys to convince us that it's the best place there is. The childish dream will cling to you with strong and sticky fingers. It is in nobody's interest but your own, and perhaps your loved ones', for you to leave childhood behind. *So, stay childish!* the skateboard industry screams.

It's no coincidence that the cutoff age for the world's most desirable market is thirty-four. There's simply no profit in adulthood.

* * *

Thoughtfulness does not mean *strategy*, a term of business owners, athletes, and military generals. It means awareness—paying attention to your self's place among your setting, the very large puzzle of which you are only one negligible little piece.

Without awareness there is no gratitude. Without gratitude there is no humility. Without humility we are children, lashing out and wailing.

Thoughtfulness, in a word, means growing the hell up, not despite being a skateboarder but *because* you are a skateboarder. Finding within the activity the very skills to make the transition possible. In Reynolds we saw someone who had done just this, and whom we rightly refer to, still, as The Boss. Justin Regan, the former brand manager for Emerica, put it best: "That's how he simplifies things down. If you want what he's got, do what he does." More and more those days, we were coming to understand what exactly it was that he had. And it looked to our eyes the same way it does to his—pretty damn good.

Or perhaps our bottomless interest in Reynolds is even more basic. Perhaps, ultimately, the reason we love him is the reason we love anyone we've known long enough to see change. We see a life like an arc over time, or a graph. We see the past and the future, a line characterized by peaks and pits and occasional spirals, a shape like something we'd like to skate. And that he's alive, still, and healthier than before, mutes our fears. Looking at Reynolds, we're reminded that transitions are OK. Skateboarding is going to be OK.

This requires repeating: skateboarding is going to be OK.

CHAPTER NINE

On This Ugly World

On December 14, 2012, I drove the familiar 292 miles from Chicago to St. Louis with a friend of mine named Maggie who I had known for years but had spent very little time with alone. I was driving down for the premiere of a local skate film the following night, and she was visiting family. If I recall, we left early enough to beat Chicago's outbound Friday traffic on I-55. It was raining, and I don't think either of us knew what to say for those first hundred or so miles, so we didn't say much. Earlier that morning, a young man had shown up at an elementary school in Newtown, Connecticut, to shoot and kill twenty children between six and seven years old, along with six adults.

We listened to NPR and kept the fan churning against windshield fog. I had my big dog in the back seat, and she kept checking to see if Maggie and I were OK. This dog, man. She knew things. Her radar for human shock and sorrow was remarkably well tuned, and her teeth back then hadn't gone yet, so the breath of her panting was only hot, not sour. She sat forward with her legs just behind the center console, sometimes licking my face, sometimes resting her head on my right shoulder. The radio kept saying the same words about a tight-knit community and the massacre in its heart. Rain thumped onto my Ford's roof and brake lights glowed ahead. We would shift for a time to music until it felt wrong, then return to NPR to hear the same interviews, or interviews so substantively similar there was no telling one from the other. *The community*, we heard, *will have to pull together and move on*.

Once we did begin speaking, the circumstances led us to talk in ways that Maggie and I never had and haven't since. In fact, when I saw her the following night at the premiere, we steered fairly clear of each other. But for those three hours, we spoke at first sparingly, and then in torrents as thick as the rain's. Spoke frankly and without any of the normal guidelines. She spoke openly of her long-term boyfriend and whether they'd get married, the concerns she had, and the source of those concerns that traced deep into her past. I spoke of K, who I'd been dating for a year and assumed I'd marry, though why, why marriage, I wasn't sure. We confessed and spoke of arguments and sex. Deep and secret fears. I know that I cried at least twice, and would like to say, without it sounding dramatic, that we could have spoken of anything inside that car. The three of us were a family, and we spoke as a defense against the death cult of the country whose so-called heart we were driving through. The conversation might have led to any outcome. We might have skidded into traffic or pulled over and stepped nakedly out into the storm. Veered wildly off course and started over with a shared life or two entirely new and separate lives.

None of that happened. The dog kept us safe, and I dropped Maggie off at her parents' and saw her the following night at a nightclub that was filled to capacity for the premiere. And what I'd like to say, here, is that the energy inside that crummy-ass, two-bit club was uncannily similar to what we'd experienced in the car. It was a family—pain and loss and catastrophe were only rumors delivered from some distant planet. The whole of the outside world stood in stark opposition to the interior world of skateboarding.

Looking back now, it does seem that this was my biggest confusion during my early attempts at writing about my life's most fun thing. The world, I knew, was ugly. Skateboarding, I believed, was beautiful. Nyjah's affront was a matter of cold efficiency out of place. Nike's scheme was an invasion—skateboarders had been dazzled by shiny trinkets and wooed by extra leg room on flights abroad. There is a barely hidden wish for revelation that I hear when I look over these chapters, an old hope for a kind of reverse rapture whereby all but the most devout are taken away.

CHAPTER TEN

Making Up Legends in the Era of Zero-Budget Skateboarding

2012

Skateboarding is about nothing if it is not about itself. We are the people on the street talking to ourselves without shame or remorse. Even as we're doing it we are watching it done—it is beneath our feet, it's the crew at the spot, the park strangers and unknowns we turn to see whenever we hear wheels in the distance. Every act is allusion and every trick is a reference, and we are ace students of our own history.

Anytime we talk about skateboarding, our goal is to name and connect distinct parts into some kind of whole. For example, I say, "Isn't it amazing, the way we can raise and lower our standards without any guidelines, depending only on circumstance?" And every skater will know how this goes—the way you applaud a friend struggling to land a trick that for you is a warm-up. It is a strange and formless competition that is also total support, and we all know it; a ground-floor joy at the mere fact of our activity's existence.

So, in support, I decided to drive through a low, soupy winter haze from Chicago to St. Louis and attend the premiere of a local video called *St. Losers*. A couple years back, a trailer claimed *St. Losers* would arrive "Summer 2011." This was bullshit, of course, but the type of bullshit we forgave, because the teaser was sharp and seemed to capture something about a city that is difficult to explain. The final product wouldn't arrive until a rainy Saturday night in mid-December, more than a year late, at a scummy and disheveled gallery space squatting dead-faced on the developing blocks that people in St. Louis watch closely with guarded optimism.

What do you know about skateboarding in St. Louis, Missouri? Do you know that since early 2009, the city's best spot has been an expansive community DIY project beneath the Kingshighway Bridge called "Shitside" that you aren't supposed to call "Shitside" even though "Shitside" does everything that a good name should do? Do you know that in the summer, the St. Louis air weighs on your body and soul like a great flaming guilt that you will never outrun? Watch *St. Losers* and you will see Rust Belt decay and wild, nameless plants growing through splayed blacktop in thick, bushy mounds. You'll see spots that VX footage[1] portrays as interesting and fun but have almost uniformly shitty, rough ground with oil slicks and deadly cracks and miserable, awkward run-ups.

What I am saying is that *St. Losers* satisfies the basic task of all skate videos in that it promotes a product. At heart, it's all product; skateboarding lives and dies by product; its veins course with seasonal releases of constantly updated product. What's refreshing about *St. Losers* and other videos like it is that there's nothing beyond the video to buy. Its only real product is the city where it was filmed and the people who live there. With Alex Kehoe's opening kickflip to stair rumble in the Kiener Plaza fountain, *St. Losers* stands its city naked before you, knobby-kneed and gaunt and ready, for better or worse, to suffer your gaze.

---

1   The party line case for the continued use of Sony's VX1000 in 2012, nearly two decades after its release, and even still today, is that it is light and nimble and has a microphone perfectly suited to the varied percussion that skateboarding makes. Also true is that skateboarding is a collector's avenue that fetishizes and revels in the archaic, and delights in prolonging life by way of electrical tape and obstinate will.

Alex is flow[2] for 5Boro and skates like it, slashing onto walls
and cramming tricks into barely sufficient space. His feet are quick
and light and he has what the city has forced upon him, which I'm
going to call *vision*. And when he ollies from a private residence's
front porch, over its concrete railing and clearing the sidewalk
below to land in a sharp and crunchy bank that coughs him down
a quick curb into an old and haggard city street, it's clear the kid
has another quality rare for his age, which is grace.

In fact, the entire video exudes a kind of authorial gracefulness
for which Gabe Kehoe, Alex's older brother, deserves more praise
than he'll get. Gabe speaks of a simple aesthetic, "Not a lot of extra
bullshit"; but that's humility for you. Consider, for example, Gabe's
choice to follow his brother with a local legend of small stature and
wizard feet named Joe Jackson. Like any local legend, Joe's part
cannot do him justice, but credit Gabe for coming close, and for
recognizing the role context plays in a full-length video. History,
after all, the oxygen without which skateboarding wilts into something lifeless and ugly, is only as compelling as the shapes formed
when it's set into relief with the present.

See also Gabe's choice of the video's ender, which goes not to
Randy Ploesser or Drew Etzkorn but one Joe Herbert, an aging
St. Louis mainstay who's donated to skateboarding two tired knees
and truckloads of salvaged materials that made the city skateable.
Joe's own ender, appropriately, is a switch hurricane[3] across a ledge
that did not exist before he found it and glued the angle iron
onto it. Whether you enjoy *St. Losers* will hinge in large part on

---

2   A state of unofficial sponsorship beneath amateur and professional and
    derived from the slang verb for the product distributed (flowed) from
    the skate companies upon a hill to promising young skaters down in
    the muck.
3   A frontside spin into what amounts to a backward feeble grind, which
    I realize doesn't help much if I don't explain "feeble," but I really do
    think "hurricane" conveys the degree of this trick's extreme torque and
    off-kilter lean, and as for switch, let it mean unnatural, harder than it
    needs to be, done with the wrong feet.

your response to these two Joe-ass dudes from Missouri of whom you've never once heard. Welcome to our new era of zero-budget skateboarding.

The next step is, of course, to debate whether this development is good or bad for skateboarding. For most of our history, ours has been a blunt-tool discourse based on a kind of Fisher-Price ethics. Shop decks and blanks were "bad" for skateboarding. Increased popularity and contest purses are "good" for skateboarding. Real-time scoring rubrics and fantasy leagues? "Good," says Rob Dyrdek. Tony hawking discount boards at Target and Walmart? Good? Skateboarding, I mean to say, has a long record of denying the vast gray desert between these two imaginary poles where the actual world takes place.

But the other word here is every bit as problematic. We say "skateboarding" and nod, yes, because it's obvious. This obviousness, though, is dangerous. By now, we have all heard some version of this refrain: "Despite our previous resistance, we now believe that Corporate Entity X should be embraced because it gives back to skateboarding." As if, that is to say, skateboarding needs anyone's help. As if there were no skateboarding before the smooth, perfectly poured plazas and contest tour circuits. As if skateboarding were some emaciated street dog living on table scraps and spare change. Yet this is the way the industry will speak of itself when convenient—we are happy to massage and torque and compromise the term "skateboarding," splitting it at the seams. For any of this rhetoric to work, "skateboarding" must mean a lifestyle. Fashion choices. A way of mind. And still the rest of us nod yes, fuck yeah, *skateboarding*.

So, the word has been stretched like the industry it sometimes denotes. And with this growth has come conflict: one does not have to be Trotsky to see a growing class divide among the ranks of skateboarders. (Bomb the corporations, some holler, because they ain't skateboarding. Burn the factory down and let God, who skates Indies, or Matt Hensley, who is God, sort them out.) Indeed, the rich are crazily rich, considering their profession. We've got a few we could call middle-class—they have pro boards but not pro shoes, perhaps, or a pro truck with, like, Orion. Then we have a swelling, anonymous army of unpaid, unsupported kids who are always better, always improving, and making movies that are weird and innovative and sometimes just astoundingly good theater.

Whether what we're seeing is something new or a renaissance of a simpler age, a pastiche or nostalgia film, we watch these zero-budget films and our expectations are loose. We are pleasantly surprised. It's an altogether different experience than watching Girl and Chocolate's 2012 skate blockbuster *Pretty Sweet* for the first time and worrying you won't like it, or won't be able to say why you don't like it, or being confused and unsure and feeling like you've been chumped, somehow, though you've no idea by whom. That somewhere, somebody is laughing. Here is what interests beyond skateboarding do to "skateboarding."

Except, how could it not be good? We see them drinking champagne in Aspen. They show us their new cars on Instagram, and they are always grateful to skateboarding. And since I'm a skateboarder, too, it's even sort of like they're thanking me personally. And that feels good, sort of.

Randy Ploesser does not drink champagne, but he is very smart. "You get a stronger sense of who skateboarders are when you see them skating at home," he told me. "Something about digging for your own spots in a place that you've skated for years; it appeals to me way more than seeing guys being carted around on tour to the best and brightest spots the world has to offer."

Today, you can click to see Randy's part and others because this is the magic of the age: access free of charge to new products, endless products, every single day. You will not, though, know the feeling on that mid-December night in St. Louis, Missouri, when the gallery lights dimmed and the assembled crowd exploded with all hands and voices rising, the thunder of this city's support like something to stand back and behold.

Gabe says it wasn't complicated: this is the way the city works. He gives us Hi8 and 16 mm shots of the city, the grain of film the only real stylistic signature of an otherwise level-handed production. When stood next to its closest coastal peers, *St. Losers* will feel subdued. The best explanation I can give for this is probably, again, humility.

The three and a half minutes that Randy Ploesser filmed for his hometown's nonboutique strip mall shop is bookended by two ollies. The first, over grass, is large. The ender, over and across a small nation of cobblestone, is impossible. Tucked between these is a concise and convincing argument on behalf of the middle-class professional skateboarder. He wallies into feeble grind on a rail that bounces when he pops out. He torques a frontside tailslide into a switch 5-0, and does a nollie front-bluntslide that makes less sense the more I watch it. His board flips a total of eight times and he skates one tree, plus several other spots that are not even remotely Things Someone Should Skate. He grinds a very tall rail out of a steep bank that is barely as long as his wheelbase. The rail, when he pops, is at his chest. But it's that ender ollie that's the real story. He's down on the riverfront, the bank of the mighty bitch itself, cold and muddy and choppy in the autumn wind. We watch him from above, pushing hard in a jacket made by a company that no longer exists, and shoes that arrive only sporadically to his door. Gabe cuts to a side angle. You can't really make out the nature of the bump of the weird drainage sluice, but Randy soars out of it and over a field of old cobblestones, and the board tilts beneath his feet as if it can't quite believe how long the ollie is taking. Then we see it a second time, from above. Neither is describable in writing and neither can even remotely be *scored*. And if you've ever seen Randy skate, you know he can do all of this, no matter how little sense it makes, because this is the odd and bizarre and distinctly unmarketable beauty of skateboarding. This, Randy's video part, his jacket, the wind and the sluice and the board tilting beneath his feet, these are what that word *must* signify, somewhere in all the rest.

The beauty of these homegrown videos is the way they reveal the worlds inside the world, a rich landscape of subcommunities that define their own "skateboarding." They remind us that we can recognize and respect legends like Eric Koston while also understanding that he no longer requires our support—he's in other hands now, and they are soft, supple, and very rich indeed. But young Ishod Wair does, and Sean Malto, too, regardless of their footwear. And Steve Nesser and Jake Johnson and Gilbert Crockett and the bucketful of other pros actively invested in the communities that made them.

Because there are exactly two ways that this life reminds us of our communities. The first is the morning of December 14, is catastrophe. The seas rise up and the levees break and despair sets in and we mourn what's been lost. Candles are lit, prayers muttered, and we appeal to that invisible framework for a return to blessed normalcy. *The community*, we're told, *will have to pull together and move on*. And, miraculously, communities do.

The second is the evening of December 15, is celebration.

Here is the point. We get exactly one go on this boat float, friends. The river moves one way, and like it or not, there is no undoing what's done. But look, a bunch of us are already here, and have been for years. They've stocked the coolers and huffed air into the rafts and are happy to share—someone brought meat and someone else brought plastic forks, charcoal, and the greatest part of all this is that you're invited. Everyone is invited. Enjoy the scenery and be witness to the performance that is always new and always improved. But be advised: to participate in this good-time float trip you'll have to chip in. People are going to capsize and will require help. You might be asked to stand guard while someone takes a shit in the woods. And damn right you'll have to ante up for those beers.

So buy *St. Losers*. Buy *Red and Yellow*, *Worship Friendship*, *Sabotage 3*. Buy a shop deck and a Send Help board. Buy Brimley. Buy *This Machine Kills Fascists* and *Hoephase* and *Videophile*. And if you will not, at least spare us the self-congratulatory bluster for the moral smoke screen you've crafted to feel good about your choice, the faux rebellion and righteousness. That you've numbed yourself to community does not make your hands any less bloody. We're either in this thing together, fucker, or we're tunneling for the core.

On the night of December 15, 2012, there were shots poured into little dentist cups and low-grade American beers served in stretched aluminum cans. We watched a rough draft of a video that you can purchase at any second by clicking the proper links and sharing basic financial data. You do not even have to stand up or put on pants. By now, select parts can be seen online. These will likely breeze through the squinty purview of skateboard culture at large, disappearing quickly into the archive. Some will see the video and be part of the conversation. Most will not. But on this rainy night, we heard the clatter of wheels over the deep, fatal cracks that run like nerves across our old and busted city. There were men and boys and girls and even a few women; all told, we packed four hundred bodies into an underfunded and poorly run gallery-cum-nightclub, ranging from parents to scumbags to those rare heroes who are both.

Because this was Missouri, goddamn, and this was a night to look into a shattered bathroom mirror and believe in our defects, our gravel streets and chunked concrete, the overgrown lots and clearance aisle vacancies.

We celebrated in a way that was itself a thing to step back and behold. This is the reason Gabe documents his city, and why you do as well, why we all do. This is why I've bothered to write it down. All that we're ever doing is making up legends.

PART TWO

CHAPTER ELEVEN

On the Obvious

(ONE)

My still-wife K and I sit together in the sun, up among the barely budding trees at midafternoon. It is windy and crisp, and the sun is distant but extremely comforting and kind-seeming. From the terrace we can watch the neighborhood go about its cautious movements. We see the neighbors out front with their boy and his grandparents. He's got his little toy skateboard and mohawk helmet. K is beneath a woven blanket with white fringe that sways a crisp shadow on the concrete. Spread across her lap is an ancient and very soft dog with foggy, empty eyes, bumps across her body, and a murmurous heart.

The big dog has passed by now, my perfect friend. This dog's name is Mimsy and today is the seven-year anniversary of her adoption. I came out here to put together a new board, and now I'm using the sun as an excuse to clean out my bearings. Despite having worked all morning, despite the glory of the afternoon and a wide-open schedule, I feel myself dragging. The other night, I argued with an old college friend, Tom, who the quarantine has brought back into my life for weekly poker games after years apart.

Like others in these months of downtime, Tom is a nonskater newly intrigued. I am the person to whom people like Tom talk about skateboarding. I have become the great receiver of links to skate-adjacent content and fielder of all relevant questions. Tom and I argued over whether skateboarding is a form of exercise. He insisted, you sweat, don't you? And I issued a scoff drawn from the very depths of my soul. If there is exercise it is by happy accident, secondary to skateboarding's purpose, which is fun. But out here now in this beautiful day, I'm not particularly driven to go push around. It is strange—I sense that I *should*, and it all feels a bit the way exercise feels, duty driven, like maintenance.

Seven years ago, Mimsy had no musculature and nipples so distended that they hung almost to the ground. She looked, I recall thinking, more like a musical instrument than a dog. For a time, K insisted that she would only foster Mimsy, then foster whatever dog needed her next, and so on. But Mimsy is special in her needs, and her face is…unreasonable. Impossible. She is a small, gray, and terrifically cute shih tzu, and from the moment she arrived it was obvious to anyone nearby that K was going to adopt her permanently, but for a time, she seemed intent on pretending otherwise.

So, I am thinking about the obvious as I pop the rubber shield off of the next bearing, preparing to drop and swirl it around in the little metal bowl of brake cleaner at my feet. The shields do what they're supposed to, but there is some debate whether their obvious benefits against dust and grime are worth the trade-off of the better, louder sound of going shieldless. The sun when it is like this is nothing short of a gift. I hold the bearing up in the light so I can see the seven balls that make the thing spin. It's easy to forget this part of a skateboard's equation, the fifty-six tiny metal spheres without which nobody goes anywhere. A global pandemic has us encased in this home with little freedom to stray, and I've become curious what it means to know something or someone too well.

(TWO)

For a time, I lived with a received editorial note rattling inside my head. Whenever I believed I'd escaped it, I'd hear a cough from the dark, rear zone of my mind. When a writer is so struck by editorial feedback, it generally means that the feedback is true, and that the writer knows it. Such knowledge is rarely pleasant. The only way to move on from this unpleasantness is to work your way into some kind of peace with the note. This is one step of what we call growth, becoming a better and more adroit and sensitive writer.

I'm not certain that all artistic growth comes from crisis, but much does, and much of what I aim to create in my classrooms are moments of controlled, private crises that will plant themselves inside students' heads and haunt them. Of course, coming to peace with the difficult note or lesson, the crisis, does not mean coming to agree with it. The better I understand what the writer is up to, the better job I can do providing feedback. Times when I fail to properly see what the writer is up to, I hope that the crisis of my challenge is one that they resolve by deciding: thanks, but nah. If I've done my job as a teacher, this *nah* will be the result of their earned confidence in their aesthetic project and its methods. Sometimes their *nah* is just them being wrong, which happens.

The seed of my own crisis came from an admired critic during her pass over the essay I wrote about skateboarding in Peoria:

> I honestly don't understand this whole Carnie aside. If he's serving as a juxtaposition against Wallace, he's honestly too obvious. I don't think these parts add to the piece as a whole, or say anything interesting about Wallace.

I should say that I was writing above my weight, reaching for a level of discourse befitting the journal, whose reputation was in no small part due to this critic's name on the masthead. It's true that the writing I've done for these general, higher-brow publications has been my most labored and tight. How frightened I have been, for much of my life, of being thought banal. To have my work called "too obvious" by an admired critic was like having my chest excavated and dined upon. I wanted to say *nah* but couldn't shake the suspicion that the engine of fraudulence by which I'd sputtered my way into her purview had come to a smoking and deserved end.

The truth, though it took me years to really understand it, was obvious enough that I'm embarrassed now to type it. *It wasn't about me.* The critic's comment assumed, as if it were obvious, that David Foster Wallace was my subject. But the essay is not about David Foster Wallace. It is about fun and boredom and hero worship, and the parallel endeavors of writing and skateboarding and the cheap, public simulacra of fun that end up working against the very thing they're prefabricated to facilitate. It is about quarter-pipes that drop you directly into walls. By "this whole Carnie aside," the admired critic meant skateboarding. Was this because skateboarding is it-self banal? I have a feeling that, to her, the answer is yes. She was familiar. She knew of the thing and its culture, had probably moved among skaters in the past and seen the way some refused to give it up, how they clung to the childish toy in the most obviously stunted ways.

Well, being over it has its allure. And what, really, does a book critic care of fun? Someone, please document the history of fun in world literature so we can learn to talk of it productively. I think of what Anna Karenina says to Levin, that his reputation as a skater precedes him, and "I should like to see you skate. Put on your skates and we will skate together." Very good. But is it fun? These "masters in the art of skating, who came to show off their skill"? Who "skated as gymnastic exercise"? God, no! Critics like very much to speak of the flâneur, yes, and of leisure as a class signifier etcetera as per the Frankfurt school, but fun qua fun is too obvious for their time.

In fact, were I to rank types of writers by how much fun they are capable of and interested in being, I would start at the top with essayists, adventurous and experimental and no-fucks-given, take-it-or-leave-it essayists. Next would come musicians, the lyricist, and then short story writers who also write novels, then playwrights followed by novelists, and then story writers who do not write novels, academics, poets, and then long-form nonfictionists and journalists, and here I'll just speed things up by grouping any other writer you might come across, every single other type including copywriters and designers who are sometimes asked to write and the people who write up church service pamphlets and everyone else under the sun and then, all the way down at the very absolute bottom of the list, would be erudite literary critics who suffer for *believing* that they are fun when they are absolutely not. They have three martinis at dinner parties and wake up the next day thinking, Oh what ridiculous things I must have said last night!, but they are never really present anywhere in any passing moment because they are always just above wherever and whenever it is, surely they are somewhere joke dancing right now in a safe and disengaged way, thinking of how it will all seem tomorrow, from a distance.

(THREE)

To read Borges is to read all that Borges read, which is everything. Whenever I find myself doubting—and therefore arguing most fervently on behalf of—skateboarding's importance, I turn to Borges and his three-page history of the universe, in which the sphere is recurrent metaphor for mankind's struggle to comprehend the universe, and God, and our relationship to both. The sphere, an obvious analogue for God, all points of its surface equidistant from the center. Or there is Borges's writing on the tango, Argentina's proud creation of questionable literary value. To Borges, the tango is a dance whose meaning and importance can be debated, but still "it guards, as does all that is truthful, a secret."

I also, as I am doing now, here in the sun on the terrace with my still-wife and our little dog, like to get a little greasy and mechanical with the thing itself. No skateboarder with any self-respect will let another person apply griptape to their board. For me, it is always a plain black sheet somehow offset, as I've said, so that I can thoughtlessly recognize the board's direction. Others will cut and collage elaborate patterns, shapes, and colors of grip. Some enjoy tinkering endlessly with the relative softness of the polymer bushings that control the tightness and looseness of the truck, their resistance and yield to a body's lean and thus the radius of carved turn they allow. Is it such a strange thing that I want to poeticize this object and see how it might function as a heuristic? Is it folly to wonder if skateboarding guards its own secret?

The still-wife and still-husband joke is one that allows K and me a certain proximity to the otherwise dangerous reality of our marital struggle. It is a presence, our struggle, so obvious that we could easily ignore and go on living with it for the rest of a long and vaguely dissatisfied and dishonest life together. Mimsy is blind and suffers from dementia that leads her to wandering into corners and walls. K and I like to announce to each other the times when, as we say, Mimsy is "in a strange place." This could mean behind the couch, beneath the succulents. It could mean sitting normally and facing the closet door. She is so weird, this dog. And in truth, it feels flatly wrong to speak of her "suffering" from anything these days, given the first eight years of her life spent inside of a small, filthy cage somewhere in southern Illinois, churning out litter upon litter of puppies that were taken to be sold in chain stores and other outlets.

How quickly and thoroughly an existence can change. One day, riding a skateboard is all that you can think of doing, so you rush out to meet friends and engage the most fun thing mankind has concocted, freedom incarnate. The next day, you're told, "Sorry, no more friends, no more meeting, no more engagement." Now, you are locked inside a home with a spouse, dog, and this obvious struggle you must take care to look directly into lest it become something so obvious that you stop seeing it. I can sit on the terrace and clean these spheres and know that right now the city is vacant, its plazas and ledges are unguarded and unpeopled and just waiting to be played upon. But to skateboard alone is not fully to skateboard. I have known this for years, but never like this.

Or another one: one day you're friends and the next you're lovers. How obvious, this shift, and good. But in the suddenness of that initial change, a fragility is also implanted, a precedent set, and doubts seeded. Should we have remained the way we were? We did not fight this way, before. We did not, as friends, cause each other such pain. How quickly a mode of being turns over into another. You are together, and then you're not. Married one minute. Unmarried the next. Though, *unmarried* is not the term we use for this state, is it.

CHAPTER TWELVE

Toward a Poetics of Skateboarding

2014

> *Voice 1:* What's that thing he's on?
> *Voice 2:* It's a board with wheels!
> *Lorraine Baines:* He's an absolute dream.
> —Robert Zemeckis

Nothing so comforts a mind as presumed understanding. The steadfast belief in one's own knowledge will always, and by far, outstrip the more difficult experience of the genuine object. Such, generally, is the challenge of modern alterity. I can know enough to not want to know you without knowing anything, and here the conversation more or less dies.

More specifically, it was the case in 2014 with what we call skateboarding. Sixty years since its strange birth, so wholly incorporated, so atomized and dispersed had skateboarding been into worlds of fashion, music, and endless confections of cultural debris that we had been numbed, or blinded, to the fundamental senselessness and mystery in its heart. Such mistakes of comprehension function as erasures, like staring so long through a chain-link fence that it disappears.

On one side, skateboarding has a clear antecedent in surfing, that ancient practice even Europeans have been hip to since 1870. On the other, there's a growing fleet of malnourished progeny— snowboarding, wakeboarding, trampboarding...anything today can be "boarded." We might sense an echo of the tumbling sports in the activity, as with diving, gymnastics, or figure skating. From these it was easy to envision schematics for judging its perfor- mances, and regulated competitions, even leagues, even season tickets, scorecards, and foam fingers for the family. Followed to their logical conclusion, such metrics do gravity's task for the market, working against any mysterious buoyancy and grounding the activity to sensible cognates.

Indeed, today the gerund *skateboarding* refers as frequently to the marketplace that's formed around the activity as it does to the activity itself. This is a $5 billion industry drawing on, by one count, twenty million participant-consumers. By another, it's forty million. Enough, anyway, to amass into a thick, chitinous shell. It's no wonder the activity lost grip on its language of self.

But for all of its private jargon, skateboarding's poetry has never been linguistic. It is forever embodied, its expression physical, nonverbal, and also, though this is difficult to speak of seriously, spiritual. How else to explain its sudden appearance in Uganda without even a single retail outlet to support it? And so, for the most part, serious speech has been absent. In fact, the only conveyable language of skateboarding, outside of participation and socialization in the activity itself, has always been spoken through film.

In broad terms, skate media splits time between documentation and advertisement, and their commercial evolution has skewed ever more crass and spectacular. Recent work from select video artists, however, attempts to confront the activity's basic mystery and mean- ingful meaninglessness. Nonskateboarders have tended not to look very closely at these films. They mostly do not care. Skateboarders, meanwhile, care far too much to care exactly why. In any case, it's here that an attempt toward a poetics of skateboarding must begin.

* * *

A poetics can come from any number of angles, though they'll generally end in a mixture of morphology and a kind of latent promotion for the form in question. Such was Darko Suvin's goal in his divisive 1972 essay, "On the Poetics of the Science Fiction Genre." Unlike myth, fairy tale, and the broad category of what Suvin calls "fantasy," science fiction deserved serious consideration—which is to say, academic study—for its practice of cognitive estrangement. By laying out a poetics of "significant" science fiction, Suvin hoped to separate its more legitimate work from the "debilitating confectionary" so pervasive in the genre.

Nor can we call such an effort unselfish. My own struggle with the mystery of skateboarding began five years ago, twenty-three after I first stepped onto a board, when I began work on my second novel. Skateboarding, as people before me have noted, is difficult to write about. Tempting as it may sometimes be, one cannot in good faith dismiss any of skateboarding's so-called confectionary, can't exclude and whittle toward a narrow definition of best practices. Contra Ian MacKaye, skateboarding today *is* a sport, and a hobby as well, along with countless other things: a therapy, an obsession, a conservative anti-drug. In its basic meaninglessness, skateboarding has become the tool that takes the shape of whoever's hand it's in.

To poeticize an object is to weigh its usefulness as a heuristic. Doing so requires a sense of history, which for skateboarding begins in postwar America, though nobody knows quite where or when. The prevailing legend starts with a scooter with its handlebars broken, or perhaps stolen. The fictionalized origin tale lodged within 1985's *Back to the Future* is as close as we can get. Marty McFly, having just clocked Biff Tannen inside the charming diner, flees by foot onto Hill Valley's town square. There, he commandeers a milk crate scooter from a boy, rips the crate from the base, and flees on the handleless board *much* faster and more nimbly than he would have on a scooter, managing an improbable 180-degree skid turn to grab a passing pickup and skitch by the diner's window. By the sequence's end, Biff Tannen is covered in manure and we sense that the wide-eyed boy to whom Marty returns the mysterious "board with wheels" is done with milk crates forever.

In any case, the first skateboards were flat, narrow planks of timber affixed to rigid frameworks stolen from roller skates. Their wheels were metal at first, and then clay, and their riders wove shirtless through Annette Funicello and Sandra Dee films. At the time, there must have been something uncanny about their appeal; the skateboard tapped into a long mythos of four-wheeled objects with uninflated wheels—the carriage, red wagon, dolly, and other labor-driven devices aimed at conquering space and time. By 1965, they were kind enough to disappear.

Thank technology for skateboarding's second act. First came the early 1970s realization of soft, grippy polyurethane to replace the brittle, rattling wheels of tradition. The new wheels changed the very nature of skateboard movements: now there was friction to lean back against and leverage into sharp turns across schoolyard embankments. Suddenly, there was style to the activity, tucked knees and dropped arms, along with a new factor of progression. Bigger and faster, of course, because this was America. But also stranger, with previously unconsidered lines finding new expression across bland schoolyard blacktops. Style did this. These were hitherto unseen, even unconsidered maneuvers harvested from the ether or revealed in private dreams, and their expression meant a process of reinterpreting the landscapes of Southern California. And with the region's record droughts came restrictions on how and when property owners could use water, leaving hundreds of swimming pools unfilled, vulnerable, and fertile.

Quickly, then, did the *Geist* of skateboarding shift, or more accurately, emerge. What in those first years had fit awkwardly into a de facto rubric of athletics—a sport to be timed and judged for athletic merit—became in the 1970s something more rhetorical. The ethos was the punk scavenging for revolution by way of repurposing. Whatever prefigurations of the object we had seen, never before had they been deployed creatively. To use novelist, Marxist, and Weird-theorist China Miéville's term, what emerged was something counterposed to the comfort of the uncanny. The activity, new, unrecognized, and bounded only by imagination, was *abcanny*.

For the forty years that followed, two forces—one internal, rhetorical, and senseless, the other imposed by the external marketplace and institution of sport—waged a sort of weaponless war. In the 1980s, the venue shifted to constructed ramps and parks, and the arguments receded as once again the culture embraced the language of competition and commercialism, the fluorescent decadence of ready-made half-pipe spectacles. But beneath this reflective surface grew a new, parasitic zine culture, one that would become the backbone of DIY independence that would prove necessary in the coming decade, when skateboarding's private golden era overlapped with the nadir of its social standing. How simple it was in the 1990s! Skater fags were fags and jocks were jocks, and from this rigid order came a hateful but firm harmony. This clarity diminished in the millennium, as skateboarding's outcast aesthetic moved gradually toward that threshold of cool to eventually bleed back into mainstream culture. Here it has stayed and swelled and lost much of the revolutionary impulse it once embodied. This, we acknowledge mournfully, is the nature of commoditization.

* * *

We know on first glance that skateboarding, in its dominant form of street activity, stands apart from ball and net athletics. It seems uninterested, too, in velocity and stopwatch performances. But the first challenge to the rubric of sport begins even lower, at a semiotic level. You and I could, if we wanted, go and shoot lazy jump shots at a netless schoolyard hoop, or go to the driving range and smack buckets of balls into the green void. We could take our gloves to the park and throw grounders and pop flies and apply tags to invisible runners. But for any of these to qualify as *basketball*, *golf*, or *baseball*, we would require the structure of competition and order of rules.

Systems such as these have no bearing on skateboarding, in which even the most negligible acts, no matter how brief or private, are simply *skateboarding*. Consider: between my home and the nearest skate park is a well-paved boulevard with sewer caps embedded into the blacktop every half block or so. A source of joy for me is to push down this boulevard and pop tiny ollies over these sewer caps, sometimes barely scraping my tail, other times popping hard and pulling my knees up to my chest. These are not tricks proper, just ways to see and engage with the street's reality. This is not, as athletes might call it, practice; I am not training for a future event. It is travel, yes, but the joy has little to do with the scenery or distance covered. In the purview of skate competition, this pushing down the boulevard, the most fun I have in any given day, is not a scorable act of skateboarding. And yet this fun *is* skateboarding—it is worth zero and it is worth everything.

In a world increasingly data driven and surveilled, skateboarding lives beneath scoring and resists all datazation by establishing everything as a performance. It deflects the surveillance state by its primal devotion to documenting and sharing itself, monitoring every possible development, repetition, and failure. It preempts the onslaught of observation by embracing it. To preempt is to deflect, but also to admit defeat. Luckily, skateboarders are shameless—in this way, they're the perfect actors to play the role of themselves.

Our potential heuristic now approaches what literary and cultural theorists today speak of, with a smirk, as the so-called authentic self. It wasn't long ago that Zadie Smith swung the "myth of authenticity" ax to split the tree of the Western novel in two. But a skater, whether standing on a stage, behind a camera, or at a keyboard, sees and thinks and performs precisely as what and who he is. What other memberships function in this or a like manner? Parenthood. Romantic partnership. Citizenship. Does artistry?

* * *

To date, the most complete attempt to theorize skateboarding has been Iain Borden's *Skateboarding, Space and the City: Architecture and the Body* (Berg, 2001). Borden, a professor of architecture and urban culture at The Bartlett, University College London, treats the activity of skateboarding as a Lefebvrian practice with potential to become its own sort of architecture—not of construction, but by the "production of space, time and social being." He traces the history of skateboarding into the 1990s street skating movement, and speaks of the way this "oppositional subculture" rethinks architecture "as a set of discrete features and elements…recomposing it through new speeds, spaces and times." The gears of capitalism create spaces in which behavior is prescribed and easily accounted for. Skateboarding's opposition is thus a compositional process, partially of the individual body, which is recomposed against the "intense scopic determinations of modernist space," and partially of a deeper critique of urban life: "Production not as the production of things but of play, desires and actions."

For primary sources, Borden dove into a trove of skateboard magazines both American and British. His book is spotted with action photographs taken from these mags, but the static nature of the photographs is Borden's limitation. Because movement is the core of skateboarding's character, and because it is always performative, a poetics of the activity must engage with the visuals and sound of its primary expression: the skate video.

Until very recently, the standard procedure for these films relied on the radical convex of an extreme fish-eye lens. This resulted in a center-heavy obsession with the skater's body, distorting all scale and limiting environmental context. By contrast, today's most compelling skateboarding films aim not only to capture the play of skateboarding, but to enact what Borden calls the "positive dialectic that restlessly searches for new possibilities of representing, imagining and living our lives." The Panoramic Series from

Philip Evans, for example, relieves the actor from the full burden of attention. Here, Evans follows Phil Zwijsen through his hometown of Antwerp. In two shots between 0:33 and 0:43, we see Zwijsen's feet pushing hard from the screen's right to left, our only audio the ambient clatter of wheels over sidewalk seams. Then the camera resets, and we see him harness his labor by appearing in from the right once again and speeding up a bank and onto a wall, landing, and adding a quick no comply[1] that eventually finds him, once more, reaching the frame's left. Breadth, here, the film's aspect ratio, upends the common assumption of skater violence against his chosen terrain. The relationship we see is nuanced, even symbiotic, and exists beneath the trick itself.

Or consider *Quik* by Colin Kennedy, in which one of skateboarding's dialectic relationships—between stasis and motion—achieves a relative synthesis by way of the director's technique. At first, we observe the city as a local might, shot in passing through a car window. The film's only skater, Austyn Gillette, appears only after the environmental context, resulting in a portrait not of one or the other, but both. The subject is, as skateboarding's always has been in practice, the interactions between city and individual body. Alongside recent work by Mike Manzoori, Evan Schiefelbine, and select others, these films find energy beyond the progressive trickery of athletics, or the documentation of extant geographies. They combine the skateboarder's practice—creative, productive—with a distinctly nonskateboarding meta-awareness of the activity's potential for meaning. Their grounding within the *Geist* of skateboarding is obvious: There is nothing a skater spots more quickly than the fraud, or the tourist. These are films made by skateboarders who have lived within the activity's world, and who choose to

---

1   A term for the family of tricks whereby a skater plants one foot on the ground to serve as a point of pivot to spin, or point of leverage to force the board against and over an obstacle, so named by the genius Neil Blender for its overt refusal to comply with a parking block's principle task of stopping motion.

leverage the activity as a tool to understand itself. How long, they ask, must a toy endure before it becomes something else? What does it become, and does this mean it has ceased to be a toy?

* * *

Even still, Thomas Campbell's *Cuatros Sueños Pequeños* arrives as a thing unique, exhaling in one long, sustained, dreamy breath the artist's own approach to skateboarding poetics. Noted today for his sculptures and paintings, Campbell's earliest work came in the 1980s, either as skateboard photography or teenage zine making, depending how we define "work." In any case, the artistic impulses that have shaped his life were themselves shaped by skate-boarding. Without it, he's not sure he would have been a creative person at all.

Shot on 16 mm film, *Cuatros* is, on one view, a return to the form Campbell discovered in 1995's *A Love Supreme*, a languid profile of New York City for a skate shop on Lafayette Street in Manhattan called Supreme. In Supreme's only full video project before 2014's *Cherry*, Campbell exhibits what, for the time, was a unique agnosticism for tricks. Instead, significance is found in the granular warmth of the film, what Campbell speaks of as a dance. Campbell's projects—film and skateboarding, along with his painting, sculpting, sewing, living—are regressive and analog mechanisms.

But here the commonalities between his films end. *Cuatros* opens with Javier Mendizabal moving in and out of focus as he prepares himself for bed. There is no dialogue in the film, and no audio beyond the film's score, which is an instrumental rock affair of the expressionist sort, with leitmotifs and refrains but no clear structure. Mendizabal's first dream opens from a perspective very low on a concrete bridge with red metalwork reaching toward a sharp blue of nearly cloudless sky. Mendizabal comes rolling toward us. Then we see time-lapsed clouds rolling in, viewed somehow from above.

We are drawn through a parade of naturalistic images that have little relation to skateboarding. Mendizabal rolls down a mountain road through verdant green forestry and we watch first from the hillside, then from road level, and then from a helicopter above. Seaside, he dives headfirst into the surf and the sun through the water glimmers like birth. His board is tethered to him by a rope. He emerges, leaves a wet footprint, then descends a walkway alongside a massive set of stairs. He pushes in front of a stunning Spanish monument.

In fact, it's not until nearly three minutes in that we see our first proper skateboarding trick. It is a quiet, impressive ollie across a double doorway set in the natural transition of another bit of Spanish modernist architecture. From this point on, Mendizabal's character engages in what might be a quest, or tour, or even retreat through forest, desert, ocean, and sky. Each shot lasts a matter of seconds in a sequence that, like the music, lingers here or there but lacks a clear through line.

Wonderfully, there is no possible map or atlas to Mendizabal's travels. The search, if it is a search, is for what? Beauty? Check. Occasionally we're shown his sleeping face fading in and out of screen, the sheets of his bed ruffled but his girlfriend asleep peacefully. It is all quite beautiful. But what else? It is never exactly confusing. The search continues and is not, we cannot say that it's in vain. It's a dream scrubbed of all psychoanalytic debris, all leftover fibers of exhausted meanings. There is no argument, per se, but you can feel something working quietly beneath the surface. When we see two figures, one presumably Mendizabal, wearing winged costumes and romping through mountains, we presume the second small dream has begun. Good, we think. Here we go. But this is only a flash before we're following Mendizabal through a series of snaking half-pipes and other pathways. Is there pain, here? He falls, is jostled awake before falling quickly back asleep.

At seven minutes we encounter Madars Apse clapping powdered palms that he holds open to the camera. In real life, Apse is a gangly, blond, and very talented Latvian skater known for irreverence. He and Mendizabal find each other in a Spanish alleyway that we see from above, from the ground, then again from the rooftop vantage point, before they descend another bridge as a pair. Their familiarity is certain; I think of DeLillo's truants gathered outside of the Polo Grounds who "have found one another by means of slidy looks that detect the fellow foolhard and here they stand." This, I think, is how skateboarding works, a tribal recognition I've never quite described. Where did Apse come from? From skateboarding, that active somnolence that recombines extant selves, that revaluates space and time. We infect each other's dreams.

The other discovery we witness is Campbell's, and thus our own—we're discovering this landscape along with his dreamers, and his filmmaker's treatment of the relevant lines and colors is quilted with the skaters'. At times, his compositions take the point of view of the fugitive nestled among the rocks who hears something coming and cannot resist looking, even knowing it could be his end. It is as if discovery were a synonym for fate. It is as if skateboarding's own mysteries are playing out in front of our eyes.

In terms of tricks, *Cuatros* offers, by my count, one every twenty-one seconds—fifty-two total, an even split of twenty-six per dreamer, spread over eighteen minutes and forty-two seconds. This, to be clear, is a laughable rate in terms of mainstream skate media, and turgid even alongside *Quik*'s one trick every 14.32 seconds. But who says trickery has to be the point? Who says there is any point at all? Instead, we are trapped in a labyrinth of alleyways with a disheveled and frantic Apse. First he has his board under his arm, and he's running. Then the board is gone and his frenetic movements get more desperate and awkward, like a grounded bird. The light is low and pale, and still we've no map. Our host, the sleeping Mendizabal, has eyes that turn to clocks running backward. Madness reigns, and all of us, Apse included, search for release.

The *Fin* arrives soon enough, in what might be its first nonironic appearance in the history of skateboarding. But not before Apse takes over the stage of Mendizabal's dream. He is a pale giant, younger and more agile than the original dreamer (and filmmaker, too), the film's final reflection—thus the anxiety of replacement familiar to any skater over the age of, say twenty-four. Our mysterious noun, *skateboarding*, does indeed signify a dialectic between artistic play and competition. We cannot avoid comparing Mendizabal and Apse, nor are we warned against it. The spirit, though, cycles beneath trend and capital, a dream space where the natural world, architectural monuments, and urban space-times overlap. Apse's switch stance ollie of a double set of stairs is an act of avian mimicry. His kickflip firecracker[2] is a dream maneuver, a thing of insane imagination that opens, or reveals, a second dream world that is Apse's own expression—this time, yes, inside the other.

* * *

Roberto Bolaño called surrealism "something convulsive and vague, that familiar amorphous thing." If indeed there is ever to be a poetics of skateboarding, familiarity will have to play a role. Suvin's argument for science fiction's value was a matter of cognitive estrangement. Campbell's film documents and creates ostranenie by the re-presentation of a familiar world as captured by, and portrayed through, the glance of the radical dreamer. In fact, what *Cuatros* does better than any film I've seen is remind us that skateboarding's heuristic usefulness is ontological. Its topos is not "there is a world inside the world," but rather, "there is a world the exact shape and texture of the world that you know, laid seamlessly over top of it, and you, for some reason, fail to see how beautiful it can be."

---

2   Sharing a taxonomic family, perhaps, with the no comply, a firecracker sees the skater cascading down a set of stairs so that the board's tail clatters against each step, making a sound like a well-rolled tongue. Were I forced to name this family I'd probably offer something like "unserious" or "halfway jokey" and promptly duck and cover.

Convulsive, vague, and conveyed by slidy looks. Campbell's subject is our ineffable, binding thing, that lurking, trembling essence that he can only render by images and motions of the surreal. The artist whose art was born from skateboarding has made an object about skateboarding that conveys this birth and mode of being. Skateboarding infects the filmmaker infects the musicians infects the viewer. Viewer goes out skating. Skateboarding is self-perpetuating in this way. It is always itself and something else, it is infectious, it is comprehensive and sublatable to the core. This is how the infinite comes to be—once born, skateboarding can now never die.

But the dreamscape of *Cuatros Sueños Pequeños* is not an expression of this infinity. Rather, it is mimetic. "What world is this?" asks the skateboarder. A familiar one we have seen so many times that it's rendered unseeable. More important, "What is to be done in it?" The second answer, like Campbell's film, is incoherent, and thank goodness. The second answer is anything at all.

CHAPTER THIRTEEN

On Nostalgia

Time, it is said, is the only true gift. Outside of necessities like breathing and sleeping and being the person who responds to "Kyle Beachy," I don't believe I've done anything in my life as much as I have ridden a skateboard. Now, daily, the activity grows more difficult for me to do, and I would be lying if I said this doesn't concern me, doesn't test my capacity to live healthily with dread. So, I have taken, as we do, some comfort in revisiting the past. But cautiously.

Let me describe the car that I drove around suburban St. Louis between 1994 and 1997. It was a turquoise Honda Civic hatchback, the VX model, with a vanity license plate that I am not presently compelled to disclose. It had a manual transmission and a profoundly effective audio system that my friend Rob installed for me. Rob, also, is the reason I returned to skating after that dark year of 1991 and why I am currently a skateboarder. The installation involved two amplifiers. One ran power to the two midrange 6.5-inch speakers in the doors and two 5.25-inch speakers that we cut into the Civic's rear side panels. The other amp was larger, and powered two 12-inch JBL subs built into the custom carpeted box that we built to fit glove-like into the slim trunk—beyond the speakers, there was no trunk. In the three years that the car was mine, its roof grew dimpled by the suck and heave of the bass—I would flick a quarter onto the roof and watch it bounce.

It was my rumbling little aquatic pod. I say turquoise, but the official Honda name for the garish hue was "Tahitian green." On certain days I would flip open the limo-tinted glass of the rear hatch and drive around with a kind of cycling hat's bill, or fish's flipper, feeling the pleasant rip of fresh air. In this way I minimized the burden of air-conditioning on the car's stock battery. The demands of the two amps caused the car to whine ascendingly, you see, whenever the engine revved hot. Air conditioner, headlights, any extra strain made for a squeal that could drown out cicadas. But this was a minor sacrifice in the name of emergent selfhood. I was a small kid into high school, but old, having gone to kindergarten twice. Getting my driver's license coincided with my only growth spurt to speak of, before sophomore year.

It is a fine line to toe, but rather than tell another story of white suburban appropriation of Black culture, I'm trying, instead, to speak the case of a white suburban skateboarder during years when skateboarding *itself* was devotedly appropriative of Black culture. This distinction might strike you as specious or hollow—that is fine. Mine is just one identity that early-nineties skateboarding played a hand in creating among its predominantly white, male practitioners. I was fourteen in suburban, white St. Louis at the time of the Rodney King verdict and ensuing violence. So I, too, found Ice Cube's *The Predator* to be the next step in Public Enemy's and N.W.A.'s dispatches from a different world, but I also had H-Street's video *Lick* on heavy rotation, with Marcelle Johnson skating to "Now I Gotta Wet 'Cha." I had Plan B's *Virtual Reality* and FTC's *Finally* introducing me to Bay Area backpack rap. If I can be said to have understood either skateboarding or hip-hop at that time, then I understood them in concert. Rap in those days was built from braggadocio lyrics, a series of gauntlets thrown at imagined adversaries—listen to how dope, how nice I am on this mic. You, meanwhile, are garbage. Wasn't this skateboarding, too? Look, everyone, at what dope thing I'll do next. Wasn't this stoke?

In those years, I lived with my mother in a modest ranch house in the deepest recess of a fairly steep and smooth incline called Stoneyside Lane. Between our driveway and the neighbors' was a strip of zoysia that made for a decent gap to skate, growing progressively wider as it moved toward the basketball hoop and garage out back. My mother and I had bedrooms on far ends of this house. She and my father had divorced—he stayed in San Diego, where we'd all moved between sixth and seventh grades. Perhaps not coincidentally, this relocation overlapped with that year of 1991 when I stopped skating altogether. Then, halfway through seventh grade, she and I returned to St. Louis, where all of my friends and joys and everything but my father still lived.

I can recall to the most minute detail the conversation when I learned of their separation. Dad and I were playing tennis at the extremely competitive and borderline abusive club that was once at the top of Mount Soledad. I was hitting and moving well enough to take four games from him, and then he called me up to the net between sets. I say "between," but our match was done at that point. And I can recall leaning my forehead on the window inside the airport shuttle van as my mother and I left that house and my father stood in the driveway and I gazed out at him and felt my life's first real sorrow, a sadness complicated and made real by an inextricable glee to be going back home. Anyway, I often left the Civic parked on the street rather than in the driveway, so that on nights when I decided to sneak out I wouldn't wake her.

It is no great mystery the way that nostalgia goes about its work. Gasoline cost ninety cents per gallon. One night I snuck out of the house and successfully snuck into a girl's house to have sex for the first time. Our friend Lyncha gave us free Taco Bell in the drive-through, and I had a shitty job shucking oysters then a shitty job catering weddings, but on Tuesdays we'd sneak out from our school's parking lot, evading a security guard named Glen, and go buy or try to steal the week's new CDs. It was all rap, then— *Blowout Comb* and *Tical*, with *All Eyez on Me* released the *very same day* as *The Score*. And I recall thinking that of all of this, the best of the new freedoms in adolescence was having a place to finally listen to music loudly. These were days when changing a CD meant steering the wheel with one knee while flipping through the massive booklet in your lap.

And skateboarder was I, now, by choice. Of all the models of identity at my disposal, I had opted and opted anew each morning to be a skateboarder. From this one decision trickled down every other, head to toe, from posture to music to my interactions with police. The denim sold by skateboard companies Droors and Blind segued seamlessly into Tommy Hilfiger jeans and Nautica rugbies, broad and colorful knit collared shirts. I had two classes of shoe: one the suede Pumas and classic Stan Smiths, the other patent leather Jordans and Air Max 95s. In other words, my skateboard shoes and my fly guy shoes, with apologies for using these words, but this was it, this is when I really started misunderstanding race. Which is of course the only way white people come to understand race at all.

In those years, my school took part in one of the nation's most substantial desegregation programs, whereby kids who lived in the city—mostly Black kids—could elect to ride a bus each morning and afternoon to attend out-of-district and better-funded suburban schools. That did not stop our common area from being split down the middle by a row of columns with a white side and a Black side all but labeled. So, I am going to suggest something that won't make sense: I believe I was nostalgic for the period even as I was living it. Another way to put this is: I understood the dream that I was inside of. Whatever kind of person I was, or thought I was, I know that I sensed something glimmering beneath the surface of this...thing. I caught a glimpse. It was a pathway, a sneak machine, a tool for slithering into and out of places other people like me didn't go. Remember that this was Missouri, where boys like me wore loafers and linen and pinched dip into their bottom lips and hung Confederate flags on rumpus room walls, took their Jeeps out mudding, and listened to Skynyrd. We said "the hockey team" to refer to the all-whites in their needlepoint belts and Gamecock hats.

In other words, skateboarding was a way to move through space and time. I do not mean to suggest that it made me somehow more generous or kinder or in any way better than my classmates—most of the time, what skateboarding provided me was an answer to preclude any further questions. It was a way to be a person, and I settled into this way and all that it deemed valuable. One such value: to go, to move, to stray. And, too, the value of Black culture by way of hip-hop. But there was no revolution to be found in skateboarding's racial dynamism, no real education. In this 1990s defining era of street skateboarding, young white skaters saw the way dope overlapped with stoke and were, in effect, charmed into a fantasy of equality. It is no wonder the "I don't see color" analogues continue to float through our culture in the form of "we're all just skaters." The dream has its obvious allure. Most dreams do.

CHAPTER FOURTEEN

Pretend We Haven't Grown

2014

We know by now, even the most dire and morose of us, even grumbling Bobby Puleo hunched inside of a small room crowded with art and trash, even as he laces up his dead-stock Ipaths and layers himself against the New York winter. Bobby knows and Ricky Oyola knows, too, and maybe even Birdo by now, wherever he is.

We spent years watching in cold terror as they came reaching their huge invisible hand for our favorite toy in the whole wide world. They were too strong—they snatched it and now they're using it to sell whatever they think it might: shoes, of course, and clothing, but also headphones, knives, and scarves. We have not liked this. We have groaned and protested righteously.

And yet, the activity hasn't died like we feared, or even suffered the slightest injury. Has it? Look, it's been dispersed to distant, strange corners of our globe and psyches, where it continues to morph into different shapes and colors of deformed and perverse glory. Consider the expeditions to post-Communist Bosnia and Herzegovina or the Amazon basin. Consider the ditch tribes of the American Southwest, fluorescent and flamboyant and utterly without care. Consider the frank interviews of professionals willing, all of a sudden, to speak openly and honestly, and their new, strange projects for which "bottom lines" are a hilarious concept. Consider the liberation of a postboom declining marketplace.

And there's even a certain amusement we feel, isn't there, for the most crass and commercialized events they've concocted for the sake of sales? The Street League experience is, if we're being honest, actually fucking awesome, the way Las Vegas is awesome, or Times Square, or a huge crowded Walmart is awesome.

Maybe now's when I should tell you that I am on drugs, namely a whale's dose of hydrocodone because my left clavicle has been splintered into four pieces that are jagging into my flesh whenever I move even slightly. I am home from work all week, immobilized and horizontal on the couch while I await surgery, trapped inside a lonely private universe of pain.

We know that skateboarding is a noncapitalist act that has, in the past, shown the potential to be an anticapitalist, revolutionary act. Recently it has also proven useful as a hypercapitalist act. And maybe it's this breadth of possibilities that leads to our endless disagreements and arguments over its most inane details. Does this person who dresses this way and used to dress another way rule, or does this person suck? Is this collaboration tight or weak? Define *tight*, define *style*, define *gay* while you're at it. Is wearing nail polish gay? Is hugging gay?

But these aren't real debates. These are only excuses to project inner demons onto someone else, is all. Which is only to say that we each suffer our opinions and want, sometimes anyway, to convince others to suffer them with us. Back there behind all of our chatter, skateboarding is barely listening. Skateboarding remains perfectly fine no matter what we say, and it will outlive us all no matter who is or is not selling its shoes.

Right now, my shoulder hurts enough that I'm groaning. Every so often I hear myself groan, or moan, or exhale in a way that contains emotional content. I wheeze like a barely open car window. These sounds belong

*totally to my body—I have no control over them or anything else. But still
I think to myself: don't be a pussy, quit being such a pussy.*

But how is that? What exactly did skateboarding do to achieve this
immunity? One simple and remarkable fact is this: there is no cheating in skateboarding. So long as it remains analog, floating between
temporary scoring rubrics and contest formats while allowing none
to stick, there will be no way to cheat. There will be no hormone or
supplement—except maybe *exactly two and a half beers*—that gives
anyone an unfair advantage. There will emerge no process to become
good at skateboarding beyond doing it for many, many hours on end.
Anyone who wants to play will be forced to bleed; doing the thing
means caring enough for the thing that your commitment outweighs
the truth of what the thing does to your body, which is create pain.

*By my fourth day on the couch I have achieved something like freedom
from time. Time, on the couch, is fantasy. Have I mentioned how much
I am crying? Every so often, I move wrong and I start crying without
any control. I am not sobbing or weeping. It is just that occasionally
my eyes start sweating. There are ways I move or sit that ignite in my
left shoulder a pain that makes me want to murder something inside of
my bare hands. I cry a lot this week and each time I do I think: don't
be a pussy.*

Not that we appreciate the pain. Maybe we get tired of hurting all the
time. Maybe we find ourselves blaming skateboarding for the pain
or the blood or for the rest of the damage it causes. Maybe you've
blamed it for how you can't find a girl, or don't see your kid enough,
or can't sit through a movie without your knees locking up.

*Another thing about pain: it's got a mainline to honesty. As an adult
who loves one woman passionately and several others platonically, I
know that "you pussy" is something one should not say, because saying
it is a small form of aggression. I know the way such small, incidental*

aggressions are dangerous, because everyone thinks they're harmless, or at least everyone who has a penis and a brain informed by his penis. I know, also, that perceived harmlessness can actually be more harmful than overt, deliberate aggression. I know that pussys add up the way cicadas add up, that these single tiny sounds become deafening, and therefore that saying pussy this way, as a judgment, as a condemnation, is an act of violence.

But blaming skateboarding is the same as bemoaning who's involved in it, or what shape it's taking—we can only maintain these for a few seconds before we burst out in laughter. Eventually we remember: skateboarding does not give a shit about us. No matter how we project values onto it, skateboarding does not care. Skateboarding cares no more about your pain than it does about your silly debates over the clothing of the men and boys who you watch doing it. We can hate it, yes, and probably should from time to time. Of what real value is anything that *only* pleases, that we *only* admire? Anything we love we also partially despise for its power over us, and if you don't know that I might as well be speaking to a rock.

So…that pussy thing. Is that bullshit, do you think? Do you think a single word rattling inside of your own private head can contribute violence into the external world? Is thinking "you pussy" enough to perpetuate our historical track record regarding men and women and power dynamics and one group's ongoing terror against the other? That depends, you might say. What's "violence," exactly? Is "violence" a description of bodies clashing and guns firing and bombs falling? Yes. But violence is also a substance that filters like mist in the air. It is waves of human radiation. It is every human relationship's atmosphere, and any time we live among other people we live inside of it, both breathing and exuding it through our pores.

So here is the secret treasure hidden inside of our pursuit of skateboarding. The activity is so terrible for us, and cares about us so little, that we can't possibly do it without loving it. Which means that even the ugliest and biggest assholes in our midst are capable of love.

And whether we admit it or not, we seem to know this by now. Six decades in and skateboarders have learned a thing or two. We still bicker, but we can't pretend we haven't grown. In 2014 we seem to be skewing closer and closer to that utopia of *suum cuique pulchrum est*: to each his own is beautiful.

Not there yet, and maybe not ever. Still and always, there is nobody more beautiful to us than ourselves, and no footage we enjoy more than our own. But pull back a second and frame the shot of you standing with this thing that you love enough to bleed for. If you love it you want it in the shot, yes? *Yes.* And this thing, skateboarding, is, if not bigger, then at least broader than it has ever been. As the range finder zooms out you yourself start looking a little smaller, there's more going on, and you watch the footage of this wide-frame shot and spot people wholly unlike yourself who love the thing, too, even if they love differently than you do; they're dressed like fucking weirdos and it's all very weird, this big shot, and now it turns out some of them *don't even have penises* to think about, or think with, and Jesus what's that like? What would *that* do to the pain experience? Suddenly, we're not thinking along the old rutted patterns, and it might feel odd and it might hurt, but we are up for it because we're bleeders, aren't we. Look at our shins and elbows. And so this is nothing, really, it's going pretty well, so why not zoom out a little more, just back it up slightly more and see how it looks.

CHAPTER FIFTEEN

On Narrative

Whatever the personal challenges of the work and my difficulties along the way in treating them—the incremental ego deaths, the preference, always, to be outdoors on a skateboard rather than inside on a laptop, the latticework of doubts and trembling fears—the *artistic* challenge of my second novel had always been clear: to merge the energies of skateboarding with those of narrative. A story is a movement through time tracing a path from one set of conditions to new, somehow different conditions. Meaning is made in the differences between conditions and the path of the quest between them. And how do we conceive of a quest, any quest at all? A quest is a framework based on shortage. What does this character want? Why do they want it? The quest is the natural outcome of a desire born from a lack, even when the shape of this lack is not always obvious. The best of our lacks are those that reveal themselves along the way.

In the field of writing pedagogy, imagination and subjectivity are largely seen as goals in themselves. To teach story is largely the process of filling out a character's desire and imagining a compelling network of obstacles to that desire. But what of the quest that is premised not on lack, but abundance? Tunnel into the mind of the skateboarding subject in the thrall of their activity and you'll find that every single thing they want already exists beneath the very wide and endlessly deep tent of this huge, encompassing world. Ask a skateboarder what they want and they'll go to the window and point a finger outside: "That." And, lacking a lack, the standard quest gives way to less linear types of movement. We see repetition and redundancy, spirals that tread over familiar paths, meaning derived not from change but rather constant, shifting tensions between body and place, stasis and movement, physical risk and private, nonmonetary reward.

But then, occasionally, the sky would clear. Like one day in 2015 moving through San Francisco with the camera, and then another day, weeks later, sitting down in the chair with coffee and the giant Word file all disarranged and unfinished and flawed in every conceivable way, with the photos I'd taken weeks prior up now on the screen. I'd start in on some writing and feel just the tiniest presence somewhere behind me, I heard the fucker and I stared into the screen with the little black keys under my fingers and there it was: an undefined, overexposed, blown out sky presiding over a culture out of place and a place out of use. The spot, after all, was a bridge. China Banks, the famous China Banks. And beneath the bridge there are men who slap cards onto overturned cardboard boxes while others crowd around to watch, and through those red columns of the gate that separates the bridge from the neighborhood you can see the women doing their handkerchief dance in smiling semi-unison. And to know, looking at the bricks in the photo, that the banks are so steep and so rough as to murder a skateboard's nose and tail. And in this small reciprocity between the board that's blamed for the city's destruction, and the symmetrical destruction the city wreaks upon the board, there is the sound of a resonance that calls you back into the thing, deeper this time than the last.

Which is to say that much of my desire to write about skateboarding has grown from my own lack, which in turn has affected the ways I perceive the activity, along with its films. We are always, after all, looking for what we want. That resonance of creative damage, of the strange physical discourse of a city's people and cultures, unison and discord, of games and dance and angled surfaces. That was the energy I wanted. On many occasions over the last decade that has meant an aversion to stories and a suspicion of those who would tell them cleanly. Stories, I mean, that are effective and meaningful, the well-designed objects that diminish rather than honor mystery. In skateboarding as elsewhere, the most competent and elegant of our storytellers have been brands.

One way to define a poem might be: a poem is the opposite of a brand.

One reason to write them might be: to affirm authorship as the province of human beings.

CHAPTER SIXTEEN

A Most Mundane Perfection

2015

Following the Chicago premiere of *Propeller*, the long-anticipated first full-length skate video from Vans, I could have reported a handful of facts about the film, at most. It was overwhelming. I know that the film was long and crowded with beauty and amazement. I know that I enjoyed it very much. I know that when a certain angelic transition[1] ripper appeared on screen, my wife leaned over and said, "What's up with this pretty little surfer?" I know that afterward, people around me wanted to discuss favorite parts. I recall thinking: Isn't it odd, isn't it even sort of *disappointing* that after all these years we haven't come up with a better word for the individual sections of a skate film than *part*? I know that in bed that night I felt strange and haunted by something I couldn't immediately name.

In 2015, I happened to be a person who often wore Vans shoes and never ever wore Nike shoes. This was my choice, about which I'd thought long and hard, and I wasn't then and am not now interested in convincing you that I was "right." You're either a grown-up or will be soon, so I trust you to think about it and make your own choice. I happened to really like the Vans product, especially

---

1 In the original of this essay I used the term "tranny."

the Gilbert Crockett low, a shoe I'll wear into the apocalypse. I also appreciated the idea of Vans. Of course, we have a convenient name for this chemistry between product and idea—*brand*. And for those of us who believe that the history of the late twentieth century is a history of war between capital and the individual, since roughly 1950 the prevailing weapon in this war has been the brand.

In both product and idea, the Vans brand leans heavily on the notion of history. Listen to Doug Palladini, vice president of global marketing: "I believe that for Vans, our heritage fuels the progression." Or: "Coming from that platform of authenticity and our heritage, allows us to progress in a really meaningful way." If language like this weren't so outwardly nauseating we might be more inclined to wonder over the logistics of balancing heritage and progress. I'm most interested in "meaning," which here and elsewhere is code for narrative. When a brand says "meaning" they mean the story it tells about itself. It's a story that you, consumer, either reject or choose to inhale and embody as part of your own.

For fifty years, Vans had defined itself as the great common denominator of American culture. Unlike others, Vans could claim that skate culture adopted them, rather than vice versa. Such a meaningful history was not wasted by the brand's mouthpieces. Steve Van Doren would say, "This is not a team you can just buy and throw together." Jeff Grosso would say how "other brands"— by which he and Steve and everyone else at Vans meant Nike, though they wouldn't say so, because that was not, is not, the Vans way—would "try and rewrite their history by trotting out some old photos of some old guy wearing their shoes back then but you know what? I was fucking there and I didn't see them anywhere. They weren't around."

And now into this narrative came Greg Hunt and his *Propeller*, which left me impressed, giddy, and not totally sure how to separate Hunt the filmmaker and Vans the brand. Unlike Ty Evans, who films skateboards, isolating and slowing their rotations with a fetishist's obsession, and unlike Bill Strobeck, who films skateboarders, zooming always closer to see faces and fingernails, Greg Hunt films skate spots. In fact, he films the settings that comprise the spot where skating occurs.

Hunt is an image maker, catching the angles and shadows and geometry that surround the activity. In 2003, this made him the perfect filmmaker to introduce the mega ramp to the world in DC Shoes' own first full-length release. It was the video's finale and the beginning of a new era in scope and scale to skateboard stuntery, a part that would include Danny Way setting two world records for skateboard air: length (75 feet) and height (23.5 feet). Capturing all of this, Hunt's subject isn't Way exactly, but the shapes cut out of the surrounding valley, the contrast of skeletal beams with the green bundles of desert brush along the dusty ground. It's the moments of alignment between Way's flight and the hilltop ridges behind the ramp, with the sky a pale, lineless vacuum above. It's those two Masonite pathways carved for parallel drop-ins leading to two sprawling gaps, the one on the left dwarfing its partner on the right, shot from a helicopter above.

If Alien Workshop's 2009 film *Mind Field* feels heavy today, that heaviness is Chris Carter and Mike Hill's branding work, not Hunt's. The toy robots helpless and writhing on their backs or disabled. Those oozing metallic porcupine spheres of death. When Hunt shows us each rider's face in profile, shadowed or otherwise colorless, it's the shape he likes, not the expression or attitude conveyed. He's more interested in Heath's shape moving between columns, or Dill carving a casual turn in front of a fountain before even more columns. It's that murmur of birds throbbing shapes above the triangle of an angled roof. Whenever a spot in *Mind Field* can bear it, he will zoom out and present it whole. Those we see up close are schoolyards, anything indoors or under cover. His preference is always outward, distant, opened.

We might compare any of this to Benny Magliano's vision of Alien Workshop after Hunt left the brand. It was camerawork that made Magliano's 2010 *The Cinematographer Project* entry feel new—not one single shot remains still. It's all kinetic and disorient-ing by design. The eight-minute section is always building and it's effective as hell, like a determined assault, rising from start to end. Where Hunt is rooted and appreciative, Magliano offers controlled mayhem.

In many ways, *Propeller* is the fullest expression yet of an artist who began his career under Ty Evans before setting out to dis-tinguish himself. Hunt's HD is broad and clean, with little interest in wringing drama from the activity. As for brand obligations, he's been consistent in claiming independence. When Chops at the Chrome Ball Incident asked him about brand identity in *The DC Video*, he said plainly, "I didn't really think about the brand identity." About *Mind Field*, no, he said, Mike Hill basically let him do his thing. And now to *Concrete Skateboarding* he says there were no overall brand messages conveyed by Vans. Was there any involvement from Vans marketing? "No, none."

The skating in *Propeller* is incredible, as anyone but a devout fool would expect. There are not surprises, exactly, but a barrage of tricks that render surprise moot. The flop of Rowan Zorilla's wrists and noodle of his legs do look wobblier and more likable against the rigid forms of a Hunt composition. Trujillo and his volcano rides, Pfanner squeezing through a doorway to lipslide that green rail, and so on; each skater is blessed with a fresh batch of frames. Dan Lu earns every stitch of his wool sweaters by sheer joy alone, forget skills, and Kyle Walker's Knausgårdian 50-50 registers as one more very, very long grind. It's quite literally all impressive. Gilbert Crockett's part is every bit as worthy of isolation as *Dylan.*,[2] and playing them simultaneously side by side opens a kind of barely alternate dimension in which mirrors aren't quite flat and identities bleed into one another.

But this isn't an occasion to explore such possibilities. Not the time

---

2   More on *Dylan.* later.

to deviate from the axioms Skateboard Videos form—introduction, part, part, part, etc., roll credits and cue bonus footage. This is Greg Hunt, who was raised on the era of *Sick Boys* and who *as such* was chosen by Vans, historical manufacturer of the most authentic shoes in skateboarding, and on whom VF Corporation is banking rather hard to progress their heritage in a really meaningful way. How could Hunt feel anything *but* pressure, given his client? Is such a thing as "artistic freedom" even possible in a case like this?

My personal answer is: no. To this one viewer, *Propeller* feels like a perfect representative for Vans, a perfect representation of a skateboard film, but not quite a compelling representation of our time. Something about the model, the form, feels wrong. The novelist Zadie Smith has described a certain brand of impeccable literature, tight and neatly constructed, the reading of which fills her with a certain strain of disappointment. For Smith, it's "a powerful, somewhat dispiriting sense of recognition." It is surely the case that we've been trained to expect this video, *Propeller*, and that in terms of those expectations it is rather flawless. Our receptors are so established, though, that this perfection becomes its flaw. "It's so precisely the image of what we have been taught to value…that it throws that image into a kind of existential crisis." Perhaps, then, it was not shrinking budgets or *the internet* that was killing the form of the full-length skate film. Maybe, after thirty years, we were ready for the form to evolve.

But could *Propeller* have been any way else? Vans might have chosen Russell Houghten or Chris Ray to direct, though I'm not sure how radically that would have changed things. Mike Manzoori would have done something else, though not necessarily something more. Dan Wolfe, too. But "more" isn't even the issue, is it? Is it insane to ask what a Ryan Garshell Vans video would look like? Or a Colin Read? Probably they would not look like anything.

This is the story of Vans, after all. Or part of it anyway. It's a selective history as all self-told stories are. And aside from TNT's bloody chest and lower back, and that brief glimpse of AVE's blackened Caine Gayle tee, it is almost totally clean. It is pristine. Greg Hunt's *Propeller* is so good, so pleasurable, that it never seems to struggle. In this way, the Vans brand has been presented as less, say, Anthony Van Engelen and more like…Curren Caples? A kid who, if he sweats, and that's a big if, he sweats meticulous beads of vulcanized waffle sole. That is well and that is good, but for me, the story lacks mystery. It lacks surprise. It lacks, as I might say to my writing students, guts.

In this sense, I'm most impressed by *Propeller* as a reflective device, a tool for my ongoing struggle with my desires and beliefs. Didn't I ask for this? If not explicitly then by continuing to choose the authentic heritage of Vans footwear? Somewhere along the way I seem to have gotten the idea that a skate video should challenge its viewers in some way. But why? Need these films disturb? Need they converse somehow with the filthy, mysterious, unframeable conditions of the world in which our skating takes place? For all that propellers suggest the movement of air, I find it difficult to breathe inside this vision of skateboarding. I keep wanting someone to open the windows and check on the outside world. Agnosticism to the mess of it all isn't necessarily, I don't think, a hostile act, but it sure feels insular.

CHAPTER SEVENTEEN

On How

Now I find myself unsure which to describe—the warmth of our love or the fury of our conflicts? First, is there even a difference. Second, if they are not the same, which will paint a better portrait of the bafflements our marriage has produced? Which, conflict or love, provides the more useful lens to understand skateboarding? Or is that backward—is it skateboarding whose lens is useful to marriage?

My problem with New York is that there is no space. Whenever I go, I feel a certain breathless tension, a vacuum of time. Early in 2014, K and I navigated this overfullness by deciding we wouldn't see or even contact the people we'd otherwise feel obliged to. But still, I sensed unease between us. Something had changed since K moved into my home, our home, and spent those first weeks nursing me back from a shattered clavicle. Someone attuned to the cosmos might note the inauspicious timing of this sequence, the injury having occurred two days before her move-in date, the potential prevision of my incapacity to help and my great, pressing need for assistance with even the most minor of tasks. At minimum, none of it augured well.

I will tell you what I can remember without aide. We caught

a cab to Chelsea for an evening of *Sleep No More*, the immersive, promenade theater that combines *Macbeth* and Hitchock's *Vertigo*. When our number was called, we put on our masks and allowed ourselves to be separated—she had been once before, and I was happy enough to wander solo. I spent too much time moving between floors, afraid I was missing important scenes. After the show we had a cocktail, and something between us soured. It happened quickly. Then we were in the cab and arguing, moving from West Twenty-Seventh back to our Chinatown hotel. I remember feeling confused, attacked, and righteous, and our voices rose until she was out of the cab, storming into what must have been Columbus Park, and the driver was eyeing me in his mirror.

Now, when she and I recall this night, we do it from among the damage that the scam has wrought. The scam of marriage, I mean. That no love is successful until it has reached this destination and is ushered inside. The scam of the wedding industry, the pressures of grandeur, the great singular assumption of most any story that's ever been told. I myself spoke of the scam on that first date after she'd shaken our world. After years of friendship it seemed that, oops, she'd fallen a little bit in love. Sitting there over tacos, completely down for what was happening, I said, if we do this, if we cross from friendship into this other thing, it's almost certain we'll get married.

But the scam was working differently on her. So, when I spoke of our marriage as a clear eventuality, she felt herself kept on line. The schedule was mine. The responsibility to speak with her father, mine. It was my task to find the friend to design the ring and decide when to present it to her ceremoniously. For me, this meant private machinations and silent righteousness—by the time we were yelling in the cab, I'd already spoken to her father and the ring's delivery was only weeks away. For her, it meant living in a kind of Casablanca, robbed of volition, with nothing to do but wait.

And so immense were these forces that there was no space to discuss or even think of how a life together might actually look. So obvious was the answer that we never even considered what sort of questions we should have been asking. The scam of marriage is to foreclose on any other futures. It is nothing short of fascism. And submitting to it did not solve anything whatsoever.

When we argue, K will at times deliver a comment that feels intended for someone else. She will roll her eyes or speak in a tone that conveys a quilt of nonverbal meaning, and so dramatic will it feel to me, so richly performed, that I will wonder, and have at times asked, who exactly she thinks is watching. My counter-performance is to make a show of looking around as if expecting to find an audience.

I have a friend, T, with whom I've spoken of arguments like these. He and I share some qualities, let's say, and his wife, also T, is nothing though I suppose maybe a little like K. Anyway, T, my friend's wife, is given to acts of dramatic departure when their arguments reach a certain pitch. I should say that I admire this move, exiting as performed synecdoche or allegory—a tactic that both is and is not without threat. T himself can be a little fierce (he's a CEO and she a social worker), and his play at such times is to call her bluff. So, here she is, moving through their large apartment with the panoramic window overlooking the river and Manhattan on the far bank, her voice sharp and pointed, her movements toward the door like a moth's to light. He stands near the couch, breathing hard. His feet shuffle like a wrestler's.

"I'm leaving," says T, her bag and keys suddenly within reach. "Fuck, *fuck* this."

And T, raising his brows like oh, sure, this familiar scene: "Get milk."

I'd like to point now to two other lines of dialogue. For context, recall that between 1932 and 1954, as William Faulkner was writing some of the most lasting and challenging novels in the history of American literature, he was also working in Hollywood to support his family. Among his projects was the adaptation to screen of Raymond Chandler's novel *The Big Sleep*, a film Roger

Ebert described as a kind of ode to process over results, means over ends, *how* over *what*.

We open with Philip Marlowe arriving at the mansion of General Sternwood. When he's led into the greenhouse, Sternwood orders the butler, Norris, to prepare his guest a drink. And so he asks Marlowe, in both the film and novel, "How would you like your brandy, sir?"

Raymond Chandler has Marlowe answer, "Any way at all."

It's Marlowe in a nutshell, the entirety of hard-boiled in a nutshell. Quick, quipped, and assured. His answer reveals a fierce literalness that speaks to the idealized objectivity of his field, which is truth. Both Chandler and Faulkner were modernists, of course, inasmuch as they believed in a capital *t* Truth whose discovery could bring resolution to the suffering of their plots. Marlowe's answer is also an assertion of his perspective, the eyes behind the first-person "I" that narrates the novel. The General's subjunctive inquiry opens up a door of possibility: *How?* In his reply, Chandler's Marlowe widens the view to reveal a door hung on a frame without walls—it's all possibility to Marlowe, it's entirely open.

Now, here is the way William Faulkner's Marlowe answers how he'd like his brandy: "In a glass."

This is better. I'd argue that it is much better. Why is it better? Well, *The Big Sleep* was Chandler's in 1939, which gave Faulkner—who by 1939 had published eleven novels—five years to improve it in time for the 1946 film. Chandler's best work was still to come. Furthermore, to write well in the third person is simply more difficult than writing in the first, and Faulkner was a master of third person narratives, their variances of voice and perspective, the characters they animated. Faulkner—we needn't stutter on this—was a better writer.

The more interesting question, per Ebert and our work here, is: *How* is Faulkner's line better? Voice is one word for it. Style is another. But to my eyes, the difference is a matter of space. Faulkner asks the reader to navigate a certain distance between the words and their meaning—which in this case feels so clearly implied by the words that we might mistake them for working literally, for functioning directly and obviously, were it not for Chandler's example as counterpoint. *In a glass.* There is work to be done, still, and room to do it. The audience has a role.

CHAPTER EIGHTEEN

Clearing a Space
for Meaning

2015

In the late months of 2015, skateboarders found themselves with unexpected and sudden access to *Boys of Summer*, a strange film that arrived the way skate media had begun to, with very little warning. It's still there if you want, free of charge to watch or download and even consider, if considering is your thing. My friend David says BoS imitates everything before it but not one thing specifically. To me, it is a tribute film that feels like the happiest eulogy ever written. It was made by Jeff and Charles. Jeff's last name is Kutter and he never returned my e-mail. Charles is a French bulldog.

Another way to put this is to say that *Boys of Summer* is a warped, fun house reflection of the blockbuster Mountain Dew film from earlier that year, *We Are Blood*. Both are arguably too long. Both take several years of footage and arrange it by logic independent of sponsors and profile, resulting in films that owe their form and effect largely to the aesthetics of the individuals who shaped them. Warped reflection of, or perhaps antidote to. Together, they present a useful portrait of skateboarding midway through this decade.

Ty Evans is an evangelist, and *We Are Blood* was his most extravagant sales pitch until his next. This time his hero is Paul

Rodriguez, with his deep wholesomeness and perfect teeth, a face you'll recognize from the billboards. Ty has given Paul a script to read and a story to tell about an RV and some friends. But forget Paul for a second—actually, the story is about us. Who? "We" are the inclusive pronoun, and "we" are also blood. All right.

And who are *we*? Mainly, Ty wants to tell us, we are single-minded and best understood in comparison to normal people. Normal people are nonskaters who see in terms of "form, function, and progress." We, then, are those who think differently, which for Ty means with a total focus on skateboarding and skateboarding alone. "All we see," says Paul, "is something new to skate." Not form. Not progress. I might have appreciated being on the right side of this them/us framework as a child, or maybe even just a few years ago—now it feels just determinedly reductive. On a sunny Los Angeles morning Paul wonders, "Why do we do it?" A very good question! *We Are Blood*'s answer? "Because we have to—it's in our blood, it's in our DNA." Ah. We've got ninety total minutes of this sermon, so strap in.

It's a fine controlling metaphor, OK, and one that gives Ty a chance to magnify a drop of blood to fill your entire screen. The blood drips in slow motion, which has become a kind of Ty Evans trademark as he grows more and more hell-bent on branding skateboarding and delivering it to the masses. Techno-fetishism is part of this. Fill the stadiums, chant the slogans, and we've got ourselves a rally. And of course, nobody alive creates spectacle like Ty Evans. His one-two finale in *We Are Blood* arrives, first, with a wholly contrived nonsession on a helipad towering over the Persian Gulf. Then we rise to our feet and cheer our hand-some prince of marketing and promotion as he leads a massive crowd of nameless youth who flow through Los Angeles streets like water.

Or, *cough*, like blood. Because, like blood, crowds will clot and clog openings, restricting the flow of meaning through the world. A crowd, says the great American novelist, is good at exactly one thing: being a crowd. Why do we do it? Because we *have* to. Against the fatalism of crowds, some of us, the humanists, hold fast to an endangered being or idea that we call *the individual*. Unlike a crowd, the individual chooses. And, on occasions when the individual makes a series of choices in a certain sequence, that individual is creating art. Art, so chosen, increases the flow of meaning through the world.

* * *

From its opening shot of Kirk Gibson and the voice of Vin Scully, *Boys of Summer* seems, at first, to be a kind of ode. Gibson limping is the focal point of every sandlot daydream: the pinch hitter, bottom of the ninth, both legs injured. *Boys of Summer* is this daydream updated: a massive, rotating cast of heroes and ascendant stars. It is a bulky package, a marathon of shifting images spackled together by a consistent mood, which is Don Henley's mood, the Traveling Wilburys' mood.

But is it a story? Not even remotely. *Boys of Summer* is a nonlinear object; it is shaped strangely and you sort of don't want to touch it because it might fall over. Since they're not busy selling us anything, including the awesomeness of skateboarding or some notional *we*, Jeff and Charles have cleared a space for us to have other thoughts as the movie plays.

Thoughts about what? We might as well start with dicks and asses. Early in the film we're primed by Alex Olson's naked frame in the shower, playing demure as always. After that comes an unpredictable series of dicks and asses: Harvey Keitel dick begets Dolemite ass, a faceless bicyclist's dick, Federico Vitetta's ass, and finally GG Allin's dick. Why? Are Jeff and his dog Charles making some kind of joke? Is it a joke about them or about us? Is he reminding us how much time we spend watching and studying the male form?

We're used to old movie clips in skate videos, and in *Boys of*

Summer we might identify some themes running through them. Here we see men fucking, fuming, killing, vamping, crashing cars, and shooting guns. Women are less prevalent and way less interesting—they are victimized, sexualized, or lying dead while a man sits at the bedside and berates her corpse. Is this misogynist? Or is it a statement about casual misogyny? And yo…what about those dicks and asses?

Mostly, it depends how you choose to interpret it. The living women we see, the few friends and girlfriends who make it into Jeff and Charles's project, are there only long enough to light a fart or pee standing up (though to be fair it is a *pretty long* pee). Maybe none of this makes you think about gender as a concept and perfor-mance. Maybe Jeff and/or Charles had no intention of making you think about gender, or maybe they weren't even thinking about gender themselves. But they did clear a space.

Flashes of old skate footage pop up to create a strange echo of some clip and we recall Don Henley singing, "Don't look back, you can never look back." We remember some friend or message board poster or Slavoj Žižek arguing that nostalgia is a disease or injury, like a limp. But who's to say we can't revisit memories and pick from inside of their sticky goop certain solids we might have missed the first or second time through? Who's to say when a series of events has been exhausted of its capacity to help in some way—to soothe, or comfort, or reveal the secret mysteries of cosmic time and human death?

And those old skaters, like Gonz and Carroll and Dill and co.? How does their footage possibly stand alongside, say, Na-Kel's eruptive and glorious pop shove-it over the rail? Well, not every hero needs a monologue. Some among us appreciate the essential fact of age, the great and basic weirdness of continuing to be, and doing it differently as time goes by. We are happy to see old men playing at the game of boyhood, same as those farting women. Much of the footage feels old, too. Dylan Rieder's picnic ender is perfection and a testament to something, surely—past or future or illness or recovery, something that tests simple language. Something humanist.

And what's most obvious, here, and what could easily go unmentioned, is that nobody in *Boys of Summer* is pretending to play. Not once does it feel like a session has been arranged to please the camera. The session exists; they're skateboarding here or there and someone nearby happens to pull out a tiny, powerful phone. Sometimes the result feels like a married man's *Cherry*. Sometimes it feels like the happiest eulogy ever written.

The San Francisco essayist Rebecca Solnit has argued about the "tyranny of the quantifiable." There in a city whose streets have been overrun by a crowd of powerful financial interests, she reminds us that we require language, among other reasons, "to describe more complex, subtle, and fluid phenomena." Beyond the slogans, beyond the pat, familiar narratives of personal ascent and technological salvation. "It is difficult," says Solnit, "sometimes even impossible, to value what cannot be named or described." It is the humanist's task to account for this strangeness, to produce and consume and traffic in the conversation of strangeness. To name what they're doing and describe it and by speaking it this way practice its revolt against the status quo of consumption.

I am suggesting, I guess, that whatever skateboarding is or might become depends on the way we speak of it. Of course, it is first about skateboarding being done, and skateboarding being consumed and marveled over and celebrated over drinks. So, perhaps, yes, consider the toast as form. One by one, we'll stand and speak of skateboarding and not necessarily in that neat, marketable line of a story. Leave stories to the brands—we'll start with the toast and move to other, more interesting shapes. Like a collage. Or a fugue. Something vatic, a prophecy, or some form of the ecstatic. None of these will move units the way a story moves units, but they will move. They'll remind us of that appreciation we all share for emptiness, for the odd nonspaces where our strange form of play occurs in the wild.

Here is another way to describe what makes a *we*. The sound of the cracks that we hear beneath our wheels and recognize from three blocks down the street. We are the ones who love the sound, or think we do. Except it is not the sound but the spaces that make it. These are the slivers, the tiny chasms that, if we choose, we can wrench apart, sink into, and even pry open for others to follow.

CHAPTER NINETEEN

On Younger

Every so often, I'll look up and find myself standing before a classroom of graduate writing students and think, No, this can't be right. The sweat comes immediately. My eyes will dart to my notes and I'll see, OK—I am supposed to be here because I wrote that first novel, and then I sat next to a more established novelist on a panel, who I quickly asked, half jokingly, for a job. And I became a visiting writer and then put my name in for the full-time position and cetera, cetera, years passed, and here I am. Tonight my notes indicate that this is to be the class when I go through a very basic introduction to phenomenology.

"Which, since we're writers, we can usefully think of as the objective study of subjectivity," I say, advancing the slide. I remind them that subjectivity is the basis for all human art, particularly our practice of writing. Human judgments and human perceptions are the raw materials of narrative. Emotions are the building blocks of plot. Characters are their desires.

"But what is emotion?" I ask. "What is judgment?"

Please do not read my surprise at finding myself up here as a statement about the seriousness with which I take this work. As long as I've been teaching, my course prep has been, like the notes beneath me now, extensive. And now, it seems, a student has asked about the wound on my hand.

"My what?"

They point. There, the open and semibloody wound on the palm of your hand. "Did it…has your skin just, like, peeled back?"

"Oh. That is nothing," I'll say, considering my embodiment briefly before accelerating us back to tonight's topic: The phenomenology of judgments, perceptions, and emotions. Or the sense-making that we all do as humans, and which we specifically explore as writers. I introduce Edmund Husserl, outline the basics of the intentional object and the four central processes by which Husserl said that human beings come to understand the objects of our intentions: perception, memory, retention and protention, and signification.

The first two and fourth of these are no trouble—they understand what it means to see, to recall, and to discuss. Protention and retention require further illustration. So, I tell my students to watch closely.

"Ready?"

At this point I underhand a piece of chalk into the air, aiming for the projector, which it strikes. The chalk falls to the old blue carpeting. Once it's landed I ask them: did you follow the chalk's flight? Yes. And did you know without really considering where its path out of my hand would take it? Did you sense that the chalk was going to hit the projector before the moment of impact came? They nod.

"Well there you go," I say, wiping my dusty hands together and wincing, due to the wound. "That is what Husserl called protention and it is a gee-dee miracle of human consciousness."

Their reading for tonight was Brian Evenson's collection *Fugue State*, and we're focusing on the story "Younger." It's the story of two girls who recall two rather disaligned experiences of a single day that they shared together as children. Years later, the younger of two sisters continues to call her older sister on the phone because she wants to revisit and understand what happened one morning when they were left at home alone while their parents were away. Unlike the older sister, who "sorted the world out rationally and in a way that stripped it of all its power," the younger sister has always "felt things more intensely than anyone else."

It is just a morning, though, from their past. A handful of hours that were either perfectly unexceptional or totally magical, depending on which sister you ask. The sisters agree that they played together, but the younger recalls more than pretending. Her memories include a prevailing strangeness that led to a "giddiness…a feeling they had stepped beyond the known world."

So, the story's conflict is a matter of perception that becomes an issue of being. For the younger sister, the day simply *is* a different day than the day that *is* for the older sister—for the younger, this was the day when something unexpected and incredible happened as they played familiar games with familiar toys on the same, familiar floor. "This time," the younger sister recalls, "anything could happen.... They were building a whole world up around them, full of things more vivid and slippery than anything the real world could offer." We picture the older sister on the call's other end, a universe away, exasperated and bored.

"So," I say, stepping around the table and sitting on it. "Which sister do you believe?"

Now they discuss. When one speaks, the others return to their books and search the story line by line for evidence in the narrator's favor. And my mind wanders a little, here, to the Bolaño paragraph that I've got taped to my office door, from page one hundred of *Woes of the True Policeman*, one of the unfinished novels that was pushed into the market after his death. It is a total mess of a project, but hidden in that mess is one perfect paragraph about what the character Amalfitano's students learned. They learned that a book "was a labyrinth and a desert" and that "true poetry resides between the abyss and misfortune and that the grand highway of selfless acts…passes near its abode." The paragraph ends with the most important of Amalfitano's lessons: "That reading wasn't more comfortable than writing. That by reading one learned to question and remember. That memory was love."

When a class has gone well, I'll often find myself winging it, which can be dangerous.

The toy horse, I say, in words similar to but not exactly these, is inanimate and unresponsive. But then one day you look down and see that it's come alive in your hands. In a story about boredom and excitement, the younger sister is in possession of a kind of double sight that precludes boredom. And just as a double seer can never be bored, nor can she ever really be lost. The map changes with her, warps to her, and brings her pleasure. To me, the answer is obvious. The younger sister will always remain younger, until the day she becomes the only.

By now, the class can just about hear the older sister's impatient voice over the phone, rationally bored with the redundancy of it all. I want them there on the line with her. I want them frustrated. I want them to demand more from her and, when she inevitably won't give it, to hang up and forget the older sister and set about their work. Was it Emerson who demanded readers who didn't want to know a piece of writing, but wanted to enter it? It was he, anyway, who claimed to "unsettle all things." Now I'm the one looking at my semibloody palm.

And so, I say, or imagine saying, the younger sister is youthful, yes, but it's a youth unrelated to time. Innocent of the exhaustion that would bemoan the obvious, the younger sister is our hero, and the world that she sees glitters before her.

CHAPTER TWENTY

"Nearly"

2016

The original uncut tape begins and ends with kids on BMX bikes. The footage in question appears only briefly, like some small, out of place island. It feels accidental, a lapse in otherwise nonstop BMX action. The time stamp in the corner says 1986, and almost all of the tape is of boys on bikes under mostly blue skies moving in fluid, uncompressed analog NTSC video. They're going at a jump they've built in the middle of some vacant lot full of pale dirt and small, motley stones. You don't wonder where they are or which one you're supposed to watch. Each shot is canted slightly this way or that because the hulking VHS camera has been propped upon something nearly level, or leaned against the leg of a folding chair.

Around minute sixteen this all changes. A line of static falls, and the video shifts to a closer, handheld shot of a single kid, no bike to be seen. He's standing at the top of a steep and roughly kid-high concrete embankment that sinks from ground level into the dug-out ramp of a supermarket loading dock. Odd faced and skinny, the boy has on a baggy bright red tee and long cutoff jeans. How minimal he looks under his clothes, frail, staring down from the top of the incline. He's awkward at age nine, with a nose too big for his face and face too big for his body. And between him and the drop he holds what seems to be a novelty skateboard by its own comical, sharply rounded-off nose. The board is circa the tape's time stamp: early, directional, with old plastic rails guarding a graphic of a skull that's being trespassed by a snake. The tail of the board widens as it goes, like a whale's flapper. Concentrating now, the boy bends to align the tail with the incline's edge, then he stands and we see his awkward face crunch into a smile. His eyes are wide and appear to have been stolen from a large bird. But he's not frightened, standing now with the tail under one shoe, balancing it nearly perpendicular over the nearly vertical slope. Soon the camera shakes a little and then the boy goes for it, stepping the other shoe onto the board, leaning forward and rolling, if you can call it that, down the wall.

At which point, failure. Awesome and singular failure. The boy slams into the cement face-first before his hands can catch himself. He stands quickly back up and he's all right, he's alive; this is the activity for which boys have been manufactured. But there is blood suddenly, everywhere. One hand goes to his mouth and he looks at the camera and yells...something. Then the boy waves. Not to the person holding the camera, exactly, but rather the people he seems to know are waiting, or will one day be waiting, on the camera's far side. Meaning us.

He waves, hustles to retrieve the board, lifts his red shirt to wipe more blood from his face. Then he screams sharply to the sky. He moves to climb the wall again, an immediate glutton for something we don't quite know. Then the clip ends and we're somewhere dark, briefly, a home or hallway, and then suddenly we're back outside in the field watching another parade of regular boys riding regular bikes.

So we rewind and set the player to slow motion and watch the clip again. The strange, ugly boy is on the top of the steep incline and the huge board is under his left foot. It's 29.97 frames per second we watch at quarter speed as he breathes deep, heaving breaths. What before was a negligible shake of the camera is tremulous at this rate, a tectonic denial. No, the cameraman tells the boy, do *not*. Then the boy's right foot steps onto the board and he leans forward, committing fully. There is no doubt anywhere in his body. If anything, his body effects a kind of death embrace. The angles seem so wrong, now, here in the stuttered transition from incline to ground. Frame by frame he is pitched forward. The moment of impact is terrible, nauseating, but he's rising almost before it is over, and then he's up and the blood blooms from mouth and nose at once. The hand inches to his mouth, and this time you can see what's happening.

He's not waving. See how he looks to the camera with eyes showing mania and revelation, and notice this time how these few seconds of bloody failure appear to have revealed to this boy some kind of truth, the origin of a noise that, before this, he sensed but only from a great distance, like some siren ringing two or three states over. Pause it just right and you can nearly isolate the very moment of understanding, but it happens just after one frame ends. By the next the boy is already besotted with joy. Staring into, or through, the camera, his large nose spews blood. Then comes the yell, and it makes sense now: The wave is not a wave. He is throwing what's in his hand. A tooth. He's lost the tooth forever and throws it at the camera before picking up the board and lifting his shirt to his face, roaring into the sky a brief prayer, or protest, or perhaps oath.

CHAPTER TWENTY-ONE

On Bafflement

When we perceive the obvious from even the slightest of skews, we see that it is, in fact, issuing a request. For? Generosity is one way to put it. Radical openness is another. A sort of simmering faith in both the object of our perception and also our capacity to perceive it in new ways.

The process I'm describing is a kind of return to that obvious thing still in our midst. A second and third and often many more attempts to resee and reconceptualize a thing driven by a faith that the qualities that made the thing obvious might still serve some purpose, might still yield new meaning. The philosopher Richard Kearney has formulated a term, *anatheism*, which in its prefix (*ana-*) signals "a critical hermeneutic retrieval" of that which has come and gone, a return to the old thing for new guidance toward understanding the world. Kearney's formulation is exemplified, he says, in the poet Gerard Manley Hopkins's description of the creative activity: "Aftering, seconding, over and overing." And so, a retrieval and revisitation by way of repetition: an over and overing practiced in a way, says Kearney, that is repeated "*forward*, not *backward*. It is not about regressing nostalgically to some prelapsarian past." In Kearney's case, the thing being retrieved is God after Nietzsche's declaration that God is dead.

In our case, that thing is skateboarding after it has been corporatized and commodified and drained of all subversion, reduced to athletic spectacle. Skateboarding's theology has been composed in magazine and video texts that have, for decades now, remained faithful to the forms that have come before them. A decade of looking newly has begun to yield new objects and understandings. By our own over and overing we can, I believe, formulate a conception of skateboarding's sacred obviousness, its everyday quiddities, that will escape the cosmic gravity of nostalgia and mythology and perhaps propel it into a new orbit.

And so, by unfolding the obvious, by spinning it in our palm and staring deep into its core, we see that its resistance to our gaze is a type of bafflement. And to *be baffled* is something rather else than to *be confused*. As it emerged in the late sixteenth century onward, to *baffle* meant to disgrace, foil, and hoodwink; in short, to cheat. Over time, the word shifted into a usage less specific to the criminal, a more general action of bewildering or confounding. It has always carried an air of defeat and confrontation, which has calcified into its most current meaning: to frustrate or foil. Which means also an air of victory, if you can hear it that way.

The word *confuse* comes into common speech around this same time, also as a transitive verb. But during the nineteenth century its dominant use changes to something more like to mix, to make disorder where once had been order. And from this meaning it acquires a use as a common noun, *confusion*, an everyday state we can speak of today without creating the least conversational friction. To be confused is to be befuddled. To be confused is, in a sense, to be alive in the third decade of this twenty-first century.

To be baffled is something rather more extreme and less spoken of. It requires a greater humility, perhaps, to admit defeat in this way. Or perhaps greater pride to think one's personal challenge is worthy of such an old, archaic set of letters. What's more, bafflement hides in other terms. Like, do you see it there at the end of Joan Didion's most famous paragraph, to open "The White Album"? It is what remains when the stories we tell ourselves in order to live begin to crumble. Bafflement is the failure to establish the "imposition of a narrative." Bafflement by another name is Didion's "shifting phantasmagoria," all of that chaos and disorder, the primary mysteries of existence.

Or, even better, it is there in Marilynne Robinson's majestic and perfect *Housekeeping*, a slim, slow novel that appeared in 1980. Her narrator is an adult Ruth, recalling not only her own childhood, but her family's history back through generations, trying to riddle what would make her mother leave her and her sister, Lucille, on their grandmother's porch before driving her car off of a cliff and into the town lake. There is, of course, no question less answerable than, "What would make someone take their life?" And yet, here we are every single time it happens, peddling our meager theories.

So there's bafflement in the framing of Robinson's plot, and even more so in the craft of her story, its form and style. What at first reads as a standard first-person reflection is, upon a better read, revealed to be a kind of subjective omniscience. Her sentences, long and subordinating, define *Housekeeping*'s world by a meticulous, polished ordering of relations. Ruth's is a syntax of total control, which leads, due to necessary ignorance of much of what she's describing, to frequent hybrids of certainty and doubt. She'll tell us how "it must have seemed," to a character, or "would have felt." And always reminding us, "I think." But the lake's depths cannot be charted. Bafflement has prevailed, and Ruth is left with only myths and her imagination. "Say" that this happened, she insists at the novel's climax, bobbing in a small rowboat upon the selfsame lake that swallowed her mother. "Say" that this were the case, she pleads, sorrow surfacing for the story's first time.

As a character, Ruth is what we might call flat. Also, static. The grand totality of her desires center on comprehending her mother's incomprehensible choice. But with Ruth it is not a matter of what but rather how. Over and over again, she collides with bafflement, and in the end, this longing that is her narrative folly—the suicide's hard epistemic limit—gives form to the novel we're holding. Her quest takes the form of memories real mixed with memories imagined, and they deliver her only to where she is at the story's beginning, baffled. Beginning storytellers learn that desires and obstacles create plot. Ruth has no desires, only needs.

But a true need, understands Ruth, "can blossom into all the compensations it requires." Plots, at their best, confuse just long enough to provide surprise by their ends. Or if not surprise, at least a *frisson* of completion, the spark of the circuit closing. Existence, meanwhile, baffles. Let me go further: any story that provides answers is a lie. "Though we dream and hardly know it," says Ruth, "longing, like an angel, fosters us, smooths our hair, and brings us wild strawberries."

To traffic in the baffling is to maintain a certain endurance for that which doesn't yield much, maybe any, result. It is in this sense a sort of gluttony, or masochism, or at the very least a strange appreciation indeed. On a sunny afternoon, instead of riding my skateboard, I sit with my wife and dog and stare into my Swiss-made ball bearings that are soaking in a shallow dish of brake cleaner. I watch little particulates of grime swirl in the fluid, which is toxic. Mankind went fourteen hundred years believing a Ptolemaic astronomy of spheres that located the earth at the center of the universe. I am only speaking of wood and metal and plastic and grease, bits of silicon carbide glued onto paper that adheres to the top of a board. Say, though, that it is more. I think it must also be more.

PART THREE

CHAPTER TWENTY-TWO

On Bitul Z'man

These are days that find me talking to myself, and not always in a charming or funny way, though nor is it mournful. It might be repeating words aloud while sitting in my little room or pacing the dark hallway when my wife is away. There is a Hebrew term I've learned, *bitul z'man* (ביטול זמן), which translates literally to "cancel time," or "destroy time."

To speak is to act. Language is action and language is the reason we're here. These are days that find me pacing, speaking this Hebrew term and acting out what it names.

One does hope, after all, to achieve some basic kind of sense. So, once you get it out you go over it again, you "worry" the thing, verb, and fashion the thing into that favored shape, a story, knowing well the iron grip that stories have upon today's meaning, upon sense, upon audiences and time.

First there was the substance, earth, with its vast crust rutted and rolling, with hills and valleys mountains and deep ravines, with terrain of every sort. Then came man,* who, soon enough, set out working to flatten the *earth, to build stairways from low to high, to bore great holes and carve the pathways that we would eventually level, pave, and make smooth.*

If you would like to transgress (or, from another perspective, fail miserably at) story, one good way is to start too soon.

For by then, we had learned to propel ourselves and our things from one end of the earth to the other. We devised a fleet of different vehicles, some very fast, others very large, and some very strange. Not everything we did made sense.

Transgression and failure. Have any two things ever looked more similar?

Language is action is language is action is the reason we're here. And did you know that until the late fourteenth century, the noun *stair* was used as a collective plural? Like *deer*. As in, *a mellow set of long stair*.

Language is *stair* from the Old English *stæger,* from the Proto-Germanic *staigri*, which comes from the Proto-Indo-European *steigh*—"go, rise, stride, step, walk."

So? And? Well, action is language, and you will find yourself staring in the direction of your obsession. And? Compose a lyric if you like, though few today will search out a lyric, so instead, narrate the action as if it is passing before your eyes. Like:

> See the boy moving through the cool shadows and flat light of Bayside fog. It is September and you can hear the perfect clatter of brick beneath his wheels. Boy. Called as much. He is the self behind a thin, paltry mustache, wearing those loose-fitting khakis, a windbreaker billowing in the breeze that whips across the Bay and snakes through the city like nature's favorite rumor. (But what is he doing?)

This is better: Desire / Obstacle, Desire / Obstacle, Cause cause / Effect effect.

See the boy push to the federal banks, be chased away, to the library, be evicted, and finally (there is no finality here, the activity is ongoing) to the famous three up, three down in the Mission, where he discovers an elderly, confused woman sitting in his way. He makes a weak attempt at communicating. She spits at him, tells him to screw. The boy thinks, Come on, lady, for fuck's et cetera.

Staigri from the Proto-Indo-European *steigh*—"go, rise, stride, step, walk," source too of the Greek *steikhein* "to go, march in order," Sanskrit *stighnoti* "mounts, rises, steps," Lithuanian *staiga* "suddenly," Old Irish *tiagaim* "I walk," Welsh *taith* "going, walk, way."

Language is obsession, another attempt to comprehend. What strange activity. Is it meaningful, what this boy is up to? Replace *boy* with *girl* and what then? Replace *girl* with *person*, replace *person* with *self*. The city is an argument we've composed in language tactile and rigid, imposing, and firm. *The boy / the girl / the self is scavenging the city.* Scavenging? For what, exactly? *They are out there, scavenging.* But for? Everything, every thing.

Language is activity, and I hear the word *protest* come wafting from the back, a suggestion. *See these selves protest on top of the toy.* OK…but protesting what? And to what end? No thing. No end. In the end, perhaps what *they* are doing is giving. Language is action, is a gift to the world. *The boy, the girl, the selves that are neither and both believe in the practice of generosity even if they would not in one thousand years describe it as such.*

Language is the reason we're here. The performer and pedagogist Mathew Goulish has written, "I don't know. I proceed not knowing." Say these words aloud. One morning, awake early, I encounter this line in a slim volume published by a small and homeless local press, and I think, Yes, this is it exactly. Language is not knowing, going, walk, way.

CHAPTER TWENTY-THREE

Good Old Street League

2015

For all that we sing of unlikely upsets and unbelievable out-comes, it is not surprise that keeps us tethered to sport; we come for the games' basic, unerring predictability. No other audience *relies* like a sporting audience, and whichever exact voids of ours these contests fill, what matters most is that they fill them regularly, on tight and well-posted schedules.

I can recall July 2015, sitting at a friend's house in Mid-City, Los Angeles, drawing lines in my notebook. I'd been staying in the house for a week, researching and occasionally writing the skateboard novel I'd returned to after a year away. The logic for this was practical: I was soon to be up for tenure, and of the two long fiction projects I'd begun, this one was much closer to completion. Also, I believed that writing these essays had given me the space I needed to see its story more clearly. I'd found something of the form I wanted, based on a kind of weave of different temporalities. Anyway, the year that had begun with my wedding had merged with a one-semester sabbatical to prepare the manuscript so it could be sent out to agents in the fall.

It was my second trip West of the year—in May, I'd ridden the California Zephyr from Chicago, arriving in Davis fify-six hours later. Why I'd done this was, first, because I'm a romantic, and second, because my father had a part-time consultant gig at UC Davis, where he kept an apartment and, more importantly, where Andrew Reynolds had filmed the magnificent kickflip ender of his 2010 *Stay Gold* part. So, it was a 2,400-mile pilgrimage to stand before an ivy-covered and trail-rutted hillside between an academic building and the sidewalk below. I marveled, breathed deeply, and snapped photos, knowing it was worth it. I watched teens skate a nine-stair rail outside the chemistry building, saw one of them front feeble it, clapped, and went back home to write. Later, I took another train into San Francisco and skated China Banks and Fort Miley and felt the jolt of uncanny time, spiraling me into my teenage dreams of these selfsame places. Weave of temporalities indeed—I jotted extensive notes that felt profoundly fruitful and traced my day-long walks on a foldout tourist map. I suppose all of this is romantic, too.

I'd come to Los Angeles for a second week of similar work and tourism. I looked at the sharp foliage in Santa Monica, stared at shops and gas pumps and overdressed visitors lining up for afternoon tapings at CBS, sweating in the sun. I stood outside the SAG building on Wilshire and walked under the Levitated Mass, and now K would arrive the following day, at which point my fruitful research trip would transform into a family trip to my in-laws in Valencia. So, I was feeling the creep of impatience as I sat there drawing lines. I'd gone to college not far from here, and it was easy to recall the question I took away from a certain Wittgenstein tutorial my senior year: What is it, really, to be the way that we mean when we say "waiting"? There is no action that accompanies such a state, no behaviors to signify it. One can *perform* waiting by checking a watch, glancing quickly to the door, or phone, or what have you. But what is the difference between sitting at that table and drawing lines when I'm *waiting*, versus when I'm just sitting at the table drawing lines? It is a term we agree to use, a language game.

It is also an internal state of being that can, at times, alter my perceptions of worldly phenomena like the ticking of my host's old clock, the silence of my phone. A professional skateboarder and friend had promised that he'd be in touch "sometime in the morning." Eventually he and I would go out skateboarding, or so I believed. One never knows, really, with skateboarders. They are not people on whose arrival and life performance I generally rely. And yet theirs are the shoulders onto which Nike and Monster Energy and the so-called International Skateboarding Federation[1] have loaded the task of stabilizing skateboarding's rocky track record with organized competition. There are, after all, only so many skateboarders in the world to sell to. The hunger for contest is a much lower and far more common denominator. I, for example, can cop to standing once on the banks of a river as a thin but fanatical crowd cheered a race of rubber duckies down the rapids. It was not a fanaticism for one ducky over another that kept me there, but the contest of it. Like everyone else at that river's edge, I was cheering for the chance we'd been given to cheer.

Competition is a form (a *how*) certain to generate an audience beyond the niche and subniches of whatever happens to be the competition's material (its *what*). Organized competition regulates and manages desire, flattening it from the spikes and troughs of human behavior into a form more predictable, which is to say useful. Which is to say harvestable, profitable, or, if you like, exploitable.

Anyway, my friend, whose lateness was totally unsurprising, had graced me with some free time to draw lines in my notebook, one after the next, until I found myself looking at what I'd drawn and thinking of Berlin, a city home to the world's best-trained

---

1   In June 2017 the ISF would merge with the Federation Internationale de Roller Skating (FIRS) to form World Skate, a compromise of warring international egos made for the sake of earning recognition from the International Olympic Committee.

dogs, dogs that will traipse obediently and joyfully behind a bike, watching for their keeper's hand to give the sign to cross a busy street. Where bicyclists have, as a man told me, a conversation with drivers, not a war. And where they've built the confusing, beautiful, unphotographable Memorial to the Murdered Jews of Europe, a name which is itself a surprise, the starkness of that signifier and the admission it contains: murdered. The monument, somehow, had appeared on the page beneath me as I sat there waiting.

It is a monument that one comes upon and experiences first from without. Soon, this experience unfolds into a choice: Will I walk into and among its stone pillars? The monument forces this choice by way of obvious invitation. And if you do descend into it, you'll likely discover among the pillars children running and laughing in a way that, at first, feels just exceptionally wrong and out of both place and taste. Then it dawns on you that the designers of the memorial had to know this would happen. There is, after all, a slight gradient to its ground that compels acceleration. Scour the world complete and I bet you will find no better venue for a game of hide-and-go-seek. Which means the juxtaposition is not only unsettling but deliberately so—we turn a corner and, by design, confront human play among countless tons of stony death. The play is a part, if a contingent one, of the sculpture. We are part of the sculpture.

Eventually my friend in LA called, we met up, and I drove us to the University of Southern California's Galen Center, where I'd been told my name was on a list for tickets to today's scheduled Street League event. To have this kind of access was exciting enough to override whatever reluctance I had to finally watching a Street League event. As I struggled to wrap up a novel that did justice to this strange thing of skateboarding, the perks of my so-called skate journalism were a welcome reminder that things did achieve completion, and from that completion, sometimes, reward.

From its origin, the half-pipe was always a natural vessel for competition. Here is your playing field, here is a block of time to perform whatever feats you can. You do you and we'll judge whose run we like best. But for decades, the tempestuous desires of street skateboarding resisted taming, or rather training. The essential brilliance of Street League was really only a matter of patience: Rob Dyrdek and his partners understood that what was birthed in the golden era of early and mid-nineties street skating, those hideous and hypertechnical developments, had in the intervening decades evolved to become not only spectacular but *reliable* enough that they could spackle competition around them. It took skaters reaching a certain threshold of talent in order for the system to work. The only question now was whether the skaters had achieved that plateau of predictability such that fans would tune in to the format as a source for the exciting unpredictability of sport.

Attend a Street League contest event and you'll note that they sure don't skimp on reminders of excitement. From where we eventually came to sit inside the Galen Center at the first exciting stop of this exciting sixth season of Street League, once the lights dimmed and the screens came alive with portraits and highlights of our athletes from previous seasons, it was, in fact, exciting—despite my long backlog of cynicism and doubt, and I mean that truly. I have been to World Series games, have sat in the United Center and heard the fierce devotion of Tommy Edwards calling "Your Chicago Bulls!" over the Alan Parsons Project. And if there was one SLS-based surprise for me, it was how genuinely energized and hyped I was by the event's prompt, sudden start.

Once we'd settled into the rhythms of the contest, though, my attention strayed from the predictable skating on the course to the hubbub around it. The timing of our beer runs happened to align with the Crailtap camp's, and my friend, the professional, knew them a bit. So, I was able to meet Rudy Johnson and Rick Howard, men whom I had spent my entire adolescence staring at until my VHS tapes gave and then broke. I watched big Nick Diamond extend one arm to shoot a goofy selfie like the thousand other goofy selfies in the arena. Ryan Sheckler posed statue-like for a dozen photos featuring his same lifeless, million-dollar smile. That Christian Hosoi's wife was wearing her husband's rising sun Vans Sk8 Hi's wasn't surprising, but did strike me as a minor and sweet detail. I was unsurprised but amused to see the other Huston siblings get stopped by children to sign their incidental names onto posters of Nyjah, their brother.

As far as the stage itself, well. There is still the principle challenge confronted by all attempts to regulate and market skateboarding to a world that doesn't understand and finds it sort of silly. I mean that age-old puzzle of valuation, difficulty, style, and taste. Despite a host of commendable efforts, human desire remains a slippery thing to manage. One spectator will hunger differently than the next. And so, then, how to determine a thing's value? How to regulate and apply something like a typical sport's score?

"Nine is too much," said the aging Rasta to my left when Evan Smith, as the broadcasters say, *entered the nine club*. "What he's doing is a, what, like a vert trick. Half-pipe trick. Street skate is about the flip."

Earlier, my friend and I had run into Evan in the Galen Center hallways. Maybe, I thought, the judges were taking into consideration that Evan had (perhaps) eaten psychedelic mushrooms? And I found myself thinking again of the Wittgensteinian framework of language games and states of being, of the phenomenology of *waiting*. What was it, really, to be in the state we call *skateboarding*? Obviously, the activity presumes the state of being—to do it is to be in the state of it. But consider writers and other artists for whom everything is work. To live a literary life is to be writing even as you are reading, as you are walking; it is an encompassing and inclusive hermeneutics: all of living informs the development of the work.

So, I wonder. When I watch a skateboarding film, can it be said that I am *skateboarding*? Anyone who identifies as a skateboarder can describe the strange, poltergeist-like phenomenon of feeling one's own body move along with the figure on screen, a kind of somatic empathy or mutualized motion—this happens particularly when we watch someone skate a half-pipe or bowl. So embedded, or rather embodied, are the motions of pumping the curves of transition, so ingrained are the shifts of weight and bend of legs required of these ramps that to watch someone else is, in a very real way, to feel your own body infected. Something more than just watching is taking place. And what is that something if not *skateboarding*?

I am suggesting that the obvious lines are in fact blurred. Am I skateboarding when I take a break from the activity to sit down in the grass and watch my friends? I am still of the session, sharing the world with my friends, am I not? I holler encouragement, I react, my body reels and rolls as they try and fail, and fail, and fail. And when they land, I exalt. How is this not skateboarding?

Or during the car ride on the way to the spot, or the train ride downtown as we discuss other media we've consumed and imagine what we'll do once we arrive. When does *skateboarding* begin in this case? At the car door or train station? When I tell K, Hey, I'm going out skating, and take the steps down to the street? Or when I wake up and think to the day that's ahead? Or that constant activity of my rear mind that keeps me looking through any car's window with a winged predator's eye, noting stairs, a granite ledge, and considering run-up space and traffic patterns? The more we acknowledge the blur of lines that supposedly mark the (obvious) beginning and ending of a session, the harder we have to work to see *skateboarding* as anything short of a way of being.

The best thing about watching Evan Smith was knowing that he *might* have been on mushrooms—the possibility of such a sub-version was one of a handful of offstage skateboard amusements that made the contest palatable. The jumbotron, the format of the contest, the empty seats prestocked with signs care of the event's major sponsors and their endorsed athletes—these were market artifacts relatively recent to the world of skateboarding.

Well. "Algebra," wrote John Barth, "is easier to talk about than fire." Like a lot of Street League stops, the Los Angeles winner would not be decided until the final trick. The competitions they've arranged have all been uniformly tight, and will continue to be so long as their proprietary scoring algorithm functions as it is designed to. On this night, I heard later, because by then we'd vamoosed, Luan Oliveira would win and be cheered by the fans. Nyjah Huston would lose and find himself booed. I'll leave up to you to decide which of these, if either, is surprising.

CHAPTER TWENTY-FOUR

On the Technology of a Secret

Back for a moment to firsts. I have on occasion told the story about my first ever concert having been a November 1989 date on Mötley Crüe's Dr. Feelgood tour. At times I've spoken fondly of the opening laser show that exploded into "Kickstart My Heart," the six-minute Mick Mars solo, and the darkness that followed, a total, enveloping darkness that was cut suddenly by the pulsing of overhead lights and of craning my little neck to discover Tommy Lee, with electronic drum kit, floating above us.

That my mother didn't actually permit an eleven-year-old me to attend the Mötley Crüe concert when I had the chance seems, now, reasonable. That my actual first concert was the June 1992 stop of Rush's Roll the Bones tour is backed up by the T-shirt I came home with and the profound tremors of nostalgia I feel today, cueing up a video from the tour online. I am not sure, therefore, why this Mötley Crüe lie has persisted. Perhaps due to the profundity of my desire to have gone to the earlier concert. Maybe somewhere along the way I decided (wrongly, it seems to me now) that the lie was more impressive than the truth. Or maybe it's just that I've enjoyed telling the lie, knowing it to be lacking in any real consequence.

Research on lies and lying shows that we all tend to be worse at detecting them than we think. Men especially tend to believe they're better liars than they are. I myself am a tremendous sucker, trusting to a fault, but a very good liar, good enough to fear their temptation and strategize my life into a shape that I can go about living without having occasions or need to tell them.

I should admit something else while we're here: I have in the past been a dishonest lover. Secrets are not lies but will, if they're important enough, sometimes require lies for their keeping. As any dishonest lover knows, the secrets we keep of our cheating have a way of scouring and eroding the many fantasies, some grand, some slight, that we like to construct around the truth of a doomed relationship until the truth itself is so unbearable, or bearable, that the secret's original cause wraps its mouth all the way around to its tail and achieves the work it could have done much more easily, and less messily, had we only been slightly less craven at the outset. In other words, that which is doomed is doomed.

But not many other secrets for me, really, unless we count the big glaring secret that we all keep these days, the one about our private selves in an age of eager and unending techno-social performance. That fantasy, I mean, of authenticity and what exactly we're up to every time we click to share.

* * *

The virus has forced the city to close all parks and insist on masks anytime we're outside. By May, we've begun emerging in stuttered, cautious steps, gathering at closed schoolyards and parking lots. It reminds some of us how it used to be, before the skate park displaced the downtown plaza and other public spots as the go-to meeting point for any given day. A nearby Ross Dress For Less, its windows boarded, sees its expansive lot transformed into a low-impact festival of curbs and parking blocks. For the most part, we keep a safe distance. One of us has a wife undergoing chemo, another provides care to his aging parents. Some wear masks, some don't, but there is ample space to claim and create distance between ourselves, if we are mindful.

I return to riding my bike to Roberto Clemente Community Academy in Wicker Park. Behind the school is a broad region of concrete slab framed by hip-high brick walls, including three walled islands of grass and trees and mulch. When I first moved to Chicago, I lived only two blocks from Clemente. At the time, it was a street spot proper, a natural schoolyard with benches along some of the walls, no augmentation required. By now, it's become a hybridized form—the benches have been replaced by more skate-friendly designs, and a number of homemade obstacles have accumulated to fill the slab. There are ledges and little wedge ramps to move and combine and lean onto stairs, a couple orange traffic barriers weighted with enough rubbish to sustain a board's impact without sliding out of place. The ground is shit but there's something for everyone, and we all continue to wonder how long the school will let this go on.

Is it fun? God, yes. The creaky old ramps take me back to a time of driveways and green lawns, and the different pods of crews that gather there remind me that skateboarding in 2020 includes middle-aged women in hockey jerseys skating with their daughters. There is shade and grass, and between the slabs certain seams stick up enough to bump with your front wheels and hop, a subtle trick of physics that was called, as recently as last year, a "Chinese ollie." There is a step whose outer corner has been ground over time into a rounded and blackened ledge just about anyone who can ollie can get onto for a grind with the most perfect, ageless sound in the universe.

We have touched on the difference between going out skate-boarding and going out filming, between means and ends and how these relate to skateboarding as a practice. What we have not discussed is the great, necessary dishonesty of all skateboard media. I mean these artful strings of accomplishments with scant or no acknowledgment of the labor and failure behind each contingent clip. Into the nineties, "slam sections" bundled the most spectacular failures into a concentrated, though deeply curated, confession. By the turn of the millennium, Bam Margera and Johnny Knoxville's *CKY* and *Jackass* expanded failed stunts into their own medium. Suddenly the slam section felt quaint and fell out of vogue. It wasn't until the release of Emerica's *Stay Gold* that a new format, the B side, returned our focus to the struggle.

Now a standard practice for any major video release, the B side compiles raw, or at least raw*er*, footage, generally without music. We see the tight pattern of repeated motions and distractions of the outside world—pedestrians, cars, water, or flower pots dropped from apartment windows above the ledge. The sunlight changes and the shadows shift. The skater's clothing will change, or we'll see them land multiple versions of the trick, dissatisfied for one reason or another. In these we are given a sense that time is passing, and because all meaning is time-dependent meaning, the B side cracks the door ajar to something more mimetic or authentic to the skateboard activity.

Though, still, this is not quite it. The only way to really know the labor behind a clip of skateboard performance is to sit and observe, as I regularly find myself doing these days at Roberto Clemente Community Academy. Which, because it is not a skate park per se, slips through an ever-widening loophole in the debate about what does and doesn't "count" as street skating worthy of filming. Part of this debate is aesthetic—footage of all-gray concrete parks set apart from civilians and litter and deep sidewalk seams and the rest of the outside world looks terribly bland and boring—and part concerns that aforementioned labor. With its shitty ground, old stairs, and the waist-high walls that young legs can pop all the way up onto, Clemente is just naturally occurring enough that people will film there in good conscience.

Sit at Clemente long enough and you'll see a kid try a trick, fail, and then push energetically back to try again. You'll hear the filmer say "You got this," or "Right here," and show the skater how it looks in the camera's little screen. See the kid stay on the ground a little longer, hear the frustration emerge in sharper forms. They'll stop pushing back to the starting spot—now they walk slowly, talking to themselves. They'll throw and go retrieve their board. You'll see the filmer stand from their crouch to stretch legs, walk a circle, check their phone. Stay and you'll either see the thing made, feel the joy of that moment built upon the ascending misery of their labor, or see the skater succumb to the frustration, sit down to roll a joint, take off their shoes, and lie in the grass while everyone else goes about their business. The process can take hours, and if I filmed it I can promise you would not want to watch. We much prefer the dishonest version.

* * *

In late 2016 I recall thinking a great deal about this social secret apropos Brian Anderson, the tenth-named *Thrasher* Skater of the Year, who had just become the first openly gay male professional skateboarder. The news itself was not a surprise—in fact, it had been an open secret for at least a decade. Still, his announcement, on video and distributed online by Vice, does appear to have sparked something of a sea change within our unabashedly homophobic industry and culture. No real change is linear, of course, but it would be difficult to survey skateboarding in 2020 and fail to notice how much more interesting, more inclusive, and more queer it looks than in 2010.

To wonder how a secret such as BA's could survive in a culture like skateboarding for as long as it did, how this officially historic detail of Brian Anderson's personal life could remain in the official dark when rumors were circulating in the late *nineties* ("The whole industry knew," said Ed Templeton), is to undermine the nature and volume of labor that BA must have exerted over those years. And a labor that became even more strenuous when Instagram entered the world in 2010. Ten years later, as some of us weigh our own inevitable departures from the platform that has become so central to our lives, it's easy to forget how vigorously some pro skaters resisted this new arena of promotional labor. Take David Gravette's reluctant dispatch upon joining Instagram, posted, of course, to Instagram on February 22, 2014 (which, *sic*):

> I am sorry! To anyone who supported me and backed my choice to not dive on the bad wagon of self promotion and anti socialism that stems from social media. Never thought this day would come and the feelings of hypocrisy are replacing my last threads of honor. Possible the only thing that could bum me out more than joining this cult, would be to have to return to the real world and see how far my eye brow tattoos, high school education, and previous employments of paper boy and working at the skate park could get me. So that is what brings me here, cause it seems that the amount of followers a skater has might be more imperative to gaining or keeping sponsors than a lifetime of skating. i feel like i am still pretty young at 26 but have watched the world of skating i grew up with, and loved, transform into something I sometimes dont want anything to do with! but beneath all this internet bullshit and big corporate companies taking every last slice of the skate industry pie, is that I am still paying my bills doing the god damned funnest thing on earth! so am gonna try and keep that going and adapt to this shit the best i can…

More than most industries, skateboarding discovered in Instagram a natural extension of the often-uncodified labor of the skater professional. To be "sponsored" has always meant riding, wearing, and otherwise repping the gear a company sends in boxes to your front door in lieu of payment, often with the explicit understanding that a skater will sell some of that gear. How natural, then, to extend the labor of repping to a platform designed for exactly that.

So it is natural to confront social media platforms as a new demand of servitude and a restriction of freedom. But what struck me in 2016 was thinking about social media in terms of the secret BA had been keeping. Clinical studies have long shown that keeping a secret creates psychological demands—anxiety, stress, and depression. More recent research reveals that secrets take a physical toll as well. We tend to think of this suffering as it relates to the labor of suppressing the secret from others; we conceptualize *the secret* as an object, and imagine the contortions required to keep that object from sight. But secrecy is also a private experience, a way of being beyond the object, the state of knowing a truth and sitting alone with it even when not actively hiding anything. So, as often happens, a question of epistemology, the secret and who knows it, bleeds into yet one more question of ontology: secrecy as a way of being.

I could imagine the new freedoms Brian Anderson might have experienced, the gusts of relief, the eliminated labor, the sudden exposure of new and sensitive and pinkish truth, as soft as an infant's skin. But if we are to imagine secrecy as a way of being, and if we are to agree that social networking is an integrated part of our twenty-first-century world, then the photos we saw on Brian Anderson's IG feed of Lady Gaga and a stunning, shirtless Brian, the photos linked to articles in *Rolling Stone* and the *New York Times* about his announcement, are noteworthy not only for this one man in this specific situation, but to ourselves, our time, and our relationship to performance. This, it seemed to me, was an entirely new dimension of liberation that social networks have given us—the flipside of their massive, at times paralyzing ethos of deception.

The critic and novelist Lauren Oyler is among the not-unfew critics and novelists to have written about the damages of social media. In her review of Jia Tolentino's *Trick Mirror*, she begins with the obvious masochism of hate-reading to highlight what she calls the no-less-masochistic mechanics of sharing: "I offer a small part of myself up for judgment, requesting acknowledgment of my existence even as I seem to empty myself willingly into the crowd, putting myself at its mercy." Oyler's reminder to Tolentino is that we enter into this "dumb," "pathetic," "masochistic" relationship willingly—nothing is forcing us to share the way we do, over and over again. It is a matter of agency.

Held up to the special case of Brian Anderson in postannouncement 2016, this and other arguments about *the way we live online now* reveal their limitations, blindered as they are by that assumed masochism—quite a sweeping projection to foist onto, say, activist collectives, isolated people who lack access to communities of support, and as a matter of fact an entire population of users who do not suffer the same internalized pitfalls endemic to literary critics and novelists. I am not interested in redeeming or rescuing social networks or the internet from their ugliest devices. But I do wonder if we've assumed too much about the relationship between technologies and truths, the development of new venues for truth-performance through the venue of these technologies, truthfulness as a way of being. I'm thinking of my own secrets and those old, doomed romantic relationships of mine, back when I was dishonest. These are facts. So, what is to be said, now, of the healthy and challenging love of my committed marriage and the new species of honesty my wife and I continue to discover each day? Surely my existence is less stressful, less anxious, by this way of being that avoids unfaithfulness and the labor it would take to hide it from my wife. It would follow that the same goes for the much smaller infractions, the secrets that are not *kept* but are more explicitly parts of my selfhood. I mean those fears, deep ones, and vulnerabilities, the entire catalog of private, sacred scrawls and notes and beliefs that comprise the library of my depths. To have the technology and occasion to share all of these, I mean. Marriage as that technology.

And skateboarding, as technology? On the day that my wife and I were separated by the strange ontologies of the Palais de Tokyo's famous courtyard, we did eventually make it inside. Among the exhibits we saw was *L'Usage des formes* (The Use of Forms), a study of mankind's relationship to the world by way of tools, curated by Gallien Déjean. "The tool," read the exhibit copy, "like a prosthesis, is precisely this extension of the body that enables man to interact with his environment and to thereby pass from a state of nature to a state of culture." We moved from *Homo faber*, by which man creates tools to control their lives and environments, to *Homo ludens*, by which man "playfully misappropriates" these same tools to find new uses for them. And here came the second surprise of the day—a familiar series of films playing on loop inside a video installation room. Or, no. Not a surprise anymore to encounter a loop of *CKY* episodes screening at this impossibly contemporary art museum in Paris, "an ode to absurdity, to the loss of meaning, able to trigger that very specific laugh that seems to mock pain."

A tool, then. And one that has, along the way, facilitated quite a bit more than its fair share of heteronormativity—in 1998, a Birdhouse amateur named Tim von Werne famously had his *Skateboarder* magazine interview spiked by his sponsors for having spoken openly of his sexuality. And would you like another open secret? How about a culture of boys watching other boys' bodies more closely than they watch anything else, appraising and mimicking each turn and twist down to the phalange? And working tirelessly to overcompensate for this close study of the male form by performing an overblown and totally boring masculinity rooted in homophobia?

In *The Argonauts*, Maggie Nelson engages theorist Eve Kosofsky Sedgwick's desire to reclaim "queer" so that it could address any number of transgressions and subversions beyond the scope of sexual orientation. "She wanted the term to be a perpetual excitement," says Nelson, while retaining "a sense of the fugitive." Skateboarding's technology has always involved a queering of space and sport, even as it was also a source of great gendered cowardice and fragility.

How magnificent this thought, that all technological complexity will, whether intended or not, cede some small space to human honesty. Small at first, negligible and easily missed spaces, which might then, BA-like, expand, grow, and explode upon use. What a pleasant prospect for a minor salvation, I think. For us, at least, and perhaps technology, too.

CHAPTER TWENTY-FIVE

A Day with Chaz Ortiz

2017

1. MAKE FRIENDS WITH CHAZ ORTIZ

It might be hard for any skateboarder who has followed the skate industry in the past fifteen years, but I'd like us all to try to imagine that the most recent Chaz Ortiz footage was the first Chaz Ortiz footage you saw. Imagine you'd never seen the child with too-big ears and that slick, camera-ready smile. Imagine instead that the grown-up Chaz arrived on this planet fully formed at age twenty-two, innocent the last decade, with "Metropolis."

When I asked Chaz Ortiz if he ever thought about the ways his standing was burdened by his past as a contest kid, his reply was like a lot of his replies during the day we spent together. It came quickly and felt more honest than it should. I was sitting in his new and immaculate kitchen with a notepad, watching him while two round bulldogs slobbered at my feet. He said, "Dude, I think about that all the time."

Alas, Chaz. It was 2017, and everyone had already decided who you were. Age twenty-two and your story was inspiring to many, grating to a few, and in any case, already long. At age nine he got on Zoo York and started hustling victoriously through contests. He wore his hat the way he did. In 2010 Zoo turned him pro, and for years he shouldered the bulk of that iconic brand by way of big, visible logos and outsize expectations to collect clips on trips with the team. If you were among the legion who followed and double-tapped for Chaz Ortiz, it was not necessarily the story you loved. It was the laser flip, the composure, the being young and being fly.

Nor was it the story of Chaz Ortiz that bothered people like me. Bothersome had been the planetary sphere of his head, and the way he kept this tiny head motionless and totally squared above his feet, always in complete and bone-chilling control. His kickflip, which was a quick, negligible add-on to whatever else he was doing, like a side salad or pickle. It was the photo shoot/charity event of him sweeping leaves with supermodel Kate Upton in Fort Greene Park. The way his board seemed almost helpless beneath him. The life-size ads of him in boys-wear department stores across the US. How, over ten years of coverage, his smug little face had been grinning at me through the screen, like together the two of us had just done something wrong and I was the only one who got caught.

But if it weren't for that decade, it wouldn't be 120 degrees of floor-to-ceiling windows and five conspicuous trophies lining the space above his kitchen cabinets. Chaz Ortiz was Chicago's first and only celebrity skater, and when he invited me into his home, I told him two things up front. First, no interview. I was not a journalist in any real sense, just an aging skateboarder who had come to talk shit and get a sense of what he was about.

Second, that his "Metropolis" part represented the first time I'd been compelled to watch a Chaz Ortiz part more than once. I did not hide my lingering distaste for his early career because, as I told him, it seemed to me that something was different about "Metropolis" and I wondered what exactly that was.

After eight hours together, I can tell you some details to convey what Chaz Ortiz was currently about, now that he was no longer a child. For one thing, you couldn't always tell whether he was paying attention. Like a lot of skaters, he spoke in a casual, nondiagnostic way about ADD. He kept pacing his apartment and opening up a drawer to look for something he wanted to show me. "I like to keep shit," he said, pulling out the handwritten note that came with a bottle of Lil Wayne's new rum, Bumbu. The rapper's handwriting was legible and golden: "It's the smoothest shit I've had in my life!"

Since the Gatorade skate program had been shuttered and the private park they helped pay for shut down, I could report that Chaz Ortiz hydrates his guests with glass bottles of Voss Artesian Water. His girlfriend was friendly and beautiful and their two bulbous little bulldogs were adoring. I learned but will not share the approximate number of dollars Chaz Ortiz was paid every month by Zoo York. I will tell you that the lighting effects over Chaz Ortiz's kitchen island, the brightness and color of which he could control on his phone, were not standard for the building's C2 rental units. I can confirm that Chaz Ortiz lives in a rental unit because late in the night I saw him lose a hundred dollars on a senseless bet to a guy who he'd introduce as a friend, and who I'd later learn was actually some kind of property manager.

Ah, except here it gets difficult. I've written "late in the night" because for me, it was. Not for Chaz, however, because time is relative, just as wealth and happiness and "skateboarding" are relative, and in none of these categories did Chaz Ortiz and I overlap.

Spend enough time with Chaz Ortiz, affluent professional skateboarder, and you'll be reminded time and again that skateboarding is senseless. It is a labyrinth of arbitrary judgments and ridiculous values. We care, if we care at all, about the most inane shit imaginable. The bedrock qualities of our activity—revolution, reinterpretation, representation—are surely worth considering and defending, or at least positing, but beyond these, skateboarding criticism reduces down to taste, taste, and taste.

So, it was a strange and educational day I spent with Chaz Ortiz. Having by now recovered, I'd like to suggest that it is nothing short of a miracle that Chaz Ortiz cared about skateboarding at all. What's interesting is just how obviously he did. I have looked repeatedly into brown eyes that grew increasingly squinty as the day went on, and this much I can report with absolute certainty. Chaz Ortiz cares a whole awful lot.

2. TELL US WHO YOU HANG WITH
AND WE'LL TELL YOU WHO YOU ARE

We left the luxury apartment inside of a blacked-out 2017 Jeep Grand Cherokee, the sort of car I don't imagine comes from a regular dealership. It was the tail end of February and an impossibly pleasant sixty-five degrees in Chicago. We were on our way to say hello to a friend who was in town, whose name Chaz said but I didn't hear, and then we were to go skating. I'd basically made him promise me that we would in fact skate. We moved beneath the tracks on Lake Street, then to Wacker Drive along the river. Musically, it would be trap all day long. Chaz drove his luxury Jeep like he was not quite convinced by the theory of consequence, the way I would have driven if I hadn't ever really fucked up along the way.

In the posh River North entertainment district, we stopped at the curb to stare into a restaurant with a wall of open windows. The friend we were looking for was the rapper Machine Gun Kelly, who just happened that week to hold the current number one spot on the Billboard Pop Song charts.

"Do you see him in there?" asked Chaz. But I did not want to admit that I had no idea what Machine Gun Kelly looked like, so I pretended to be real busy with my notebook.

Actually, Machine Gun Kelly was at a different spot, which when we arrived was packed full of people dressed a good healthy leap beyond my profession. Chaz was in a hooded Zoo York windbreaker, what I believed were Zoo York twill "Brooklyn" pants, and Adidas Boost runners. The upstairs level, we were told, was at capacity. Weird, I thought, and indulged a nice sustained rotation, taking in the banquettes along the wall, the pulsing daytime lights reflected in walls of mirror, the chevrons on the ceiling. At that point I realized we were in a nightclub.

For ten minutes we waited in line, something I sensed neither Chaz Ortiz nor I was used to, though for different reasons. After a moment the music went silent and a voice came over the speakers calling for a bottle of Patrón to Machine Gun Kelly's table, the cheers rained down, and Chaz got a little antsy. Soon, we were ushered past the rope and up the stairs while the rest of the line discovered new ways to hate.

I had to keep my eye on Chaz, here, because I was totally fucking baffled by this place. In person, Machine Gun Kelly looked like a wizard or high-level mage, and his two Very Strong Friends in tight T-shirts were not the sort of fellas I normally hang with. We all shook hands and headed into the crowd of packed bodies. It was three o'clock in the afternoon and I was shouldering between men with perfect cuticles and very white teeth, women who generally did not see me, and a server holding aloft a flaming sparkler. On the way to MGK's table, we had to keep stopping so Chaz could be the valuable part of someone else's selfie.

And the table was actually a couch up onstage behind the DJ booth. A guard wearing an earpiece eyed me as I climbed up there, and at this point I'm going to skip a whole lot of material so that I can report the primary takeaway of my time onstage with Chaz Ortiz, which is this: once you are up there onstage, it is almost impossible to be unhappy.

I mean this—I awoke the next morning embroiled in what had become a kind of standard, sustained funk born of, well, a number of factors. Where were those factors onstage? Who cares. Once you are onstage, the world shrinks. There was no global warming, no creeping advancement of a new American fascism. Beers arrived and had fruit in them. The people beneath me were dancing, and they were obviously beneath me. If I made eye contact, I would have seen a keen awareness in their eyes, like a reverse glimmer: I was up there, they were not. Who are you? they would wonder. What had I accomplished, what victory or deceit had I pulled off to be standing up there with the Billboard rap star and actor?

Machine Gun Kelly was dancing on top of the couch wearing a $700 tank top and some of the least likely jeans in the history of denim. Chaz was calmly next to me, seemingly accustomed to all this. I walked over to the bottle of Patrón as if it were mine, as if I'd shorn the thorns of the agave plant's leaves with a machete. I poured a round and every one of my new peers onstage took one, and we were the luckiest people alive.

But soon MGK was bored. When Chaz told him we were going skating, which in the delirium of my sudden new caste I had forgotten, MGK decided that, actually, we were all going skating. So, we packed back into the Jeep and headed to Wilson Park, where MGK could recede into the sidelines to watch his friend, the professional skater. As it happened, most people in the park that day kept their eyes on Chaz, especially the kids. I managed to push around a little before retreating to the sideline myself. Maybe it was the drinks, but I was having a hard time staying in the moment. I kept thinking of a time that I came to Wilson a couple years back with Preston Harper, who was also a professional skater, technically. We were having our standard, stupid low-impact fun when here came Chaz Ortiz with a personal filmer, doing every-try backside flips over the pyramid. The park was empty that day, and I remember Chaz trying to be friendly with us. But because he was a contest brat and famous and we were old guard and aching in ways he couldn't possibly conceive, we didn't really engage.

Back in the Jeep on our way to dinner, I heard Chaz lobbying for the night's activities. A club owner had put ten Gs on the table if MGK showed up. But MGK's agent said he's not supposed to do appearances for less than fifteen (*thousand dollars*, to sit there at some high-visibility table in a club, holding a bottle and doing more or less what we were doing up on that stage earlier—and now it occurred to me, my god, was MGK being paid to stand on that couch and dance to "My Boo"?).

"He gave Wayne twenty-five," said Chaz. "I bet he'll go fifteen."

"Will he?" asked MGK. He was a tall, stringy white dude wearing circular sunglasses who'd been nothing but friendly to me, despite a clear distaste for writers and critics. "Shit, I get five," said Chaz, and together we all laughed at the absurdity of the world and inevitability of death.

And by this point I'd become more detached from the action around me. I thought of all the pressing skate questions I hadn't asked. There had been too much celebrity. Too many tiny sandwiches of sliced prime rib. The music was too much, relentless, beating at flat, total saturation, trap, that ambition rap, always telling you how to want. Hours had passed. Chaz gave away his windbreaker to a kid at the park who was cold, and I hadn't even asked about Nyjah yet. And to be quite honest, I still didn't understand why we ever got down from the stage.

3. "I'M HAPPY IT ALL CAME TOGETHER"

But then, just as the day seemed to have gotten away, the friends cleared out. Dinner ended and it was just me and Chaz Ortiz on stools, a couple of fellas drinking beers, talking skate. Suddenly he had gone loose. He was quick with praise for his Zoo York teammate Zered Bassett, who is the best, he said, the actual best, no question. But press Chaz Ortiz on who else he likes and you would see hints of the smile that, in the past, I had found smug. It read differently now. It wasn't pride I saw, but reticence, part standard-issue Midwestern and part deference to the complex system in which he'd found success.

But the rounds kept coming and we kept talking, enough that I'm not sure what I should and shouldn't share. He couldn't do switch 360 flips down stairs. He was vocally unimpressed by a certain skate team. He had what sounded like a legitimate beef with a newish shoe company. In fact, Chaz was fluent in all the shit talk and nerdery that defined our little society.

"Why is he a person?" he said of a colleague, and we laughed until the restaurant's manager arrived to introduce herself. She handed Chaz Ortiz her card and it was like he settled into a different gear, speaking to her. I would think of this moment later, when I was plunging deep into a YouTube spiral of contest footage. Watching old Dew Tour, X Games, and Street League clips, the victories aren't nearly as interesting as the occasions when Chaz is not skating his best, which means any time he's skating like other humans do, a way that includes falling. Like, every single time Chaz Ortiz falls, the announcer will rush to explain how falling, for Chaz Ortiz, is uncharacteristic.

And how about that? Imagine someone narrating in real time what is and isn't characteristic of you. I, for one, do not even particularly like people watching me skate. To imagine a public identity, a selfhood premised on constant, unsustainable success? The bar manager had comped us a round of premium tequila. In an interview, a TV person asks young Chaz about his strategy for an upcoming contest, as if the strategy this time might somehow be different than the last time, when he either won or came very close. "Hopefully stay on my board," answers Chaz, which is not a funny joke by any measure. But then he adds that "it's anyone's game," and if you watch very closely, there's a faint, sub-radar irony in his smile: *I can't believe you have me sitting here saying this shit.*

You can see it even more clearly in the precontest interview for the 2009 Wendy's Invitational stop of the Mountain Dew Dew Tour: "This one's gonna be a little different. I'm gonna skate hard and try to take it." Which to be clear, even just typing that dependent clause is enough to make me stand up and go to the kitchen for beer: *in the precontest interview of the Wendy's Invitational.* Imagine a life beholden to very large interests that overlap your own interests only by way of the prize purse they dangle carrot-like before your eyes. How many times can a kid look into a camera and describe what it is like to win? Or, uncharacteristically, to fail?

Now I watched Chaz enter the bar manager's number into his phone and then stay on it, socializing, and I knew the day was ending. But then he looked at me suddenly and went, "Dude how did I not win that?" We hadn't talked about Tampa 2014 for an hour at least, but I knew what he meant. I told him "Steez" was going to haunt him until the bitter end and he went "Fucking Rob Dyrdek."

Josh Kalis didn't like the term "contest brat" applied to Chaz Ortiz. "He skates hard as fuck," he said. I'd written to ask about Chaz's final trick in "Metropolis," a back noseblunt nollie heel, but Kalis's defense of Chaz Ortiz seemed more interesting than NBD wonkery. "Hate on it all you want, but then he comes through with some raw urban shit. Whoever calls him a contest brat, I invite them to go to Chicago and try to film a part. When they realize how hard it is, especially in the Loop, they might change their tune."

When I got home that Saturday night, I fell onto the couch next to my wife. Oh boy, she said, you are drunk. She was not wrong. I was stunted and dazed. But more than drunk, I was weary from my travels, and I would remain this way for days to come, never quite wherever or whenever I was supposed to be. The world of our home, with its expectations and established practices of communication, well, it took me some time to get all the way back.

Spend a day with a celebrity and you learn that the only real distinction between them and us is permission. The world tells them to go right ahead, ignore the haters, do you. Permission is the stage, everything else disappears. But from whom, do you think, does this permission come? God? The universe? No, only from the people who stand to benefit from their celebrity. From the owners of those nightclubs. From, if not Zoo, then the Iconix machine behind Zoo, the world's premier brand management company and owner of a diversified portfolio of strong global consumer brands across fashion, sports entertainment, and home. Permission is a savvy investment.

"Hate on it all you want," wrote Josh Kalis, so long as you're willing to change your tune. Here is the prize of "Metropolis"—all of us having no choice but to reconsider Chaz Ortiz. And the quieting of certain harsher voices among us who have been singing the tunes he can't help but hear. Do I have to say, this is why we need voices, to speak against permission? It is permission that leads to empty banalities in precontest interviews. Permission that results in Chaz settling for a slightly bigger laser flip in each new part. Chorus aside, a healthy skateboarding culture is one that must include criticism.

At age twenty-two, Chaz Ortiz was no longer the future champion of skateboarding. Something, some combination of forces had stopped Chaz Ortiz from achieving the escape velocity that comes of full celebrity and total permission. A big part of this was his family, whose support he spoke of with love and gratitude. He was a kind, composed, and generous young man who could do just about anything he wanted on a skateboard. In two years, his contract with Zoo York would expire, and whatever Chaz Ortiz did next I imagined he would continue to hear voices, because Chaz Ortiz cares.

This part is going to sound naive and probably soft, but at a pragmatic level, caring is precisely what we require in our cruel phase of history. Because what is skateboarding without failure? What is consistency if not the smoothest, most boring surface? What is a nightclub in the daytime? What is Chicago winter when it's sixty-five degrees in February? The world was growing madder and the stage grows higher, the stage gets smaller.

The reason for protest, for raising critical public voices, the reason we hate on regular success, is to determine who among us—on either side—actually cares. Most of the people up onstage aren't going to hear you over the din of permission. Others will. That's the moment when stories, maybe, get interesting.

CHAPTER TWENTY-SIX

On Tampa Pro

Do we ever wonder why skateboarders talk so much about skateboarding? No, stupid question. Because we share it. Because speaking of what happens in skateboarding—of the clips and photos of the feats, the films that assemble the feats and present them with varying degrees of artistry, of the industrial changes and rumors and business dealings—represents a central program of our own identities. Language is, among other things, a process by which identity leaks into the physical world. Language is what we collect from the world to calibrate and fuel our engines of identity.

So, it is strange when there's no talking. Six days after I watched, live and in person, the third and final day of Tampa Pro 2018, I sat quietly in the Tampa airport, reviewing what scattered and crooked notes I'd managed to make in my notebook. Words weren't much help. Mainly what I recalled were images collected in moments of absolute proximity—standing and leaning among these figures of skateboarding and knowing nobody actually, but everyone in the same ways that I always had, which is distantly, and falsely. But: I had been granted access, and the situation was different now than a week ago. I just wasn't sure how.

* * *

As far as winning, the kid who did it that year had a left hand thing I noticed, an elevation or float, and also he made faces as he moved across the course, as if thinking very hard or doing thinking's precise opposite, chewing on the individual moment of his timed and judged runs. He was seventeen years old and not a professional. I'm not sure he even had an obvious board sponsor at this point despite it being Tampa *Pro* 2018. From what I saw, he was indeed the most consistent and I guess winning skateboarder on the course. He didn't tire or slow and I can't imagine I was alone in not having any idea who he was. His given name is Jagger.

The wristband that *Jenkem* magazine had left under my name was red, but nobody told me what that meant—I guess because I arrived on day three of the three-day affair. I learned quickly that red would get me into the spectator area upstairs and yes, it was disorienting to be inside the Skatepark of Tampa looking down on a space more cramped than I expected. It did in fact smell the way it always looked like it smelled, but unlike pilgrimages I'd made to famous street spots, nothing shimmered with any mystical or even electric energy. Well, because it's a warehouse. And it's in Tampa.

I slid into a vacated spot on the railing and immediately saw Nyjah take a few extracurricular warm-ups between the late runs of Heat 1, then return to his place on one of the platforms and not talk to anyone. He's focused but not all the way, and seven years after he was the subject of my first entry into skateboard writing, I am not sure I can do this work without resorting to language of warfare and dominance. Can I describe what he's done to skateboarding without reducing him in the process? Nobody deserves to be a metaphor, after all. Nyjah has grown beefy, shoulders wide beneath the tattoo coverage that runs from chin down to thighs. Before the month is over, he and Ty Evans will release his first official Nike part, a tripartite coalition any of us could have predicted back in 2011. The video, "'Til Death," will be a pornography of warped perspective and slow motion and spectacle and bloody pathos, and his Nike signature pro model will be made entirely from proprietary rubber polymers. Maybe one way to put it is that, in person, Nyjah looks less like a soldier than a weapon of a terribly advanced sort.

They are not lying about this "day" measurement, either. It did truly go on. Eventually I gravitated toward what I want to call the "athletes' area," which is funny because, aside from the shade of a tent and the monitor of what's happening just on the other side of the wall, what really defined the athletes' area were the coolers of Corona and blunts full of what smelled like fairly decent weed. I spotted the photographer Matt Price inside, a mutual friend of a friend who I'd once spent an evening with sitting on an old dock on a lake in Farmington, Missouri, as the outer storms of a tornado rolled across our purview over the trees on the far bank. I assumed the red bracelet had a limit but no, I just walked right in to say hi. I could go anywhere, it turned out. I could reach into the cooler next to Raven Tershy and his red-on-red Jordan 11s, their patent leather reflecting the sun. I could drink a Corona standing with Ishod Wair and Tom Asta in a way that would perfectly mimic how we'd stand if we were friends talking, and float on a hybrid cloud of my own out-of-placeness and an anonymity that functioned like almost total invisibility.

As the finals were winding down, I located Ian Michna, founder and editor of *Jenkem*, and Alex Raspa, *Jenkem*'s main, I guess, videographer. Ian, as I'd expect, knew every single person in attendance. Alex seemed to also, somehow, though it could have been just that he's a New Yorker with a camera. Between the contest and dinner we went to their hotel and I lay on the floor, already more or less drunk, thinking about age and accomplishments and the annual AWP Conference for writers that I would attend later in the week, also in Tampa. This would be the year, it would turn out, that all the writers were talking about open marriages, their own and their friends', how it goes, how well it works. And also divorce, but that is AWP every year.

Yesterday, five days after Tampa Pro and three days into the writers' conference, I spent some of happy hour with my colleague Christian at the swimming pool where most of the conference attendees were staying—he and I were sleeping at a distant satellite hotel that shared a parking lot with a strip club. At the pool, not in. There, I spotted a writer I knew from Chicago, with whom, in fact, my wife and I had gone on one of those exploratory new-friend couples' dates because I knew and liked her husband. The results were conclusive and negative. In any case, I said hello and told her that I enjoyed her recent essay about her and her husband experimenting with Tinder profiles as a kind of social experiment. "Oh," she said, "I'm glad you enjoyed my misery."

Days earlier, the *Jenkem* guys and I left their hotel to meet up with a group of women who worked for Zumiez. The conversation over dinner was heavily industrial. One used to work for Street League, another actually worked for Stance Socks, or would. The stories they told were really updates to stories they'd told in the past, and there was a lot of "Yeah, that sounds like Buzzy." They were talking about the machinery of SLS and Rob Dyrdek and ETN, the media company that was digitally distributing today's and other contests, and even dulled as I was by the day, my selfish writer alarms were buzzing and spinning and yet I just could not bring myself to process many of the words passing across the table.

I was pinched into the back row of an overstuffed minivan when I understood what had happened. I'd gotten too close. The red brace-let was too powerful, I'd come too far, my nose was pressed right up against the skeleton. Once we made it to The Bricks, I took a shot with Jake Donnelly, turned from the bar, and found myself inside a tight encirclement listening to two-time *Thrasher* Skater of the Year

Chris Cole, who was earnestly and with formidable hand gestures describing the challenges of calling play-by-play for the live broadcast.

People danced, I danced, and it was a great relief when I realized that I wasn't being paranoid. Everyone there really did know each other. From where? Here. And also there. Because all of these annual skateboard events are actually the same event. A few contests, a couple-three trade shows, a handful of release parties and that's your fiscal year—now run in it all back. The occasions are incidental, the titles shift, and the industry is the industry. On the patio out back, I watched someone film Ishod with their phone as Ishod just stood there being a person, without asking or discussing it with him. Ishod's face twisted into a perfect WTF shape as he turned to find sympathetic eyes to convey his…not anger, exactly. Mine happened to be the eyes, and I happened to have seen what he wanted me to see, but still, as he walked back inside, my thought was, That person is the best skateboarder alive.

But is he? It was a contest, after all, and my route is spiraling us back to Nyjah. That afternoon I'd watched him do a single massive, thundering nollie heel over this year's version of the tame, mellow hips common to Tampa's recent strings of arrangements. It is strange, I want to say, to build so toothless an obstacle for professional skateboarders. What happened to, like, the Radlands volcano? Well, dummy, because the purpose of this hip is primarily to facilitate Manny Santiago's every-try laser flips so his runs can go smoothly and Chris Cole can speak the words while Andrew Cannon emotes and the few of us who fit can applaud from the rafters and the athletes can ignore all of it from the athletes' area. Suddenly and with great impact I was struck by the basic flaw of all skateboarding contests: *they penalize failure*. How inane! How absolutely and fundamentally wrong to deduct points for doing that which comprises the vast majority of what skateboarders do. Skateboarding *is* failure! Anyway, I don't know where I was when

Nyjah hurt his ankle and dropped out. Maybe I was standing there watching and still didn't notice.

* * *

I drove out of Tampa early on the following Monday morning, down the Gulf Coast and into the Everglades. Just after sunrise on Tuesday morning, I woke and got myself onto the Anhinga Trail. What I will remember, always, are the sounds that fill the Glades. Nowhere have I heard more clearly the disregard for human life. It is the Mesozoic down there, man, rich with screeches and twills and calls that ring in three dimensions from great distance and tight proximity. Regarding the bench under the awning of the welcome center, I less wanted to skate it than to contribute the noise of skating to that ringing cacophony. I mean the most interesting sound that I, vulnerable and fleshy human, am capable of making, that grind of forged aluminum chewing into a concrete edge, a song both human and not, natural and un-.

I have, since about the time when I began writing determinedly, feared the prospect of becoming a miserable person. At the swimming pool at happy hour, had I responded, I might have told the miserable essayist, No, it is not your misery I enjoyed, not as I read your essay or sat with our spouses on that trial date or now, here in the gorgeous Florida sun. What I enjoyed is how, knowing that you, its author, were miserable, the essay read to me as an example of misery and conflict being harnessed into possibility, which, though your essay does not seem interested in pursuing that possibility and centering it, making possibility the perspective or spirit from which you write, does remind me that the two swirl in the same pool of creative energy. What I enjoyed, as I do sometimes, is the mirror that your essay provided.

At the time of Tampa, my wife and I had not yet begun the marital therapy that would confirm that my fear was not unfounded. It all made good sense—after eight, nine years of competition and pressure and rejection, I couldn't deny the tolls that writing had taken on me. Late one night, among writers, I had claimed that my unagented and elliptical novel about skateboarding was *objectively beautiful*, and about 25 percent of me believed it. The newer pain, which came accompanied with a host of new fears, was due to the very real toll my writing had begun taking on my wife. I should say that I reject outright the notion that one must be miserable in order to create. And I know that *people* can write without it destroying them, just as *people* can play tennis without screaming into the sky and breaking rackets. But I'd lost touch with possibility.

"Do you even *want* to be happy? I mean that as a real question. Do you believe in happiness? Is it a thing you want to pursue?"

The Skatepark of Tampa is a warehouse familiar and unsurprising, with wax caked so thick on its rails that casually scraping a fingernail along one will earn you a thick black worm as a souvenir. The vert ramp is long gone. The warehouse walls are corrugated. The course changes each year and this is a point of great Skatepark of Tampa pride. But change is the false god of this place, like so many others, the name in which the church prays while keeping a much realer commitment to the same, same, and same. They still penalize for failure and dole out numerical scores. One hundred is the best you can do.

A few months after Tampa, Ian and *Jenkem* would reject an article I sent them, one I wrote in a fury of anger and unusual output, getting done in a weekend what normally takes me two to three weeks or longer. My knee was hurt at the time, so I couldn't skate, and my wife was out of town, so I was able to move recklessly about the house without having to justify the anger or sleeplessness. It's possible, too, that I'd begun writing the article long before that weekend, as early as that seat in the airport as I was waiting to leave Florida. In any case, *Jenkem* wouldn't run it. It was nothing personal, as I understood. Truly, their hands and wrists were tied.

CHAPTER TWENTY-SEVEN

Primitive Progressivism

2018

And so, the aging skateboard legend assumed the appearance we had come to know him by, buttoning his shirt tight to the collar and putting on his two hats. And seriously, did he read or at least summarize a portion of the apology he had written to us, which I can summarize for you now: He has changed, words are not actions, he will keep changing, he denies hate, embraces love. He reminds us how long it's been since the Bad Thing he said, denies that saying the Bad Thing defines him, apologizes, expresses regret, apologizes again, declares love to everyone reading. It is general, it is vague, and written in handwriting totally on brand for Jason Jessee.

For anyone who hasn't seen them, here are the specifically hideous words Jason Jessee spoke during a 1994 interview with *Iron Horse* magazine: "My mom fucked a nigger and me and my sisters found out about it—and I'm older than the nigger!" Here are some others: "I live in Santa Cruz. There's a lot of militant lesbians here and raw faggots." In the past, those of us who didn't subscribe to *Iron Horse* in the mid-1990s might have missed this little bundle of hideous language. But every day, these days, seems to teach a new lesson in the limited lung capacity of yesterday's secrets. Everything floats to the surface. Nothing is secret.

But how about sacred? Since that interview, Jason Jessee has formed some swatstikas out of steel and pinned some swastikas onto denim jackets. He's had his photo taken wearing motorcycling gloves dominated by a big, hand-size swastika on each. He's made friends with the sort of people who visit his Instagram page to say he's their hero and complain how PC culture has run amok, or to defend the swastika's heritage and suggest that maybe Jason Jessee is the real victim here. Doesn't Jason Jessee deserve an apology for being called a racist?

* * *

I'm summarizing all this because, like a lot of you, I find this situation depressingly familiar. "My example speaks louder than my words," wrote Jessee.

But can we agree, readers, that words are not farts? Words do not gather against our interests and then slip squealing out of our bodies in ways we only partially control. And the clean distinction between words and actions is a little too convenient, philosophically speaking. We have a whole class of speech acts that are themselves mechanisms for changing relationships and power dynamics in the world: promises, insults, marriage pronouncements, christenings of children, and, of course, apologies.

But Jason Jessee's letter doesn't actually become an apology until its postscript, when he says he "truly regrets" his actions that hurt or offended anyone. For most of the letter, he's looking less for forgiveness than to *be excused*. One clean path to being excused is to admit having done the Bad Thing and then call into question its actual badness. This is why apologies that focus on "any offense caused" or "anyone's hurt feelings," or that hinge on a conditional "if" tend to feel insincere: they cast doubt on the obvious badness of the speaker's behavior. To his credit, Jessee's appears to recognize that he's done an actual Bad Thing. However, he also insists that the rest of his life, his "example" and the love in his heart, should outweigh the Bad Thing. Because many of us don't know Jason Jessee personally and have no way to know his actions beyond on-screen hijinks and, now, the swastikas and hideous language from the twenty-four-year-old interview, these arguments serve as a version of the common nonapologist's appeal to a private self that transcends and even rebukes the Bad Thing: "Anyone who really knows me knows I'm not really Bad."

By comparison, to ask forgiveness is to accept blame and moral responsibility for the Bad Thing without excuse or pointing to some mitigating circumstance. It's the promise that behind and before that act came a legitimate, concentrated moral *reckoning*. And there is a chance, still, that being "indefinitely suspended" from most of his sponsors will result in Jason Jessee showing us that he's reckoning with his Bad Things. That will mean more interviews and video clips. It will go on and he'll either learn or not, it will be his journey, and I frankly don't care too much about Jason Jessee anymore, and you probably shouldn't either.

The real issue at hand here is not Jason Jessee but the system that was complicit in putting him into his current role despite knowing the Bad Things in his past. The big problem is the prevailing silence and empty emoticons that defined the skate industry's response to his apology. Those who spoke did so obliquely, and few I talked to were willing to go on the record with any comment remotely specific to Jessee. Ryan Lay was, for a time, the only known skater who commented: "I really would prefer not to be the only person addressing this," he eventually wrote to the public, "but a lot of people in the skate community are really upset and rightfully so. They basically feel like the industry has let them down."

Jim Thiebaud posted his own apology for the role he played in the complicitness, and reached out to me to say emphatically: "Bigotry and hatred don't belong in skateboarding. Period." Hearing his voice, hearing Bob Denike's voice and Andrew Cannon's voice, it was clear that those first few days after the story broke were tough on them.

Reckonings are, by their nature, difficult things. Far easier to go the route of *The Nine Club*, who responded to a DM by explaining that they "try to avoid all that negative crap. Jason is a great skate-boarder and person who said some really dumb stuff back in the mid 90s…no need to revisit it."

* * *

The United States is a nation founded on land stolen from indig-enous nonwhites and wealth built from the slave labor of African Blacks. Modern skateboarding is an industry and culture founded on the exploits of a dozen surfers and skaters in the 1970s and the writer/photographer who made them into legends. This is the gospel according to Craig Stecyk, whose writing on the Z-Boys you probably have not read, but have definitely seen quoted. For instance: "Yesterday's heroes, the mangled messages left molding by the all-fronts media blitz and tomorrow's tragedies are all meaningless to the contemporary skater." Here, in a typically florid and alliterative sentence, is the entire mythos of the skate outlaw and their rolling, eternal now. No looking back, and no looking forward either.

But I'm not sure many skateboarders realize just how small and insular the US skateboard industry really is. The slightest look behind the curtain reveals about 120 people, 150 max, cramped into a cozy pyramid; everyone knows everyone else. Nor might the average skater realize just how concentrated the power is at this pyramid's top. In 2012, I was surprised to receive an e-mail from Dave Carnie, a writer I'll argue is second only to Stecyk in terms of importance to skateboarding. It seemed that Carnie had read my profile of Andrew Reynolds and wondered about doing something on Steve Berra. I'd have to be careful, he warned, because he'd have to give Berra final review of whatever I wrote.

When I said, basically, "Hold on, you're Dave Fucking Carnie," he explained that Berra had the power to yank advertising and thus was not someone to fuck with. He admitted that this was not very punk rock, but unfortunately he had to consider the reality of the situation.

The next time you wonder why there is no such thing as hard-hitting skate journalism, consider Dave Carnie, the most radical and subversive writer in the history of skateboarding. Consider a world in which someone so overtly narcissistic and fragile as Berra is granted control over how he's covered. Or consider other real-world practices that are missing from skateboarding—things like labor unions, or organizations that might offer any other kind of protections for pros and amateurs. Consider how fragile is the existence of all those skaters hustling for some small space inside the pyramid. A single injury—like Jason Jessee's broken leg in 1991—and they're done.

Consider how frightening this must be, knowing how profoundly replaceable you are. And considering all this, it begins to make sense that no skaters, or writers, or other industry figures were interested or brave enough even to comment on Jason Jessee's swastikas. Skateboarding's history of blacklisting is fairly short, officially, but the lessons are stark. Anyone, everyone can be replaced.

* * *

It's a good thing skateboarding has discovered the world's most powerful remedy, isn't it? Marvel as the pro skater dismisses the haters and moves fluidly on from "all that negative crap." Watch them practice gratitude daily on the apps. Feel the love of each moment. As Jessee says, "I have zero hatred or negativity in my heart for anybody or anything, only love." How could this be wrong? And anyway, isn't the swastika itself ambiguous in its meaning? Doesn't the symbol predate all that negative crap the Nazis attached to it? Everyone knows what it means and stands for, but there's always some bit of thumbnail Sanskrit scholarship that can get you off the hook if you don't want to say it.

Read his original articles and it's clear that Craig Stecyk was as interested in morality and its misuse as he was in foundational hero myths. In particular, his "Surf Nazis and Other Objectionable Material" dives hard into this contested realm of "actually." Stecyk writes of Greg Noll's 1964 film, *Search for Surf*, describing a scene wherein a group of smiling blond surfer boys take a wheeled flexi flyer to La Jolla's storm drain, one of them in full Nazi regalia. First, Stecyk rationalizes: "Whose father's footlocker didn't sport at least a samurai sword, a captured battle flag or a German officer's coat?" Then he equates the "misunderstood" Nazi uniform with "hot rodding, low riding, and motorcycling," all of which East Coast "mavens of 'appropriateness'" fear for equally wrong reasons. The only crime on display, Stecyk says, was how "the arbiters of the 'social norm' overreacted to these decidedly non-ideologically based pranks."

Keep in mind that the film in question is from *1964*, a year in which many Black American citizens were still not allowed to vote. State antimiscegenation laws stood until 1967's *Loving v. Virginia* in the US Supreme Court. This scene happened in pre–civil rights USA; these charming blond boys put on Nazi uniforms nonideologically nearly twenty years after their fathers brought them home as trophies—or for whatever other reason—from Europe's bloodlands.

This is where skateboarding began; it doesn't require a master's degree in the internet to find any of it. Of course, if you don't want to look, you won't find it. If you don't want to see Jake Phelps getting hyped by a swastika, you don't have to. If you'd rather celebrate Stecyk's ubiquitous bit on the minds of eleven-year-olds than pay $3.99 to read his 1992 article rambling about outsider art and the fascism of anti-fascists, it's easy. And no one, up until recently, would blame you if you'd rather go googly-eyed at Jason Jessee's frontside airs than hear Denver Dan say of his friend,

"When his mom fucked a black dude, he said, 'Mom, that's fucked. When she dies I'm gonna dig up her bones and surgically implant them in my belly and shit them out. And then we'll be even. I owe her nothing.'" Denver Dan said this on film back in 2006 for *Pray for Me: The Jason Jessee Film*, a documentary that I imagine Santa Cruz, Converse, and other sponsors might have thought to consider before they started writing Jessee a new round of industry paychecks.

Speak to industry figures on the phone and two things are clear: One, they claim to have had no idea about this stuff. Two, this is just not the Jason they know and love. Their friend Jessee could not also be this person.

It might be a totally retrograde and simplistic and naive understanding of racism, but it's comforting to people who define themselves wholly by love. It also offers a convenient escape. Rather than take Jason Jessee's recent collision with his dark past as an opportunity to work against the systemic forces that convinced him it was OK to rock swastikas in the first place, the industry can simply bottle it up as something "in the past" and of it. Recall Stecyk and live in the now, instead. Live inside love.

Never mind that two-thirds of the contemporary skate industry is dedicated to repackaging the past through reissues of old boards, shoes, and brands. Under the blissed-out rhetoric and ad hoc worldview is a familiar and stubborn status quo. It inhales our silent complacency like oxygen, and its exhale is poison.

* * *

Forty years after Stecyk wrote the foundations of skateboarding legend, the big question is this: Is skateboarding a primitive force, or is it a progressive one? Or more than that: Will skateboarding continue to perpetuate the old American power dynamics of few and many, of white supremacy and brown otherness, or will it work to dismantle them? Does it PMA its way into cozy selfishness or play a more difficult and labor-intensive role in the world beyond itself?

They're not rhetorical questions. The Jason Jessee apology puppet show is a good reminder that the US skate industry doesn't have our best interests in mind. As it currently exists, built by surfers, it's a machine programmed to capitalize on nostalgia and hero worship. Its representatives are men with dubious histories who have in many cases done historically Bad Things. After nearly thirty years of spending my money on skateboarding, of paying to engage in an activity and belong to a culture defined in large part by its ugliest and most violent legends, it's pretty clear to me that, inside of skateboarding, our best answer is a primitive progressiveness.

It's to say to Craig Stecyk: you don't speak for me and you're done speaking for skateboarding. It's to say to Jason Jessee: I hope you find the help and support to remain healthy and grow toward a new understanding of racism in America—and also, fuck you. And to the narcissists, the powermongers, the skaters who beat their girlfriends, who abuse and drug and rape: fuck y'all. And to the few remaining California old guard who continue to own and oversee a workplace that enforces silence and disempowers the people working in the industry? Fuck you the worst. This isn't about playing the PC police. It is direct democracy.

It's been forty long years since Craig Stecyk wrote his articles, and still we're quivering in the shadows of these old, creaky, defective gods. Forty years of wandering and barely any distance traveled. There's some historical precedent for that, at least. As the crow flies, the distance from Egypt to the banks of Jordan is one the Israelites could have covered in days. What took them so long? One reading goes like this: The generation that led them into the desert had lived its whole life under the old system of slavery and was unprepared for the responsibilities of freedom. In order to be free, the Israelites needed to wait those forty years for them to die off.

It is 2018. Next time you're out skating, have a look around. What do you see, today, but a land of milk and honey—Jewish and

Black and brown and transgender skaters, girls wearing hijabs and queer boys kissing on the steps, and so many of them skating better than Jason Jessee ever did or could. That's skateboarding today, that's our new industry, and that's what matters. And fuck off, Nazi scum, if you disagree.

CHAPTER TWENTY-EIGHT

On Pushing Boarders

What follows is a brief account of the skateboard industry fuckery that both provoked and accompanied the publishing, erasure, and republishing of the previous chapter. Because the events unfold linearly we might call it a story, one whose main character is the Skateboarding Industry. That is, the creature whose genesis was an evolutionary crawl out of the sea and into surf shops, and which in the very late eighties fell into the hands of freestyle skaters (quoth Jason Dill, "These freestyle dorks never partied, that's why they run the industry") who would, two decades later, oversee its transfer into the books of global footwear companies.

In December 2017, I received an invitation to participate in what was being billed as the first ever international conference on skateboarding, to be hosted by University College London in early June 2018. Pushing Boarders would bring skateboarding academics of architecture and sociology together with representatives from skate NGOs (Skateistan, SkatePal, the Tony Hawk Foundation) and the skateboard industry. They wanted to have a panel on the unique challenges of writing about skateboarding. I responded immediately to thank them and accept.

It was spring by the time the first rumblings of the Jason Jessee situation appeared online. After years away, his visibility was about maxed out—he had the cover of May's *Thrasher* and the final after-credits part in Converse's first full-length, *Purple*. Adidas had Mark Gonzales, Nike had Lance Mountain, Vans had Jeff Grosso and Steve Caballero and Christian Hosoi and about every known skater from the seventies and eighties *except* Lance Mountain—now Cons had their own legacy ambassador. It is hard, with such stuff, to know how closely to look, but suddenly the message boards were full of terrible, incriminating artifacts being unearthed by a kind of crowd-sourced detective project. So, I started watching and talking to people. I met up with a skater at a coffee spot in my neighborhood, a table outside, and he spoke openly and angrily about growing up Jewish in Cincinnati. When Jessee posted his apology, I was stunned by its ineptitude and the swiftness of its broad acceptance. I was also, I should note, empowered by the upcoming conference.

On May 21, I submitted the article to *Jenkem*. I was conscious to have skirted around the specifics of Jessee's sponsors. *Jenkem*'s relationship to Cons was no secret—their banner ads were fixtures on the site and they'd subsidized the production of *Jenkem*'s two hardbound book projects, among other trips and projects. The following day, I got an e-mail suggesting some fairly radical revisions to the piece, all of them aimed at having a "greater dialogue" about the bigger problems in the skate industry, of which, they suggested, Jason Jessee was only a symptom. They listed a series of Bad Things from the long history of skateboarding. They suggested I lose the anger and replace it with encouragement for the next generation. They acknowledged that it would take time to write the more inclusive (exhaustive?) article about the industry's systemic ills that they wanted. But actually, waiting a bit would be a positive because it would mean the article wouldn't be anchored in time to Jason Jessee per se.

All of which struck me then and now as a very long-winded,

labor-intensive two-step lacking the clarity of what I suspected was the true explanation, an explanation that has since been fortified by other writers who submitted their own Jason Jessee articles to *Jenkem*. I have spent some time studying irony and I suppose, in that sense, there was some interest to experiencing the effects of the industry's illness that my article had aimed to diagnose. *Jenkem* couldn't run anything about Jason Jessee. Converse would cut their support.

There is no simpler way to put this: Skateboarding has no journalism, only "coverage" coordinated to align with the plans and promotions of each magazine's sponsors. Skateboard publications are and have always been trade magazines. *Thrasher* began as a way to promote Independent trucks. A couple years later, *Transworld* was a chance to promote Tracker trucks. It's almost too stupid to bear, and until someone figures out a new model for revenue the whole enterprise will remain beholden to advertisers (who, recall, are the very companies who produce the video content that drives the culture around which the magazines orbit).

Anyway, I declined. I told *Jenkem* that if they sat on the issue and said nothing they would be perpetuating the de facto gag rules of a fucked up industry. I was angry and sensed the luxury of my anger, the security of my position outside of the industry, with my teaching career, my invitations to international conferences. The next day I visited the Art Institute. I found myself going downstairs to the photography room, where I encountered a Darryl Cowherd photo called "Gage Park Protest, Chicago." Shot during the white-led counterprotests against Martin Luther King Jr.'s desegregation campaign in Chicago, it shows a group of ten white people, young men of the so-called White People's March of September 10, 1966. And they were all so familiar, these dudes. They were flesh and living men hung on the wall, and I knew them. I thought of a moment late in DeLillo's *Running Dog*, when Lightborne, collector and reseller, holds the object of his longing and realizes, "Objects were what they seemed to be. History is true." I understood.

History is not over. So, I took a picture of the picture and posted it to Instagram with this caption:

> I spent much of last weekend writing a long, angry thing about Jason Jessee. Was too angry for *Jenkem*, too rooted in my perspective to represent theirs, and is surely too angry for other US skate pubs, and that's how it goes. So, let me say here: fuck Jason Jessee, fuck those who are compliant in harboring and protecting and loving racist white folk, thinking that positivity will somehow comfort us through all this. Love doesn't tear down systems. Heart emoticons are worse than silence. So long as we cling to the old gods as mythologized by the old lore, we're not going anywhere. Fuck friendly. Fuck respect. Fuck Stecyk and all trickle down mythology. Skateboarding is more ours than it is theirs. We're the ones who pay for it. We make the industry wheels spin. We decide what "skateboarding" means.

Well, the richest angers are those that unfold. By the time I'd left the museum, an editor at *King* magazine in Canada had reached out and by the next day, he'd offered four pages in their next print magazine along with an online feature much sooner, in time for the upcoming conference.

Then we were visiting family outside of Bristol, my wife and I there for a few days before heading off to the London conference, which would open on Friday night. The article went up on *King*'s site as I was enjoying Thursday night, and I soon fell into the fuzzy embrace of Ambien and positive feedback. By Friday morning, the article had been taken down, and I had an uncomfortable, apologetic message from Jeff, *King*'s editor, written in a series of bullet-points, which I'll summarize:

- The piece "took off right away."
- Upon seeing it, Jason Jessee had personally phoned Dave

Carnie, a personal hero of mine and former editor of *King Shit*, which became *King*, asking to have it taken down.

- Dave (MF Carnie, model of liberated and free-spirited writing, whose middle fingers gave even themselves the middle finger) called the publisher of *King* to act on Jason's wishes. Publisher got shook and obliged.

- Article quickly disappeared from the website and forthcoming print issue.

- Publisher spoke with editors at *Jenkem* about doing something that Converse would have "a final say on."

- Would I like to interview Jason Jessee one-on-one and have it released on *Jenkem*?

- We know how this looks, taking down your angry article and replacing with something that focuses so much on Jason.

Off to London, then, frankly agog at the brazenness of the access journalism I'd been offered. K and I found our hotel and drank beers and moved through the city by foot, as we like to. On Saturday, the conference's first session featured Iain Borden and Ocean Howell and Becky Beal, and I was not alone in my amazement at what was happening before us—a serious and inclusive conversation about academia, and the room was full, as it would be all weekend as skateboarders spoke of race and gender, NGOs and occupied Palestine, the whole broad world described in the unique vernacular of our toy. At the breaks we moved about in a daze, eager to talk but cautious, I think, of popping whatever dream bubble had manifested this unlikely gathering.

Our panel on skateboard writing was hosted by Ted Barrow, who has since become a friend. My co-panelists ran a gamut of approaches and views and histories, and I listened, and listened, until Ted handed me the mic and asked about the Jason Jessee article, which had over the course of a long day and a half become something of a *samizdat*. Aside from one or two pro skaters who

I knew were friends of Jessee's, it was as sympathetic a crowd as could be imagined. So, I spoke of the old, rusty hulk of California's industrial surfing core and their professed desire to move forward while trading in rereleased classic boards and beach towels of classic logos. I spoke of introspection and reflection and using our outsider revolutionary status as a way to escape that which the industry worked to ensure we'd never escape, which is itself.

Then there was applause that felt to hear much the way the notes I started receiving felt to read, once the article was picked up and published again by *Free Skateboard Magazine*. To be thanked by strangers is a precious and profound joy. I had, after all, spent eight years at this point working alone on a novel that nobody who read it, save K, seemed to enjoy reading. And so, while the story goes on, we have arrived at an eddy of personal gravity that I am going to indulge. It would take a year and more—well, it took therapy—before I could give words to any of this, but the seed was planted in those days following the conference. Many years prior, I had made a choice to take writing seriously. Quickly I developed notions, firm ones, about the ways writing and living should inter-act. Now, I can look back at this young person, as surely I could have looked back at him from the year 2018, and say, *That young me does not understand dick of the world, man.* Look at the fool! And yet, I had by some baffling artistic inertia continued to abide by the same rigid arithmetic of success, forgetting entirely that my life's principle joy has, since childhood, been rooted in a practice of failure. What damage my commitment to that fool's notion of success had wrought.

* * *

The second iteration of the world's first international skate-boarding conference, Pushing Boarders 2019, was held in Malmö, Sweden. The focus this time was more explicitly on social issues and activism. The event was larger and longer than the first, its disagreements and protests more visible, the challenges more acute. By its end, the event's organizers were depleted and asking openly for help, as were others, live and in person, for this was a theme of the event, individual mental health and the role the skate community can play in supporting and assisting those who need it. Such matters are now part of the conversation.

And, too, a more complex discourse between skateboarding's industry and culture. In the first half of 2020 that has meant being held to task for a stuttered response to the uprising against police departments in the name of racial justice and a reconsideration of the great debts owed to Black culture and Black skaters. Contra and with great personal risk at the hands of skateboard tradition, Na-Kel Smith took to his Instagram Live and broadcast a long testimonial about casual racism he's experienced in Los Angeles, in tour vans, in the industry. Has meant the growth of Unity, the LGBTQ+ collective started by Jeff Cheung, and its board company, There. Has meant girls and women representing the fastest growing market segment, and two all-women skate videos released by the two major skate shoe brands. Vans's *Credits* was filmed and edited by Shari White, cofounder of *The Skate Witches* zine and crew, and forgoes camera technology in favor of the analog texture of the VX1000 and friendship and laughter, foregrounding *these* skaters and *this* skating above all else. Nike's *Gizmo*, conversely, was filmed and edited by Jason Hernandez and can feel, at times, as distant from its subjects as the drone shots that provide B-roll. The skaters of *Gizmo* cycle through unnamed until the end-of-film credits, when, as a matter of awkward fact, Jason Hernandez's own is the first name we see.

Work to be done, still, on every front. There are abusers among us and very real dangers for those who would expose them. Skateboarding's systems can't but exist within broader US systems of racism and inequity. But our statues do not require rope to be torn down, and it would seem that each day brings new, beautiful freaks eager and capable of doing just that. The gatekeeping that has perpetuated white supremacy in publishing and Hollywood and every facet of American entertainment is finding itself, in skateboarding, newly challenged. And you can feel it, anyone who's spent time in this old creaking house. Narrow hallways have been sledgehammered to reveal new sources of ambient light. There is new space for new storytellers, new possibilities, new meanings. New standards and expectations, new tricks, new approaches to what even qualifies as such. New movements, presented newly.

CHAPTER TWENTY-NINE

A Serious Man: Mark Suciu's "Verso"

2019

So, anticipation, that terrible and excellent fever, had indeed survived into 2019. Finally, Mark Suciu's "Verso" was here, two months after it premiered to small crowds in San Mateo and New York City. Eleven minutes and thirty seconds split into four distinct movements. It's a strange shape but not unprecedented—Nyjah's "'Til Death" video was also eleven minutes, once all was slowed and done. But next to "Verso," "'Til Death" looks gluttonous, eleven minutes for only seventy-one tricks. This is a total Mark Suciu reaches by the halfway point of "Verso" and more than doubles by the end. That is because "Verso," a triumph of contemporary skateboarding, is constructed almost exclusively out of skateboard tricks.

On first watch, its opening moments can feel like the release of long-stuck plumbing. A melodica, a kind of toy instrument some play seriously, rings out, and here's Mark doing a switch back noseblunt followed by a switch back noseblunt flip out. In a few minutes he'll do front blunt then front blunt flip out, which is the way "Verso" goes about its work—by pairs, sequences, and reflections.

Filmmaker Justin Albert moves us from section to section with moments of architecture and fountains, columns and kaleidoscopes.

It's a light touch, and tasteful. There's a brief shot of a coffee cup and a Willa Cather novel, shots of Mark in profile or flatgrounding in the distance, and some scenic worldly B-roll but no real lifestyle arguments, no Eiffel Tower or heavy geographical cues. We're in San Francisco and St. Louis and Tokyo and London; we're citizens of a borderless world, everywhere at once.

So, that is one strange thing: it's a major video production with skating as the first, last, and only real point. It can feel sometimes like Mark is moving through a kind of vacuum or isolation chamber. We don't even see a high five until the back noseblunt at Blubba. "I wanted to put together a part that, to me, is perfect," he told *Thrasher*. Forget for now the tropes of the modern skate video. There is no zoom into Mark's face. There are no brushes with security or pedestrians. No fascination with fingernails, no heaving ogre growls of slow-motion cheers. "Verso" is serif fonts and modulations of pace. The third movement is all New York and Mark's commitment to surprise. We do not expect a back 180 out of a front feeble or the quick wallride after dropping into the Bronx Borough Courthouse bank— are any other feet quick enough for the cellar door chain hop?

Perfection is folly, of course. But the desire is the thing, the impossible ideal. "Verso" has been conceived of and executed, sculpted into this form. It is a single whole comprised of 150 constituent parts that are paired, woven, and otherwise combined into sequences. The novelist and critic John Barth famously argued that "virtuosity is a virtue." The critic and novelist William Gass once said, "the trivial is as important as the important when looked at importantly." If it feels like I'm taking this too seriously, it's only because "Verso" deserves it.

* * *

Back up a step and imagine that you're an ascendant skateboard wizard. It's 2011 and you, not yet twenty years old, are able to do more or less anything you want on a skateboard. You skate sizeable gaps and high, long rails and have, since you were a kid, been doing weird variations of every flatground trick there is. Lines are becoming your primary tongue. You can do at least the great majority of all existing grinds and slides and have begun finding new ways to spin and torque into and out of them. You are gobsmackingly good at skateboarding and still very young and soon to be pro and truly, from my perspective, it must be a super rad and fun way to be.

At the end of 2011, you put out the first and defining part of your career and the people love it. They croak and clap and speak in great hyperboles about melting faces and shitted pants. A few don't like it or pretend not to like it but they are the exceptions, and we all know that a lot of skaters are assholes, so you're not bothered. What does hurt, however, is how nobody seems to really get it. Not completely. They don't notice the specific kind of work you put into making the part. And this feels disappointing. Deflating, I imagine, like a totally private, secret, and unshareable little death.

Some of us sensed that Mark Suciu's five-trick nighttime line at the SF Library in "Cross Continental" was an homage to Mike Carroll's *Modus Operandi* opener. But did anyone consider that each of those five tricks might itself have been homage? Well, no, because that's not really what we're looking for when we watch skateboarding. We don't consider a skater's intent because most skaters' only real intent has historically been: *be as dope as I can be, and by being dope, get people stoked*. So, what optimism or naivete it must have taken in 2011 for Mark to have expected any of us to register the allusions inside the homage. And what a lonely existence, to speak a language nobody else can hear. No wonder, then, the dour-faced young man in the rocking chair on the porch. No wonder Elliot Smith.

* * *

I should have asked: Do you believe in meaning? Do you think that a work of art, a poem or a story or a sequence of musical notes or an arrangement of brushstrokes on a canvas or, I don't know, a video of someone riding a skateboard, can affect us in ways that alter our sense of who we are and what we're up to for the brief time we're alive?

Mark Suciu, fully grown, had aged out of the scrawn and turned bookish, wearing collars and vaguely militant jackets with chest pockets. Tim O'Connor says he looks like someone who "flosses twice daily, smells nice, and look at that hair—that hair looks like it loves to vote in every election." We noted the illogical dismounts and hyperquick 180s, the torquing, and a push that seemed, somehow, to get longer and slower as it went. There was something a little other-worldly or at least suspicious about his talent. The worst we could say was that his skating can feel clinical or terse. Four- and five-trick lines helped by stretching him out a bit. A narrative arc helped, too—of the *Sabotage 3* sessions, Brian Panebianco told me: "At that time he was figuring himself out, how powerful he was. That part was him testing his abilities. Now he knows what he can do."

But knowing can be paralyzing, especially among the serious. The list of matriculated pro skaters is short and it turns meager when we narrow to those who complete a higher education degree. So, it is a rare choice that Mark faced, as he described in his long 2019 *Thrasher* interview, between a skateboard career and academia. After writing an undergrad thesis on Robbe-Grillet that he planned to use for MA applications, "I was bummed," he says, "at the idea that my body would still want to skate."

The fun house was no longer fun. Look closely and you have evidence of this crisis as early as *Sabotage 4*, which is the closest that Mark Suciu has come to looking unhinged. "He was unstoppable, then he was like a human all of a sudden," says Panebianco. That was partially about illness but mostly about college and fun houses and a visionary skateboarder realizing that, uh oh, nobody will ever treat what I do as seriously as I do.

* * *

I believe I've the authority to say: Mark Suciu's writing is deft and at times lovely, shows great potential for growth, and also that skateboarding should absolutely remain his primary focus. Whatever he has thought and tried to unthink since "Cross Continental," "Verso" presents an artist at the height of his power pushing against the assumed limits of his medium. Too serious? Flagrantly so! He has doubled down on the conviction that skateboarding can be a compositional practice. He insists that the toy can be put to intentional, serious, and even meaningful use.

Form, according to the poet Robert Hass, is "the arrangement and relationship of basic elements in a work of art, through which it produces a coherent whole." More romantically, form is the way a composed object "embodies the energy of the gesture of its making." The clearest view of Mark's creative gesture comes in the fourth movement of "Verso," where we find the "ender" behind the delayed release. One announcement of the gesture is the paint-dripped sign bearing an X of lines from AB and BA. Another is the basic-ass frontside fifty that's so far beneath Mark's abilities that it can only be a message. We see a second front fifty close the section, an anti-ender to affirm a pattern that in poetry and rhetoric is called *chiasmus*. ABBA, the formal repetition of elements in a reverse order. Think of Mathew 19:30: "But many who are first will be last, and many who are last will be first." Or Keats: "Beauty is truth, truth beauty."

In the final section of "Verso," Mark Suciu shares what only the most passionate denialists would not call a poem: the first ever skateboarding chiasmus. The sequence is important enough that had he not gotten the trick, he and Justin were prepared to end "Verso" after the Blubba noseblunt. They'd have released the ABBA section stand-alone down the road, whenever he finally got it. The frontside fifties form a pair, the first and last tricks. The second trick is a nollie front heel fakie 5-0 revert (frontside), which pairs with the thirteenth trick—the trick of famous delay—a nollie back heel fakie nosegrind revert (backside). So, the thirteenth trick is a totally fucking bonkers pretzel maneuver that reflects or inverts or reverses the second trick. The same goes for the third trick, a nollie crook, and the twelfth trick, a fakie crook. And so on, unfolding a sequence that represents a totally new realm of skateboard poetics.

* * *

OK...but why? What is the point of the secret labor Mark Suciu has put into composing "Verso"? In a word, for effect. Unified and singular effect. What Hass calls the "resonances" we feel from "a well-made thing, a passionately made thing, a thing made from full commitment." Think of the pairs—early the back noseblunt into a back noseblunt flip, later the front blunt followed by front blunt flip. The moment we have two of a thing we create form and create an energy of relation. To look into causes and trace their effects is to participate in aesthetic theory, or poetics.

I realize now that I have been wrong about the role of numbers in skateboarding. I've shunned computation because I've feared skateboarding losing its essential strangeness, its magic, at the hands of sport analytics. (This is a fear of capital.) Really, I should have been approaching it the way poets approach their own strange, mysterious objects. Stressed, unstressed: to scan a poem's meter is to map that poem's music, meaning, and effect. So, it is counting and also a type of reading that teaches poets to know poetry better, appreciate poems more deeply, and compose more interesting poems themselves. Is the sixth trick of the fourteen-trick ABBA chiasmus missing a half rotation? Does a missing rotation function like the dropped "is" from the Keats, "truth, beauty" line?

Part of the activity of poetry is this: reading poems well. It is a way to see the poet's mind. And why shouldn't the activity of skateboarding include watching skateboarding well? Each sequence and each bundle of sequences moves with "a rhythm, speed, a tone, a flow, a pattern, shape, length, pitch, conceptual direction," says Gass of language. Says Suciu of skateboarding.

Since at least 2011, Mark Suciu has desired a seriousness from a practice that has historically positioned itself against the serious and scholastic. "Verso" wears the labor of what went into making it. He is an uncommon talent, an artist who creates by way of discipline and cunning, a virtuoso. Modern skateboarding is made richer by Suciu's thoughtfulness and deliberateness, by his *pretentiousness*, if that's what you'd like to call it.

"Verso" asks that we pay it a kind of attention many of us automatically do not. Knowing this, we choose to either look more closely or let it pass before our eyes the way the rest of skating does. You are of course free to choose to watch however you please. Choice, too, is skateboarding. That one has been on the list forever.

CHAPTER THIRTY

"The Monk's Posture"

A small restaurant mostly emptied, the lighting soft and flickering, the music ambient beneath the voices of four women at the last of the night's tables. The meal has stretched the way they all expected, knowing how nights like this can go. They've spent these hours catching up, and finally the server has come to drop the check, unsolicited. But there's no pressure, yet. The air is largely uncharged.

"Well, sure," says one of the women once the server has gone. "I mean, you're right—I could. But also I do enjoy it, sometimes. It's not all—OK. So, do this for me, all right?"

She has her elbows on the table and the wine glass between them, suspended with the gentlest possible pressure. All three of her friends are mothers and two of them appear still to be listening. The third hasn't been for some time.

"Meg, for example. Hi. So, think for a second about the way Connor will play. Just incidentally, while you're out walking and he makes some impromptu balance beam out of a fence or little retaining wall. He's six now, right? So, yeah, just some knee-high fence around the little sidewalk garden on your street. And you stand there and watch, maybe a little nervous. I don't know. Proud, too, whatever. What I'm suggesting is that also, whether its conscious or not, there's also part of you that recognizes the pattern of what he's doing. You know his little private act of play taps into a historical and likely ancient precedent. Yeah, I know, thank you, nice face, Meg. But this is the part I enjoy, and why I'm not ready to walk away. Because you also definitely sense that Connor's play, though it may be silly, also taps both of you into, you know, death."

She laughs and raises her glass and the other two laugh enough that Meg, eventually, joins. "Not his, I don't mean. Connor obviously is full of life. And not yours. Both, I mean, both. Cheers! All of ours."

They are always happy to ask about her job but never about her research. One of the three, maybe, would be able to name her department. Maybe. She sees their server leaning on the bar, thumbing through a phone.

"Where I come into this is that I've been trying to argue, lately, and this is the actual detail of my work, that all of this might have something to do with the soul." Maybe she's had too much to drink. Maybe they all have. In any case, she's leaned back now in her chair, leaving the empty glass on the table. She shrugs. "Which I know is a sort of tough word for us. But watch these films closely enough and you begin to witness something distinct from all the categories people in my field have set up for evaluating them. It's not purely aesthetic, that much is clear. But it's also not meaningful in a concrete way, you know? It's not literature. It doesn't point to the world and tell us how to think. I mean really, if it's most like anything then it's whatever the sort of thing we see in children like Connor. Not play but those bigger words beneath or behind play."

She looks at the empty glass. She can feel them watching her, knowing her better than anyone. "Prepositions!" she exclaims, making a joke that won't surprise any of them.

Oh, the politeness of old friends. Oh, the concern they wear across their surface areas. Maybe, they think, she's gone off some kind of deep end after the divorce. She'd come here knowing they'd want to talk of motherhood, as in hers, and she'd bobbed and weaved well enough, she thought, but maybe her evasion had been too effective.

"What I'm *not* saying, by the way, is that any of you have to believe in this. I'm only sharing my work by suggesting, you know, maybe it's time to start asking where in this day and age we might locate something as fanciful as this soul, or so-called soul. That whether we figure it out, that maybe by the process of asking, we might end up getting a peek at some small truth about the age in which we live."

She's lost Meg, and that's fine. The other two drain their glasses in unison but aren't gone completely.

"Look," she says, leaning back to the table. "I don't mean some orb or interior essence. When I say *soul* I mean a method of release, a process of motion. I mean the soul as creation, because the human soul, as it were, requires expression." She is gesturing with both hands. "Activity. Kant, OK, Kant reduced the whole soul and body opposition to a single term, *Gemüt*, which is kind of the meeting ground for pleasure and judgment. Whatever the life force was, he said it was inseparable from the body where it is expressed. What I'm adding, my work is about suggesting maybe it's foolish to try and isolate one body's movement from the crowd that watches the movement. Meg, what are you doing?"

Meg looks up.

"I don't mind, but I mean, that's it. You've chosen to leave my audience and you've gone in there, to your phone. No, don't put it away. That's fine. I'm just saying, what if the soul, what if I suggest that maybe your soul is partially contained in the people who gather around you?"

They love her, though. She sees that. They're very old friends.

"It could be a crowd or just one person. You guys watch and listen to me in a certain way because you know me. Right? What-ever is going on here, you're involved. I'm not expressing alone, I mean. And what I've come to believe is that there are really count-less ways this expression can occur—practicing medicine, Kris, for example. Or look, being a parent. The activity could be operating a business, making art, and so on. But simply engaging in these activities alone doesn't assure that a soul will be expressed, because most activities, as practiced, represent a means to some end. Health, for the doctor. A child's well-being, for the parent. Profit, profit, for everyone else."

There was a time, she thinks, although she can't exactly recall what it was like, when she knew how to talk to old friends without frightening them.

"But there are moments that exist underneath purpose. There are means that have no ends. It's…it's not that one leaps," she says finally, as they all run fingers along the rims of empty glasses. "It's how, having leapt, one spins and flips and lands."

She looks into her own glass. Heroism, she knows, is keeping your head perfectly still despite your friends' eyes. The music is gone and the room has become filled by an almost plaintive silence.

"It is not that the monk burns," she says. "That's not what gets us. Is it?" She looks up briefly, expecting and finding nothing. "No. The real protest is the monk's composure. It's that he can sit there perfectly still, and maintain that stillness as the flames lick the skin from his charring frame."

She knows her friends are watching her, waiting for her to look up. When she does, that's when they'll expect her shoulders to rise and her lips to go tight and her head to turn, what we call a "shake" but which is not a shake, is in most cases a movement far more subtle, a matter of millimeters, the chin's slightest shift. Anyway, what they'll expect to see is apology.

PART FOUR

CHAPTER THIRTY-ONE

Seven Small Bafflements

2020

BAFFLEMENT #1: WHAT IS NOW?

I n the waning days of 2019, my wife and I set out from Chicago to drive counterclockwise around Lake Michigan. It would take us four days—our desire was to be gone from the city, away from screens, and together, likely asleep, as a difficult year came to an end.

We moved through storms. At times, our drive was treacherous and sublime and other times only beautiful. We did not succeed in answering the pressing question of our marriage but did engage in two arguments that brushed against the existential issue at hand—the first by private candlelight and the second inside an otherwise empty and bright restaurant over breakfast. We also laughed often, and sang songs that already were and songs that we made up. On long drives like that, the car can become a sort of world with its own rules and expectations independent of the extant reality it speeds through. I imagine that was part of our motivation, too.

In any case, we behaved as the friends and lovers that we are, our marital confusion along with us but no more invasive than our very old and small blind dog in the back seat. At some point, we found ourselves talking about comedy, which can be difficult. She and I have rather different responses to the majority of internet humor: regarding Twitter, she is often moved to laughter while I am mostly dismayed. But we've a common ground when it comes to a certain trend that is not a type of joke, per se, but rather a pattern of playful transgressions worked into recent performances. Examples include but are not limited to inappropriate prepositions ("Should I run about this?"[1]), bloated verb phrases ("This town is going to eat you out, and it's going to throw you out, and then it's going to wipe up everyone with you out, too."[2]), ill-suited prefaces ("No offense, but what's for dinner?" "Thanks, I hate it."), and accents that seem to come from imaginary, nonexistent lands (see: Catherine O'Hara's Moira on *Schitt's Creek*).

In the car, this conversation got me thinking about the topic that I've spent much of the last ten years thinking and writing about. And which now, unsurprisingly, I find myself considering again. Having begun, I know that "now" is going to continue until I finish writing. As reader, your own *now* will come to an end much more quickly, either by abandoning this book or reaching its end. Either, surely, will take less time than my writing. Our *nows* are unequal.

BAFFLEMENT #2: WHAT IS A STAGE?

At the corner of Chicago's Milwaukee and Fullerton Avenues, in the hot, hot, hot Logan Square neighborhood, sits Liberty Bank. To the immediate west of this building is a 34,000-square-foot

---

1   "DePiglio," Chris Fleming, December 20, 2019, https://www.youtube .com/watch?v=KpelkMBAD2o.

2   "The popular girl in the movie that the main character runs into during her shift at the dinner," Meg Stalter, December 13, 2019, https://twitter .com/megstalter/status/1205542384739799042?s=20.

parking lot where I and others like me will go after normal banking hours. Speaking structurally, the only real appeal of The Lot is the ten parking blocks arranged into a rectangle beneath the Blue Line "L" tracks that slice diagonally across the space. Several of these blocks have been rub bricked and waxed by us or others like us, and they're the most obvious thing to point to as the "reason" we come, though I'm not sure that's quite the right word.

And come to do what? I will try to describe our practice. We gather along the perimeter and take turns moving determinedly for the blocks. We stray by arbitrary routes across the space, getting our legs warm, working through familiar movements. We make cautious, early attempts at new movements. We watch the ways that everyone else moves and know that we, too, are being watched. We plug fingers into our ears when trains thunder overhead, marking the city's time. We resist the basic assumptions of this and other cities. We fall and the blacktop of the lot stains our palms and we make eye contact with the others. So much of what we're doing, in fact, is watching. We stand or sit with our prior movements lingering in and about our bodies like an odor, or glaze of sweat, a residual shimmering of the soul. We watch and laugh and applaud and we recoil when someone fails, like there is a string between the failing body and our own.

I am not being coy, or only coy, in avoiding the common name for this practice. To be honest, I fear the way its name will trigger assumptions of the very sort the practice aims to upend. It is a performance. Each human performer stands upon an individual stage that is elevated four inches or so from the pavement, on wheels. As is common to theater, the performance that we are watching, and that we are doing, occurs in the body onstage. Less common is the way each body will manipulate the stage on which it stands. These manipulations in fact would seem to represent a radical mode of experimentation. For example, we regularly spin our stage a half rotation beneath our feet, like this:

STAGE → ƎDⱯꞱS

Or a whole rotation, like this:

STAGE → ƎDⱯꞱS → STAGE

We'll flip the stage, like this:

STAGE → ꙄꞱⱯƆE → STAGE

In short, it is a theater of transgression and trespass. The architectural historian Iain Borden has written about our practice as participatory architecture, a system of behaviors that "challenges the notion that space is there to be obeyed."[3] The assumed normative purpose of the parking block, for example, is upended by our use of it. The language of theater allows us to go further: by engaging the block as we do, sliding and grinding our stages against it, we infuse the block with a new purpose. It, too, becomes a stage.

BAFFLEMENT #3: WHAT DO WE FEAR?

Adults fear death (this is why we invented literature). Children, unable to comprehend death, find a suitable surrogate in adulthood. Skateboarders, in the meantime, worry only over that apocalyptic moment after which we'll be forced to stop skateboarding. This, we call terror.

BAFFLEMENT #4: WHAT DO I WANT?

When I was young, before I understood my self or my body, skateboarding taught me what it means to long. Even before that longing was complicated by adolescence, skateboarding shaped my dreams, wrote the algorithm of my desires. I modeled an identity after young men who lived on the plastic tape inside the plastic cassettes scattered

---

3   Iain Borden, *Skateboarding, Space and the City* (Oxford: Berg, 2001), 231.

across the carpet in front of the television. Years later, I would, for a time, love a ballet dancer who liked to point out other women she was certain were dancers based on their turned-out hips. During my first visit to the myofascial therapist I hoped might help with my chronic neck and back and knee pains, I stood before her for three seconds before she nodded and said, "You're regular footed?" I am. And it seems that when I stand still, my left leg, which on a board is my leading leg, bears almost the entirety of my body's weight. One thing to say about this is that it's not good for my body. Another is that the cause of my left leg's burden is a thirty-year record of habitually pushing my skateboard with my other, right leg.

I am still amused each time I recall how new it is. It was not so long ago that skateboarding did not exist. In attempting to write about it, my approach has more or less hewn to the shape and methods of my topic. I circle the thing, jab and poke at it, then back away to sit for a time and watch. I can summarize the conclusions I've reached during this decade of work thusly: skateboarding is weird. I fear sometimes that its wonder, the meaninglessness that is the source of its mystery, is also its vulnerability. Capital loves nothing the way it loves a void to fill. The market is the seeping fluid that fills any fissure or space or hollow. The stories our culture's industry tells about skateboarding—and with capital it is always a story—tend to be composed in a language of winning and losing.

It is just so much easier to speak of the rings that spin around skateboarding, its offshoots and reverberations, than the activity itself. There is the culture and its effect on popular fashion. There are media objects produced about the activity—films, photographs, articles—and a global skateboard industry that grows and fluctuates between creative autonomy and corporate control. There is qualitative academic research devoted to skateboarding's applications in social work, philanthropic NGOs, and education. In all of these cases there is always a satellite device, a conceptual tool or metaphor that limits the strange object and renders it comprehensible. For me, that conceptual tool has been literature.

BAFFLEMENT #5: WHAT IS USEFUL?

Almost certainly, you are familiar with the basic shape of skateboarding. You have a skate park nearby, you have taken your child there, you have watched and perhaps rolled cautiously around yourself. Whenever exactly the next Summer Olympics do come, skateboarding will make its premiere as an Olympic sport. The commentators will tell you origin stories and explain things—this is called frontside, this is the motion by which an athlete executes a kickflip. OK. But if there is one thing I'd ask you to remember after our brief time together, it is that, no. Respectfully, no. To borrow Annie Dillard's voice for a moment, these relate to skateboarding but only "as kissing a man does to marrying him, or as flying in an airplane does to falling out of an airplane."[4] The strange ontology I mean by "skateboarding" does not survive transportation across the natural borders of its world. One can only experience it by experiencing it.

Now you are thinking: But that is not so special! Don't other things work this way? Yes, sort of! Dance, for one. But the comparison has its limits. Prompted to give a broad, inclusive definition of dance, one might say something like, *The intentional use of bodily movement in a manner outside of convention and productivity*. Similarly, a broad definition of poetry could be, *The intentional use of language in a manner outside of convention and productivity*. An in-kind definition of skateboarding, however, would have to read: *The intentional use of a surface by a nonmotorized four-wheeled, lean-to-turn platform in a manner outside of convention and productivity*. It is, in other words, one thing to cover a stage with dirt and quite another to dance across the earth's soil.

So, we return again to the city that plays theater complex to skateboarding's stages. Here I think of the language Don DeLillo gave to the aging visionary Richard Elster in his strangest, most

---

4   Annie Dillard, *Teaching a Stone to Talk* (New York: Harper & Row, 1982), 89.

static novel, one that I love and that nobody else seems to even like, really, *Point Omega*:

> It's all embedded, the hours and minutes, words and numbers everywhere…train stations, bus routes, taxi meters, surveillance cameras. It's all about time, dimwit time, inferior time, people checking watches and other devices, other reminders. This is time draining out of our lives. Cities were built to measure time, to remove time from nature.[5]

Time is the city's most glaring assumption and source of skateboarding's most important transgression. "The temporality of appropriation," wrote Iain Borden, "is different to that of ownership."[6] But different how, exactly? I'm not sure. I do wonder, though, speaking of theater, what it could look like to somehow make a stage of time.

BAFFLEMENT #6: WHEN DID PEOPLE START LOOKING INTO EACH OTHER'S EYES?

A personal question arises: Why has writing about skateboarding this way returned me to thinking about marriage? Is it only that both are mysterious, or is there something else they share? Two additional passages might shed some light on the matter. The first comes from the poet Dan Beachy-Quick:

> A transcendent moment may be a simple concept: the mutually creative point at which a world expressed and a world received coincide in time. I speak out the world within the reality of subjective time that makes my world possible,

---

5   Don DeLillo, *Point Omega* (New York: Scribner, 2010), 44–45.
6   Borden, *Skateboarding, Space and the City*, 241.

and you listen from your own time, from the depth and singularity of your own subjectivity. Transcendence occurs when my world becomes real for you and thus is no longer merely mine, while the perception of this world is no longer merely yours. In becoming real for you, my world gains from your otherness, from your not being me. You shape it as you listen to it.[7]

For the second, I turn again to DeLillo and the other of his two small late-career novels about time:

She framed his face in her hands, looking into him straight-on. What did it mean, the first time a thinking creature looked deeply into another's eyes? Did it take a hundred thousand years before this happened or was it the first thing they did, transcendingly, the thing that made them higher, made them modern, the gaze that demonstrates we are lonely in our souls?[8]

I feel us getting closer. It is a fusion of perception and recognition. It is a merger between performer and audience, one that upends the assumed separation between these two roles. Moments are fleeting. Moments are repeated. There is no story, here, to tell, only an animating principle of simultaneity. Such, as we have seen, is the temporality by which skateboarding moves. It is not a narrative practice, but interrogative.

---

7   Dan Beachy-Quick, *A Whaler's Dictionary* (Minneapolis: Milkweed, 2008), 282.
8   Don DeLillo, *The Body Artist* (New York: Scribner, 2001), 87.

BAFFLEMENT #7: SHOULD WE STAY MARRIED?

Midway through 2019, our marriage therapist suggested that my wife and I table our all-consuming, painful, and baffling attempts to decide, together, whether or not we should remain married. Give it a rest, how about, through the end of the year? In so doing she accomplished two important tasks. First, she pumped the brakes on a pattern of extrapolating current trends in our marriage into a frankly inconceivable future. By centering us in a finite and manageable time frame ("the rest of this year"), she also invited us, once we reached the end of that time frame (or slept through it, as circumstances would have it), to discover just how arbitrary the Gregorian calendar is when it comes to an activity or way of being like marriage. To recognize, in effect, that a marriage creates its own temporality.

The second and, I believe, sitting here now on the far side of that time frame, much more important thing our therapist accomplished was reminding us that such exterior clocks *will always be ticking* just beyond the borders of our mutualized world. Stick fingers into our ears as far as they'll go and we'll still hear the train as it thunders overhead. Marriage has always been an arrangement at the mercy of economic and cultural forces, a thing defined almost entirely by the way people talk about it. Earlier, I rounded up: our five year anniversary is in fact one week from today. This marker carries its own expectations—wood, we're told to buy, or silverware—conventional wisdom—if you can make it through five, a friend says, you can make it through fifty—and any number of additional norms we're to observe, and in observing settle into our roles in the story of our marriage.

But there is a different way to conceptualize all of this. When I think of those two arguments during our drive around Lake Michigan, I cannot but recall George Lakoff and Mark Johnson's *Metaphors We Live By*. By way of introducing their arguments about common metaphor framing and reflecting a society's values, they ask a reader to imagine "a culture where," unlike ours, "arguments are not viewed in terms of war, where no one wins or loses."[9] What if, instead, argument were conceptualized as dance, and the arguers performers?

Forgive me if this sounds like a brag, but I for one have no trouble whatsoever conceiving of argument as dance. Not all theater is narrative; not all engagement demands change. Who is to blame for convincing us that redundancy was a thing to be avoided? At this point it would be very, very strange for either my wife or I to claim that we have "won" an argument. It is true that a component of our dance is asking ourselves, over and over again, the same familiar question. But this question no longer seems as daunting as it once did. It was not the asking of the question that paralyzed our marriage, but the expectation of an answer. What better way is there to be than to take nothing for granted, assume nothing, and discover mutuality by this activity of regular, ongoing consummation? And what knew our therapist, anyway, of the ways 2020 would change how my wife and I—how any of us—speak of marriage? This is the way that time becomes a medium: by the activity of interrogation.

Only now do I realize what I've been doing. I've had skateboarding in one hand, marriage in the other, and have held them up to the bright light of theater, curious what their shadows might reveal. Wonderfully, it would seem that the shadows are full of questions.

---

9   George Lakoff and Mark Johnson, *Metaphors We Live By* (Chicago: The University of Chicago Press, 1980), 4.

CHAPTER THIRTY-TWO

On Animal Play

A hooded crow, which with its ashy gray frame and black accents on its head and wings and tail looks to the untrained American eye a whole lot like a pigeon, stands at the apex of a tar roof with some kind of disk clutched in its talons. The roof is snowy and the sky is gray and spaceless. A dreary day, at least outside. The clip is shot from an apartment across the street—there's a presumably male voice, female voice, and a child who giggles as the crow rides the lid of a jar sled-like down the snow that mostly covers the roof. It rides the lid down, and then, once it slides to a stop, takes the lid into its beak and flies with it back to the top of the roof. Now the crow struggles a bit, seeming to *want* to slide down the roof again, but its angle is wrong, and the face of the roof it starts to descend has no snow cover. After a few feet it once more takes the lid into its beak and flies to its starting point. (I realize now that there's a fourth voice, a baby's, that caws in the background. And there are in fact two children, I think, so five humans watching this show, plus me and 1.9 million others.) Anyway, the third of the crow's descents finishes a foot or so short of its first. It picks up the lid and flies back to the peak, presumably to drop once more into the roof. I try searching "Russian crow roof extended" and find a slightly longer version. But there are no more descents—the crow plays with the lid a bit, stands on it on the dry roof and goes nowhere, then picks at it with its beak until eventually it gets a good grip, and flies away.

It is folly to suppose *why* anyone today watches anything—to feel virtuous, to distract from cataclysm, to put to further use the chunk of plastic and glass in our hands and by using the chunk feel less bad about the chunk's outrageous cost—and it grows harder each day of the algorithm's evolution to think in terms like "choice" at all. But there seems to be some effect, some kind of nutrient we get from watching animals play that we don't find anywhere else. Once, K and I visited the Gibbon Conservation Center outside of her hometown of Santa Clarita, California. It is a largely unsorrowful place, despite the screaming of the caged gibbons. You can stand there and watch them swing about their cage on long gray arms and admire the length of their toes. They dart from a platform and reach for a rope and swing, then swing back, then hang there and piss onto the dusty ground far below.

This I can imagine felt good. A relief, at least, and also maybe more. As for the hooded crow, who is not caged and who, in addition, is capable of flight—what can we say of a bird skiing down a snow-covered roof? Is there any way to understand this without using the word *fun*?

Biologists, it will not surprise you, are far more interested in function than fun. Prevailing accounts of animal play tend to focus on the social, physical, and cognitive benefits that playful activity might offer. There's also a kind of meta explanation, whereby the purpose of play is to understand play itself: to learn to differentiate between pretend aggression and genuine threats. For example, much in recent months has been made of the super-slow-motion footage of dogs play bowing, and pawing, and faking right to go left. New technology has allowed for new observation, and now we know more than ever before the codes of dog play and what they mean for canine development. Dogs are social. They agree. They apologize. They punish.

Though, these are human concepts. So, even leaving *fun* behind, we're still using human language as we watch and interpret and distinguish between *play* and other behaviors. Safer to focus on nonmetaphorical categories, like use-value, the ways animal play provides opportunities to practice real-world skills. The baby ibex leaps across sheer cliffs and thereby learns agility and other skills to save them from predatory attacks later in life. Young chimpanzees playing with objects develop their control of prehensile hands. And so on.

It gets a little weirder as we move away from warm-blooded mammals and look at fishes, frogs, and reptiles. Adult dendro-batid (poison dart) frogs will wrestle irrespective of sex. Komodo dragons mess around with buckets and balls and will sometimes play tug-of-war like dogs, albeit a slowed down version. Aquatic soft-shelled turtles bat floating balls and bottles back and forth, and crocodilians, too, will play with objects. Invertebrates? An octopus will repeatedly pounce on a fiddler crab and release it unharmed. The social spider *Anelosimus studiosus* seems by all measures to engage in nonconceptive sex play—mock copulations.

And what to do with cases without any clear use-value? What about the baboons teasing a cow by reaching through an electric fence to pull the cow's tail? What about young elephants running after nonthreatening animals like wildebeests and egrets? Function is one thing, and these would seem to be something rather else. We know that certain animals that do not play can suffer. Ravens, for example, are very intelligent and therefore easily bored. When they're bored, they can become unhappy to the point of self-harm. Boredom also upsets research results among mice and rats.

There has been concern in this house, as I assume there is in others, about what happens when I am no longer able to skateboard. K's concern is the understandable consequence of being around me when I have broken a toe and sulked about the house, or sprained a thing, or suffered this lingering groin injury, which I ice and heat and stretch but that, the fucking thing, simply will not abate. If this is me now, then what becomes of my life when it's robbed of this practice I so rely upon? I can see her, sometimes, looking at me on the floor on the foam roller, extrapolating her experience with my current, low-forties aches into the extended truth of late-life limitations. Will I go quietly? Will I heed my body's cries, or will it require a shattered hip or ulna before I stop?

Earlier this year, my seventy-five-year-old father suffered a bad injury while skiing. That I was in the mountains with him but not, that afternoon, on the slope when he fell is one of my regrets. That I had the day prior to his fall been with him and done what I do these days whenever I snowboard, which is go just stupidly fast and carve long deep turns and more or less challenge whoever is with me to keep up is another. I can remember the phone ringing and looking at the clock and thinking, Ah, yes, that will be ski patrol, calling about Dad.

And it was. He had been collected and moved to a local hospital, where we found him. They wanted to airlift him by helicopter to Denver but could not because of a storm moving through the Rockies, so my mother rode in the ambulance with him and I drove into the storm an hour or so later, after I ran to pack some clothes for what looked to be an extended stay. The drive was treacherous and the week that followed difficult and galvanizing. We met with nurses and doctors and huddled around monitors as a finger pointed out his one normal kidney for comparison, and then the gray shapeless mass on the other side. He went in and out of sleep, his mouth at times pulled into a rictus of pain and at other times hanging terribly slack.

On the second of his six nights in the ICU, my father lay awake in his bed riveted with pain. There was internal bleeding, there was leakage, and a procedure to install a stent and a catheter. He slept better the following night, and when we talked the next day, he said that during that painful night he had discovered a way to tunnel back into memories of his father that he didn't realize were there. I had made it this long knowing more about my grandfather's

death than his life—he was a Mennonite preacher who was forced
to take on extra work selling insurance after leaving his church
due to the dispute over homosexual marriage (Grandpa Neil was
in favor), and was killed by a woman who, drunk, had decided to
suicide by driving into oncoming traffic late at night in the middle
of Ohio. My father was sixteen. Anyway, in the pain of that night,
Dad remembered a black snake that he killed with the 12-gauge
shotgun they kept in the barn. He saw images of himself chopping
the head off of a chicken, and then entered into memories of him
and his siblings plucking its feathers. But where did they boil the
chicken? Over a fire? On the stove? This memory had its limits.
Before the insurance job, Neil Beachy drove a school bus during
the week and delivered sermons on the weekend. Groceries were
delivered from the main church each week, cans of food, supplies
for the preacher and his family on location. He remembered being
a young man in Goshen, Indiana, with a paper route, waking up
at 5:00 a.m. to fold the papers, tie them, and then go out on a
bike tossing them (cliché-like) onto porches. His face lit up, talking
to me this way. He recalled Neil driving him in the winters and
helping with his route.

I have written these down here mostly to ensure that I'll remember them. One memory I will not forget, I do not imagine, comes
from that day of the procedure, following the night of pain. But
before I share it, I realize now that I have spoken of my parents'
divorce but have not yet described their remarriage after five years
apart, their second wedding to each other, held in a small chapel, by
coincidence, in the Rockies. Second marriage? No, not according to
them. Anyway, so, yes—I attended my parents' wedding. And yes,
my mother was there for him after the fall that obliterated a kidney
and cracked several ribs. She was there once we left the hospital and
I'd driven them back to their home in Missouri and left them and
returned, finally, to my own home in Chicago. She was there on
that most suffering of days before his procedure and after the night
of bloody memories, writhing and moaning, speaking in a strange

and tortured voice. And the memory I will not forget is of my mother, Teresa Sophia Beachy, née Brown, herself born in Bristol, England, leaning over my father's curled and shattered body as he cranes his neck to her and says, "Please don't let me drown."

It is strange, watching memories this way. One is tempted to try and slow their motion and study them like we've studied dog play, to see what we can learn. The way we slow skateboard tricks to understand the footwork required and thereby, sometimes, come to know what adjustments to make in our own. The way we turn back to those who have come and gone and left behind them a visual record of how they were, which is another, and maybe better way of saying who they were. But memories are different, of course. There can be no "slow-motion" memory because memory has no standard pace. How does a memory unfold? By what clock? No, in the realm of memory, time is an illusion—there is no more "now" to pinpoint in memory than a "here" to point out in a river. I do believe that once a door into memory is opened it will remain that way. This, however, has not stopped history from laying its claims to times and places both.

CHAPTER THIRTY-THREE

Inappropriate Places

2020

At first I didn't understand it, and I still don't.
—Jacqueline/Jackueline Wright,
age sixteen, August 16, 1968

They have come from Barrington and Cicero and Naperville, from Lincoln Park and Hyde Park and from Gary, even. Wearing their suits on a Tuesday, the men, and the women in their hats and jewels. It has been set up as an occasion and these for the most part are people who respect their mayor, and believe in what he's accomplished even if nobody has seen the precise shape this accomplishment has taken, yet. Big, they know. Big and important. There is some rabble, too, as ever these days. Young women in swimsuits and men in funny glasses and the like, but for the most part they have arrived on a Tuesday in August beneath a stretched blue sky, ready for history.

The orchestra is in white jackets and the accomplishment is there beneath the massive blue tarpaulin and everyone has circled around it, thousands of them, filling the Civic Center Plaza and spilling onto Washington Street, which is closed to traffic. The servicemen have raised the flags and they have heard a priest, a rabbi, and a Protestant minister all speak prayers for the occasion, and there's an obvious joke here about Picasso the atheist that the journalist Mike Royko will make in tomorrow's paper. The red carpet under the folding chairs of the mayor and featured poet and other local dignitaries and the pale blue helmets of the Chicago Police. Though we are a year, still, before the helmets become national news.

It is 1967 and though Royko will say the day was somber and serious, aren't those people over there playing in the Civic Center fountain? Isn't that a man with a Bolex climbing into the big honey locust for a better shot? The great Gwendolyn Brooks stands and declares to the crowd that art hurts. It is easier to stay at home, says the poet, and I suppose this might sound somber, if you're closed to her poem. Later she will say she admires the thing they've come to see unveiled, the massive, perplexing thing.

Eventually the mayor follows the poet and clergy and all the rest and stands at the dais. Looking so proud, so inflated you almost want to hold his shoe so he doesn't sail away, he speaks of a new representation, a new image, a new interpretation of the city's soul. He says "fine arts" like "aihrts," and, upon his death, will give this plaza its new name. When he's finished speaking, he floats from the dais to where the ribbon hangs from the accomplishment's big, artful tarp-covered top.

The granite slabs of the plaza have never seen as many feet as they do today. "A record crowd," reads the museum copy, fifty-four years later. It's a crowd packed close enough to lose yourself, to divest itself entirely of that fear of touch Elias Canetti spoke of, that restricting human thing. They shuffle and crane and Daley stands there near the ribbon and then pulls it. The blue tarp parts and slides unevenly, one side catching briefly on…what, the head, maybe? Shoulder? But eventually it falls and here is what everyone agrees came next: silence. Some accounts allow for a "smattering" of surprise but for the sake of the story, what we need at this moment is quiet. And then the silence, somehow, according to Royko, "grows," if such a wording can be read as anything beyond embellishment and affected narration. Anyway, next comes laughter and smiles, and I suppose all of these people all eventually went home? This part is harder to find in primary texts, but, yes, the orchestra stood and someone folded the chairs and rolled the red carpet and the plaza emptied and Royko's column came out the next day, "They had hoped, you see, that it would be what they had heard it would be."

But after that silence and once the laughter had died down, a new batch came the following day, and then the next, the less dense crowd. Cars lined the curbs on Washington so that others, too, could be baffled by the unveiled thing. Mayor Daley at a press conference: "I think it's wonderful. I've seen young people, old people, school teachers, and children looking at it. This is everyone's Picasso." And this is how Pablo wanted it. A gift, everyone's. He rejected all of Daley's and Daley's men's overtures to pay him for his work. The thing and all the rights to its image's reproduction: signed them over to the people of Chicago, just like that. Fifty feet of sculpture, 162 tons of steel. His gift even to Mike Royko and the gigglers, to the head-shakers and eye-rollers, even to the riot policemen of Chicago one calendar year before they'd swing batons into unhelmeted skulls outside the Democratic convention.

But more, I have to figure, to the playful. A gift from Pablo to those who experience delight. And come they would, to stand in the shadow of a sculpture that "appears to make friends of strangers" and "makes children even less inhibited than usual." A gift especially for the children who laugh and run around this strange, asymmetrical shape crafted of the same steel as the stark, towering Civic Center building behind it, Cook County's central courthouse for property disputes and other matters. Out here it is a public plaza laid with smooth granite, a public space in which to gather and take a good look at the thing nobody understands, a Spanish atheist's gift to a city he'd die without visiting and knew mostly as his pal Hemingway's hometown. And where is Royko's silence now that the children have arrived? A year later and they're still coming, falling one-at-a-time in love with their weird sculpture, everyone's sculpture, one of them now running circles around the thing to see it freshly, Picasso's gift, and getting closer and closer until eventually she ducks beneath the ropes and moves to get up onto the thing, Why not?, and feels herself grabbed by the shoulder, hooked by a guard with a stern warning and then, fishlike, thrown back into the fray.

* * *

A presence has of late come sneaking into my life. It is a vague thing, like a barely perceptible figure waving to me from a future I can imagine but not without caution. A most delicate desire, minor by any measure but also massive, in some ways. If I close my eyes I can picture myself doing what I would like to do. I stand in the middle of a gray granite sea, holding my board in both hands, glancing left and right for a clear path. Then I am running at the knee-high platform upon which the sculpture rests, my steps timed so that I get two on the platform before three quick ones up the mellow incline of steel—right, left, right. By now the tail of my board is scraping along steel, and then I'm upon it, carrying the momentum up the rest of the mellow incline and then smashing into the steeper, nearly vertical wall at the top.

I can see it in the first person, too: the Picasso's asymmetrical non-face towering before me as I sprint across Daley Plaza, huffing with the board in my hands and leaping up onto the stage, then the sculpture, my feet going from steel to board and then rising, pulling my knees up as we mash onto the fiercer wall of the statue's…shoulders, or whatever, and then I do the thing and meet the board back again on the mellow angle of the bottom bank, gaining speed on the ride down and dropping back to the granite.

All of this, now, living inside my head. A desire not just to wallride the Picasso, which I have done, which the Picasso invites every skateboarder who sees it to come and do upon its impervious and smooth and angled planes of American steel. A desire to shove-it out of that wallride. I want to run at and roll up the statue and ride the wall and then pop and scoop my tail so that the board rotates 180 degrees beneath me and then a number of degrees more. Then I'll land.

In my office, now, I can hear K beyond the door, just back from the store. Among the other things between me and my desire there is still the global pandemic to consider. We've been washing our hands and wearing our masks and have grown newly aware of our surroundings. We are being asked to engage differently with the world and with one another. This is how the future arrives, it would seem. Inside, we learn anew that we are all soft and vulnerable. The moment calls for caution and defense against an aggressive world.

What other desire compares to this one, with such tiny and private and monumental stakes? Perhaps it is like hunger. Perhaps a hunger for a certain meal prepared just so, exactly this way, by the hands of a particular chef at a restaurant in a faraway city? Perhaps it is a meal made of a rare, even extinct ingredient, or rather a meal you had in a dream once, many years ago and only remember, if "remember" is the right word, in the dark basement of the mind where consciousness cannot go.

No. Wrong, wrong, wrong. It has to be as familiar as foreign, as practical as dreamt. It should be a pull toward a mapped but unseen land. It needs to be a haunting, a ghost dispatched from another dimension or possible future, this desire I mean.

Well, by now I can tell when I have hit that wall after which nothing worthwhile will come. I had hoped to narrativize all of this. Struck by desire, I thought, ah! Here is a chance to write a good, old-fashioned quest. I will render the Picasso's historic unveiling as a scene and move between the bafflements of the past and my clear and present desire. It has been so long since I've written a story. But now, I'm unable even to analogize and make concrete this desire.

The old blind dog moves slowly through the hall. I close the laptop and stand from the desk, step out of the office and go spend time with my weird little family while we still have one another.

*   *   *

I am not alone in being affected by Pablo Picasso's gift to the people of Chicago. There is no child who sees the sculpture and does not think: I will climb that and see what happens. It is at once imposing and inviting—fifty feet tall but a thing a toddler can scurry onto, 162 tons but open on all sides. Sit on one of Daley Plaza's granite benches on any sunny afternoon and you'll see as many folks kneeling and posing for pictures as folks arms-out balancing against the smooth surface as they step onto the stage and climb its mellow, lower incline.

This matter of what it's a sculpture *of*—a cause for much debate in the early years. The face and/or body of a woman, the wings of justice, or even Picasso's beloved if indolent Afghan hound, named Kabul? It soon stopped being *of* anything but itself. It is a massive, public sculpture by Pablo Picasso plopped into the middle of a broad and open plaza laid with squares of textured but friendly granite. And like the statue, the plaza and the thirty-one-story Civic Center that became the Richard J. Daley Center one week after the man died, belong to the public.

On the day of my first attempt, the plaza is lively. There are people in and around the fountain, including a woman with a Doberman, and tourists moving across the space, sitting on the benches, taking photos of the sculpture. The *Chicago Tribune*'s longtime architecture critic, Blair Kamin, has called Daley Plaza the city's "unofficial town square," and also "Chicago's living room." I am told that before the 1996 repairs to cracking, leaking tiles that saw all of the granite pulled out and replaced with new tiles that were twice as thick, you could roll a marble from one edge of the plaza to the other, 125 yards away. It's a Saturday in early May, warm and breezy, and I've come with two friends, Zack and Dan.

I've got my phone leaned against a flagpole for one angle and Zack stands closer with his own phone. There is a quinceñera photo shoot moving nearby and a few bikers I have to watch, and also a group of four sitting on the sculpture's left half. So, I go straight at the thing's right side four or five times before it's clear that this won't work—if it's gonna happen, I'll need to run up the sculpture's left side, hit the wall at a softer angle, do the shove-it, and come down the other side. This means waiting for the people to leave, which they do, only to be replaced by the fifteen-year-old in her chiffon dress and the photographer with her assistant.

These first attempts have me winded. So, I drink water, push around the granite, watch the security guards linger between the building and the fountain, necks craned skyward because it's a stunning afternoon in Chicago. When the way has cleared, I get back to it from the new angle. Three or four tries in, it starts to make sense, but it's difficult to achieve any sort of rhythm while I wait for kids to run up and down the sculpture, photographers to pose and shoot, and to huff and tend to myself between sprints. Eventually, by try seven or eight, it starts to click, and try nine ends up basically beneath my feet but I miss it, groan, and slide down the sculpture's sun-warmed steel and lie there for a minute or so on my back, staring up at the bizarre latticework of Picasso's fancy. When I'm back up I see that the woman with the Doberman is standing with Dan and Zack, gesturing. Also, it seems that a security guard has peeled off from the others and is wandering toward me.

She is upset, this woman. Quite. So, we get to talking over on the plaza's eastern side about our selfishness, to be acting so recklessly during a health crisis. Obviously, she says, we know they don't want us here. I say, yes, but here we are, because some laws are dumb.[1]

---

1   Chicago Code of Ordinances 9-80-20: Toy Vehicles, states "No person shall ride a skateboard upon any roadway or sidewalk in a business district."

She: You're going to damage the sculpture.

Me: No. That's not actually possible.

She: Well then it's childish. You're behaving like a
         child.

Me: You know, Picasso actually spoke of the
         sculpture as a gift…

In fact, she says, voice rising, by doing this I'm exhibiting white privilege, and I say *I know that*, and by now other people have gathered, and they're on the woman's side, they seem to believe Zack and Dan and I have threatened her somehow, that she's in danger. I say, look, we can disagree about whether what I'm doing is bad. She tells a woman nearby that she was just talking to this man right here when this one came up and started yelling at her. I chime in to say that is absolutely not what happened. Her dog is beautiful and does not care for me, but there is a kindness that shines through even when it bares its teeth. She tells me that I have no concept of what it is like to work a job, and I take some exception to this, so now is when I say "Wow you are sure behaving a lot like a cop," then ask if she thinks she'll get a prize of some kind or fucking pension for all of her efforts today, and by now Zack and Dan have packed up and, well, they have the right idea.

As we push south on Dearborn I apologize to Dan for coming over during his conversation with the woman and making a big fuss. My desire, I say. I blame my desire. Actually, says Dan, we weren't talking. Actually she just came up and started berating me while I stood there and tried to ignore her so you could get your trick. Which is a thing I can believe, knowing Dan and the way most American citizens think about skateboarding in shared public space.

* * *

Now it is a Wednesday in late June 1988. Chicago, like much of the country, has suffered through a historic drought, the nation's worst since the Dust Bowl and the costliest natural disaster of all time. Corn yields fell by 44 percent, the Mississippi River was twenty feet low in some regions, and eleven states declared every one of their counties as disaster areas. The last three days have all seen record-high temperatures in Chicago—104 on Sunday, 101 on Monday, and yesterday, 97.

But still they have come, and among the crowd of a hundred or so skaters it is mostly graphic T-shirts and colorful shorts, with some fingerless gloves, some tall white socks rising from inside of high-tops, and headbands against the sweat. They are bodies and they *sweat*. They've gathered in Daley Plaza in defiance of a new law that has gone into effect today, one that bans their presence. Before coming to Daley Plaza, the organizer of today's event, D. L. Nevin, became the first person ever to be ticketed under the new anti-skateboarding law. DL looks exactly like you'd hope, wearing his *Skateboarding is not a crime* T-shirt beneath very long bangs that are the only part of his head that isn't shaved, plus a sneer that could shatter ice.

The *Tribune* will call them "sort-of-angry," and the atmosphere "circus-like," and take pains to note how Lieutenant Frank Vondrak's warning to the protestors is "good-natured." When some of the crowd breaks out to cross Clark Street and take their protests inside City Hall, the reporter follows. They chant "skate, skate, skate" until they are "bored out of the council chambers." And what a tremendous verb clause, isn't it? What fantastic dismissal.

As for D. L. Nevin, I can find only one other record of him online. It's a long essay that was originally published in Chicago's *StreetWise*, a magazine sold by people experiencing or at risk of homelessness. "An anarchist report on Nigeria" details the author's trip to help establish a community radio station and organize a general strike. I find it archived on the Struggle Site, an outpost for Marxist and revolutionary organizing. The quote attached notes that "any nonprofit anarchist newspaper/magazine should feel free to re-publish" the essay. "There is no copyright."

* * *

A few weeks ago I met up with Dan at a DIY spot that some people had built into a disregarded parking lot on the Northwest Side. It's gone now, I just heard—the owner showed up one day and didn't like what was happening on his vacant, otherwise lifeless private lot. The ground was neglected asphalt that was graveling and treacherous in places, but the spot had its charms while it lasted. At some point during my standard warm-up—a period that spans at least a half hour these days—a goal wormed into my head. I was going to do a backside nose grind along the length of the cinder block ledge that was there—a fine and serviceable and even sort of fun ledge topped with angle iron. I would backside nose grind the whole ledge and then backside 180 out—that was the goal.

I'm highlighting this "goal" language to distinguish between this DIY's situation and my breathing, living desire for my Picasso trick, which remains as I type this. This thing on this DIY ledge was not so interesting. A ledge, you see, is a ledge. It is a means to an end, the medium through which one moves to reach a goal waiting on the other side. They vary in height and shape and friction and what kind of ground surrounds them, but the world is full of ledges. They are more rare in some places than others— Brooklyn is notoriously without good ledges while Manhattan is just packed—but are these days the stuff that any street section of any skate park is made from.

On this day, my goal proved elusive. I don't know—it's not that hard of a trick, but the combination of sustaining the grind and then rotating out, something wasn't working. I'd come real close and then the next three would be wildly bad, then I'd work my way back toward my goal only to once more lose it. After forty-five minutes or so I grew frustrated and went a bit, I guess, batty. I yelled some. I raised my hands on either side of my face and said some words loudly. I picked up my board and swung a punch into its griptape and sent it flying across the lot.

I'd done the trick before on similar ledges, I didn't even really care. This rage was something other than frustrated human desire, something mathematical. Given finite minutes each week to do this thing, should we battle against the entropic forces of the universe to maintain our stable bag of tricks? Or should we venture toward something else? Do we suffer the minor, flat joys of familiar achievement or the craggy pains—and potential ecstasy—of something new?

On my second visit to the Picasso, the area behind the sculpture is filled by two unmarked white tents, what look like triage tents. But there's nobody around, and in fact it's a bit eerie as I set up my camera leaning against the flagpole and my friend Nick sets up to film the second angle. I'm excited that the tents block sightlines between my starting point and the security desk inside. But, no. On this visit I manage six runs at the Picasso before a young guard comes out shaking his head and looking unamused. My days of arguing with security are over. Or maybe what the woman with the Doberman said has gotten in there and started fighting, Kaiju-like, with my desire. Anyway, I get three minutes and forty-seven seconds with the Picasso, which is not enough.

* * *

A week or two back, *Thrasher* posted a new episode of their "My War" series devoted to the stories and struggles behind notable tricks. This one was devoted to Sammy Baca's noseslide down a long, curved handrail in, I think, Koreatown, Los Angeles. "I'd have dreams about it," says Baca of a rail he'd already noseslid on film in 2005. "It was torturing me every time." Complicating his attempts is the fact that Sammy Baca lives in Las Vegas, and would ride the Megabus the six hours to LA on a Saturday, try the trick on Sunday, "get fucked up," then hop back on the bus back home overnight, arrive before sunrise, and take his kids to school Monday. Sometimes he'd get only two or three tries on the rail before limping away. Sometimes he'd try for two hours. Every time he tried he'd end up bloody, with duct tape on his hands, stains covering his shirt. "Get fucked up, not skate the whole week, then go try again."

This cycle went on for two years. On the final weekend of filming for the video, the last possible chance to get the clip into *Baker 4*, premiering days later and fourteen years after *Baker 3*, he finally landed it. "I didn't give a fuck. I touched the wall, I touched my hand. Fuck that. I'm surviving, dog. Trying to get diapers." It took him twenty-seven visits to the handrail. Each time he went, he'd land the long, curving noseslide. Each time, it was a shove-it off of the rail that would elude him. Twenty-seven visits requiring 324 hours on a bus. "Fuck the trick, it wasn't even about the trick. Fuck that trick. It was about the fucking spot."

* * *

The history of conflict between skateboarders and private property owners is long and storied and often amusing, if you can see it, and other times ugly and embarrassing. "Please get the fuck out," says an exasperated San Francisco home owner in 2017's *The GX1000 Video*. But they do not, and soon she's confronting the skaters— who appear to have been skating either her house's yard or the gangway between her home and the neighbors—more physically. First she swings one of their boards into the step. Then she swings the board at them. This is an extreme case, but the situation of this type of collision feels for many of us familiar.

Though, the publicness of space doesn't guarantee more peaceful relations. I can imagine how the sight of a skater running up the Picasso would spark any nature of internal dissonances. Some civilians are amused. A few will take photos and even find themselves caught in the spirit of the struggle, rooting almost against themselves for the make. Most, however, seem offended by what strikes them as blasphemy. I keep thinking of that woman with the

Doberman and her eagerness to protect the Picasso and those paid by the state of Illinois to work the plaza's security. I think of the two tourist women I encountered last summer who berated me even after I waited for them to take their photos and move aside. I think of a man who claimed to be, but was factually not, a "property manager" and tried to take my friend Jesse's board.

Meanwhile, two facts remain. First, no one, save a welder, could possibly do any real damage to the steel mass Picasso gifted to Chicago, upon which locals and tourists come at all hours to step and sit and play. Second, some laws are stupid, others unjust, and all of them can change.

I manage a phone call with the generous Miki Vuckovich from the former Tony Hawk Foundation, now the Skatepark Project, about a document that forever changed skateboarding's trajectory in the United States: California's Assembly Bill 1296. Its history began several years prior to the bill's passage in 1997, when a group from the International Association of Skateboard Companies (IASC), a for-profit trade association that promotes skateboarding, began lobbying legislators to convince them that skateboarding—and here's where it gets funny—is dangerous. And deserved, as such, to be listed among hang gliding, rock climbing, football, and other activities performed on public land that are so inherently risky that liability for any injuries fall to the user, *not* the provider of the space (the city, the state, the high school). Oregon and Colorado already had similar language written into law, and elsewhere case law already supported precedents to protect owners from liability. But California's history with liability was marred by the explosion of new skate parks in the late 1970s—Miki estimates a couple hundred between 1976 and 1978 (Craig B. Snyder's *A Secret History of the Ollie* names about eighty), many of which were poorly designed and quickly built to meet the sudden rise in skateboarding's popularity. Then the fad died, and there were emphatic insurance rate spikes following a handful of injury lawsuits, all of which led to a near extinction of skate parks.

Adding skateboarding to this list of Hazardous Recreational Activities (HRA) put the activity in line to receive municipal resources along with ballparks, beaches, and bike paths. So, you can see why an industry trade association would be interested in HRA, and indeed, once it passed in California, other states followed. And yet, there is no skateboarding brand—nor even skate branch of a larger athletic brand like Adidas or Nike—that markets themselves as a skate park brand. Skateboarding's economic value is inextricably tied to the street.

So we are speaking, again, about desire. About those strange and dominating forces that, today, begin in the many new parks that have been built—by TSP's approximations, the US had 2,000 skate parks in 2005, 3,000 by 2015, and about 3,500 in 2020 (which is still about 3,000 parks short of their ideal number for our country of 325 million people, figuring one park will serve a population of 50,000). About desires that may be sparked in designated skate parks, or after-school programs, or other pro-social outlets but that will, among the few who start and who are themselves devoted, grow and change shape. Such desires that metastasize and outstrip the safe confines of the venue and insist upon returning to their rightful home in public and semi-public and privately owned spaces shared with an American public who still thinks of skateboarding as an illicit and potentially litigious activity. Desires that will inevitably lead to some degree of trouble.

* * *

Each night, the neighborhood swells with people out for walks. It has been hot for a week, but now we're all relieved by the dusk and the arrival of the cicadas and the fact that out here is not where we live. These days there is home and then there is everywhere else, and tonight I find myself moving along residential blocks toward a spot that I've skated maybe ten times over the last decade. Three of those were in March of this year, after lockdown but before they shut the schoolyards and parks. I don't even realize where I'm going until I've walked past the wooden police barricade and into the closed schoolyard. The basketball rims are back up, I see. I move around back to the playground where there's a ledge that rises out of the ground then levels at about thigh height, low thigh. But the gate is still locked, which blocks any run-up to the ledge, which means, no, not yet. I am saying that the desire for the Picasso trick is actually just one of several, one small phenomenon of the world that I move through, and that moves through me.

Once more I make my way to Daley Plaza, this time on a Thursday afternoon. Though I've had success here during business hours in the past, it's pretty clear upon arrival that it won't be happening. I take a seat on one of the benches facing the Picasso across what Blair Kamin called the "exquisite flannel-gray carpet" of granite, which today is a desert. I count ten of us, currently, including the one person sitting on the sculpture's stage. No pedestrian cover to blend into, no daily motion to claim myself part of. Plus the white tents, I now understand, are there to serve as runoff space and prevent the crowds that can amass in hallways and lobbies during daily court proceedings. The security at the tent's opening is sitting there with nothing to do, staring at me staring at the sculpture.

It was not so long ago that one could speak ill of skate parks without reservation. Having not had my own local park until the late nineties, a full decade after I'd started skating, it was easy to see them as artificial stand-ins and pale imitations of the authentic. But the conversation has changed in recent years. In Malmö, I met Lisa Jacob of the Concrete Jungle Foundation, a nonprofit that moves around the world building skate parks in environments that lack infrastructure and community spaces. Sometimes this is it—a world-class skate park where there was hitherto little or nothing for youth activity. In some cases the Foundation also introduces programs they call Edu-Skate, an interventional pedagogy premised on Self-Determination Theory and structured with skateboarding at its core. Having begun to understand the social and self-actualizing values of skateboarding, the conversation about skate parks today is largely about access, which is to say justice. As Karlie Thornton, founder of Chicago's FroSkate collective, has said. "It's ridiculous the lack of skateparks available" in Black and Brown communities like the south and far west sides of the city. "We want to impact people's lives and provide safe spaces on the southside for Black and Brown people to have an outlet to skate and let go."

Of the sculpture's finite shape, its asymmetry is perhaps my favorite part. Or the donut nostrils, and that they're the same as the eyeballs. But I cannot look at it without seeing what's not there. Seeing spirit and history and other desires, other unseen but present forces. I mean Timothy Johnson loping his long strides at it from the east so he's riding more across it than up, then somehow kickflipping off and all the way over the ten or so feet of platform to the ground. I mean Ken Keistler, the godfather of the rare no-run Picasso approach—ollie up those sixteen inches onto the platform and then (somehow) ollie again very quickly onto steel, and (somehow) maintain enough speed to make it up the incline and wallride. I mean Jackson Hennessy, who somehow scampered up onto the thing's western shoulder and dropped into the sculpture like it was a vert ramp. I mean Josh Kalis and his kickflip wallride. Josh Kalis and his boggling and improbable 360 flip over the granite bench where I happen to be sitting.

What is it, really, that leads a civilian to object to someone skateboarding in public? There is the noise, OK, and the fear that a board will shoot out of control and cause some kind of damage. But that, I don't think, is all of it. Having skateboarded in Copenhagen and Malmö and Paris and Berlin, it seems clear, if generally stated, that other concepts of public space are more inclusive than ours, more public. In Bordeaux, France, when skateboarding in public became more and more popular, the city instituted a series of repressive policies—citations, defensive and hostile architecture—common to cities who haven't yet been convinced of skateboarding's values. It took Leo Valls, owner of Magenta Skateboards, to work with city leaders to establish particular hours when skateboarding is allowed in public plazas. "If you change the policy of the city," he says, "the average citizen is going to change the way they look at skateboarding." As a result, Bordeaux, like Malmö, has learned to integrate skateboarding into its cultural and social landscapes.

American history, however, is a story of ownership. So, the litigious history of skateboarding, real or imagined, continues to haunt its public perception. It's a powerful association to shake, and one that the skateboard industry doesn't even seem fully to *want* to shake. See for example the following, taken from the Skatepark Project's website:

> In communities without skateparks, people seek the next best thing; streets, plazas, sidewalks, campuses, and parking lots eventually stake their claim as the "best place to skate around here." At some point people run out of patience and law enforcement finds itself penalizing local youth for pursuing their recreational interests in inappropriate places.

I do not know where exactly a veiled threat becomes extortion. I do know, however, that just down the street from Daley Plaza there is a very large and modern "street plaza" park, which means there are stairs and handrails and ledges, many more angles than curves. It is also enclosed on three sides, which means there is a bottleneck that allows for police officers to drive their squad SUVs through the surrounding grass and right up to the park and keep a close eye on what's happening inside.

To fall prey to the desire that keeps me coming back to the Picasso sculpture, to live with desire of the sort I have been describing and carry it as a weightless burden, is to live within an envelope of time between the desire's onset and its satisfaction. I am speaking, I think, of history. The life span of a honey locust is around 120 years, which means the one I look at now was here at the Picasso's unveiling. Was here at the 1988 protest of the new anti-skateboarding law. Was here on August 23, 1968, when the official protests of the

Democratic National Convention kicked off and Phil Ochs was arrested. FroSkate's own wildly successful No Breaks protest of July 4 this year took a path south of Daley Plaza so that it could occupy the street outside of CPD's State Street headquarters, but still began and ended in a corner of Grant Park known amongst us as a spot: the double-sided ledge over a ventilation grate. It is perhaps, I'm suggesting, not merely coincidence that so often links skateboarding's desired spaces with a history of protest.[2]

* * *

The signed statement from Pablo Picasso reads in full: "I hereby give this work and the right to reproduce it to the public building commission, and I give the maquette to the Art Institute of Chicago, desiring that these gifts shall, through them, belong to the people of Chicago."

Picasso, friend of poets, friend of Chaplin, spent his life suffering for his associations with anarchists and communists. There were files on him as early as 1901, when Paris police took note of his living with an anarchist art dealer. He was rejected in an application for French citizenship before the Nazi occupation because he was an extremist "evolving towards communism." He died having never visited the US, unable ever to secure a visa due to the FBI and State Department's suspicion that he was a communist. Picasso's American oversight began in 1945, when J. Edgar Hoover himself personally ordered a special agent in Paris to watch Picasso due to a statement he wrote in 1944, "Why I Became a Communist." From that letter: "Through design and color, I have tried to penetrate deeper into a knowledge of the world and of men so that this knowledge might free us."

---

2   E.g., Zuccotti Park, the home of Occupy Wall Street and origin point for many of 2020's BLM actions, is a playground of skateable marble, and Philly's branch of Occupy set up camp among the historic ledges and stairs of City Hall and Thomas Paine Plaza, known to skaters as Muni.

There is *Guernica*, of course, a painting so powerful that a tapestry reproduction that hung at the entrance of the UN Security Council had to be covered (Maureen Dowd wrote that the UN "plans to throw a blue cover over" the antiwar masterpiece) on February 5, 2003, before Colin Powell made his case for the invasion of Iraq. Art critic Dore Ashton said that Picasso "was a born antifascist; it was in his blood." The poet René Char called him "furiously subversive." Dominique Desanti, a friend, told the *New York Times*, "Had he known the F.B.I. was watching him, he probably would have laughed his head off. He might have put on a mask maker's red nose and made jokes about it. No doubt he would think such an absurd thing was surrealistic."

The great mystery upon the unveiling of Picasso's Chicago sculpture was one of meaning. What is it? What is it supposed to be? "Statue What You Make It," ran the *Tribune* headline on August 19, 1967. "You're supposed to use your imagination," said Mayor Daley. The idea that the sculpture was modeled after Picasso's dog, Kabul, originates with the photographer David Douglas Duncan who wrote from Saigon in 1967. He'd met Picasso in 1956 and their friendship lasted until the artist's death, seventeen years later. Douglas has written at length of visits to the maestro's home, attempting to capture the spirit of the artist that gave design to his way of life. "No individual day was ever better than any other." Some days, though, "seemed even gayer," such as the time Picasso tried to emulate Jacqueline Roque's ballet steps. Stare at the Chicago sculpture and you can see it, the great artist "mixing pirouettes and polkas and ponderous flipping and flapping of his own spontaneous invention."

It can indeed be captured, dance. The spirit of gaiety and freedom can be conveyed into and through nonrepresentational forms, made tangible if illegible, not frozen in time but adjacent to it. It is not so hard, really. If you're a genius, all you do is sculpt a thing that cannot be understood, make it large and inviting, and then—this part is crucial—you give the thing away.

CHAPTER THIRTY-FOUR

On a Decision

How to best paint darkness? Given perception's reliance on light to define shape and size and depth, how to convey the requisite details without light as a guide? One option is to center light's absence—to describe or capture the inability at the core of the challenge. The trap, as it were, the shape of the place from which no light escapes. But creating a mimesis of darkness results in a performance that is…unpleasant. It leads to a story one begins reading, feeling generous, and then quickly realizes no, no, no and sets aside, shaking their head and issuing a quick, relieved smile, grateful for this most basic freedom.

Another option: forgo mimesis in favor of something more mediated and distant. To name the darkness, I mean, and treat it as an object, a given, and to speak of it only this way, as "The Darkness." Such an attempt is less concerned with convincing or even conveying. Which means that the rhetoric of such attempts often lacks pathos, feels sterile, *assumes* that the audience can and will draw from their own experiences of darkness. Carry this personal darkness into their witnessing of the performance as if their own darkness were a water bottle or binoculars, some handheld personal aide.

I stood in the kitchen and heard K crying in the bathroom.

For the past two years and more we have spent an hour of

our Thursday nights—sometimes every other, sometimes every—speaking with a marriage therapist named Winona. I wonder, typing this now, how long that sounds, "two years." Tonight, to Winona, K and I agreed out loud that we are going to separate.

There is no failed or successful marriage, said Winona. There is only the truth.

You sink to the kitchen floor and all of the stuff of the floor—this becomes you, this is who you are now.

From the floor I wondered, What do we do, socially, with the divorced? Not any worse than we do with the childless, I thought, so I am not dropping in the American caste. Then I thought: I will move out of this country. If I can trust my parents to live well, I will live somewhere else for a time. I will either have sex with everyone I can or have sex with no one, and however it goes I'll do it in a faraway land.

Later in the night I put on *Fury Road*. "War!" the painted boys yell.

Before the movie, she and I sat at the kitchen island and took shots of whiskey. I cooked us ramen and oh boy, did I play it cool.

"Witness me, bloodbag! Witness!"

"I live, I die, I live again."

A perversity: the way a mind unleashed will scurry for the far ends of what we might call good and bad future outcomes. At one end, all the unlikely but possible opportunities and developments, hearts and bodies and gatherings in idyllic locations. At the other—and there is simultaneity to this, a sequence you could perhaps riddle but never reproduce—all the sorrows and destroyed certainties, the storms and aches, the terrible and frightful worsts that lay ahead. The result of mind is a mixed reality at once excruciating and utopic; by what evolutionary logic did we learn to do this to ourselves? Well, fear I suppose. And hope. Survival, in a word.

The next morning I am up too early; it's dark when I get out of bed. It's lightened by the time I hear her—I'm in the chair reading and taking notes, searching for whatever it is I turn to literature to find. She is weeping, breathing, a sound that only— was it yesterday?—rang like an alarm, a duty, a plea. I stay in the chair. She goes into the bathroom and her toothbrush buzzes. She weeps. My book on skateboarding is becoming a memoir, as books primarily are these days.

I do not know what to do. I sit with this for a time, studying the empty space that's normally filled by *should*. Which is kinder, which cruel? Go in or stay here? And to whom? And also, my tea is empty and the path to refill my mug takes me down our long and only hallway, directly past, or to, the bedroom door. For the first time, it occurs to me how fortunate I've been in this age of open floorplans to have lived with a hallway for all these years.

Inside I sit close to her on the bed. She is…riven. For the moment, I am only devastated. She cries, adjusts in the bed, and says she's not going to work.

We speak some words and then I ask, "What is the best thing to do with all this sadness?"

"Probably write about it," she says.

After a time I get up and refill my mug and put on some water for her. Doing this, pulling down the bag of loose green tea and scooping out a teaspoon and pouring it into the strainer, is the absolute saddest motherfucking sequence of actions I've ever done in my life. And I know that this will only retain its title until the next thing I do for her or she for me, plus here I've done the dickhead thing that I always get mad at her for doing, filled the kettle too full so it's taking the water forever to boil. I only want this single mug's-worth and I wonder what she's told her boss of all this in her message about staying home from work. Has she conveyed or hinted or said outright what we've decided?

Did we decide? We did. We said the words out loud to our therapist. If marriage is a speech act coming, then it will be one going, as well.

Gradually the sound indicates that the water is nearly there, and it's coming from above me. It seems I'm on the kitchen floor again, so I stand. On the counter, beneath the strainer, I see the remainder bits of green leaf matter, the powder bits too fine for the metal latticework, and here is a thing—sorrow and meaning can coexist (is this true of joy and meaning?), and I know because licking my finger and pressing it to the counter to collect the green tea powder that has traveled from mainland China to our cluttered shelf, I am aware of the journey and the naked symbolism of that which seems too small to matter *of course* still being matter, everything matters, and soon enough she is there in the kitchen wearing her most familiar oversize sweatshirt, an item of clothing I could not begin to approximate how long or how many times I've looked at.

This is the day following our decision, and it will, the day, go on. Soon, in the bedroom, she'll ask "How you doing, Beach?" and I will speak some words around a practical concern, money, the mortgage, a kind of protective measure for my brain, practicality as defense, evolution again, great, and stand there looking at her earrings and other hanging things that I've gifted her or she's gifted herself, hanging like anchors of a dozen missing ships on the little rack on the wall.

I'll stand in the bathroom after chewing some Tums. Then, moving toward the couch, I'll think, Why don't I sit for a second and have a little cry, grant myself that much? Soon, I'll have curled with my face in my hands and then suddenly I'll be weeping, the sounds beyond me and they'll keep coming. Pain, I will understand, is made of sound. I will think into the past and future at once—that which we've had will soon be gone and never the same, time will have folded me into it and I will be weeping, weeping, and hear her come from the bedroom and realize that I have called her to me, I've made a request with these sopping wet sounds muzzled by my hands, and she'll be on the couch with me, curled onto me, holding me as I moan and babble and gurgle time's pain into a puddle that will gather inside my hand cavern until eventually I carry my face to the bathroom to wash and brush my own teeth and see my face ravaged, hair two weeks beyond its time but the world is closed, and she'll say, once I'm back on the couch, she'll note, "We were supposed to be in Mexico right now." She had such hopes for the trip. Still (of course—what would she do, change clothing?) she is wearing her big billowing navy blue crewneck sweatshirt with one sleeve rolled a little higher on her forearm to expose the plush, worn interior fabric. Her legs folded beneath her. It is true that we are different people on the road. We travel well. Mexico might have saved us, I think magically.

I can remember the moments before our Skyped therapy session last night, moving through this room and adjusting the lighting to suit the call that I knew was coming. It occurs to me now that our last vacation, the short trip she took to join me for a few days in Colorado, will be our *last vacation*. She was there for a time then I was alone working, then my parents arrived, my father fell and my mother stopped him from drowning. What I will do, I think, is move to Denmark. I will move to Malmö, Sweden. I will find a room for the best of my books and not much else. I will live simply and do my work and ride my skateboard for as long as my body will allow and then, what. I will become a husk. I will blow away in the Scandinavian breeze, out into the barley.

Here is a meaningful detail: her big oversize sweatshirt is a Primitive sweatshirt. I mean it says so right there across the chest in big block capital letters, arced over the bear stolen from the California flag, PRIMITIVE, but this predates the skateboard company that grew out of the clothing line, and there is a way that we can look at a thing so much it becomes obvious, yada yada, we stop seeing it et cetera, et cetera.

I have written about Primitive, once. I made an attempt to describe why or rather how I enjoyed a short clip of theirs. I remember quoting Virginia Woolf: "Style is a very simple matter; it is all rhythm," because this Primitive clip was all style, its style was its rhythm was its harmony, and because it was difficult to get any more specific and pinpoint what was good, I shared more Woolf: "No this is very profound, what rhythm is, and goes far deeper than words." Good has always been so hard. To speak of the opposite so much easier.

And then, yes, this was the first time I wrote of our therapy, K's and mine, in some throwaway blog post about skateboarding, a kind of test run to speak our struggles into the world. (She is across the couch from me, wearing her Primitive crewneck. Soon she will be gone, will move into her own home and take all of her clothing and houseplants and self along.) That was—I remember now—what the Primitive clip did for me. It was a theme of our conversations at therapy, my difficulty isolating positive elements of the world or myself and extrapolating those positives into a clearer, cleaner relationship with my own desires and preferences. Because how, my therapist and still-wife and I all asked, how without seeing and knowing those positive preferences could I possibly determine the way that I would like my life to go in the near future? How could I guide my own progress without stars to steer by?

There was, I wrote at the time, a point to be made here about writing, and what it asks of the brain and body. And so the short Primitive clip made me want to try (again) writing more loosely. Try writing with lower stakes. To go overboard for a while, wildly and irresponsibly, with little regard for decorum or good taste. It is so easy, I concluded, to write from indignancy.

Her tea is steeping on the counter, still. We're in the kitchen between what has happened and what soon will. She leans into me and at this point the book I'm writing ceases to be a book about marriage. I have been thinking of it this way: *my book about skateboarding and marriage*. But it is not about marriage, was never about marriage. It is about rhythm and harmony, disharmony and witness. Time. This is what the Primitive realization does, and it is a comfort that I find in the middle of this sorrow. This whole time it's been a book about love. K and I love each other, have loved, will love each other wherever and however we live. That is the mystery of time.

CHAPTER THIRTY-FIVE

The Dylan Period

2020

ONE:

When the most beautiful man ever to ride a skateboard died on October 12, 2016, the news was covered by *Rolling Stone*, *Sports Illustrated*, and *People Magazine*. Which might lead us to believe that he was a musician, athlete, or celebrity. He was not. He did sit shoulder-to-shoulder with Cara Delevingne on the hood of a New York taxi for a DKNY campaign, was at least a few times broadcast live on ESPN, and did move comfortably among models and actors through the nightlives of Los Angeles and New York City. His was a narrow face that slimmed into a tight and mischievous smile, with eyes that conjured images from nature, cheekbones like rolling hills. His body was skinny and long, with drinking-straw hips and a swimmer's shoulders, the kind of frame onto which you could put any clothing and it would hang just perfectly right. He was twenty-eight.

So it was easy from time to time to forget that what Dylan Rieder was, above and beneath the rest, was a skateboarder. People who knew him will tell you: those haggard T-shirts he wore didn't come pre-ripped. He was a skater's skater, a rat to the core no matter how good he looked on screen. When he was on a mission, he'd be the one lying on the ground or bent in obvious pain and exhaustion, hour after hour as the camera batteries ran out and his colleagues had gone back to the hotel or out to the bar. Or, if they were rats too, sat there watching Dylan keep going and knowing that this was it, this was the behavior that gave the word its glimmer.

I did not know him. He was, I gather, a private person, which is why the two years that he spent in treatment for acute lymphoblastic leukemia remains, for many skateboarders, a cloudy sequence even still. In July 2014 he was diagnosed and began chemotherapy in hopes of achieving a remission that would allow for a bone marrow transplant from his sister. A bout of encephalopathy complicated this plan, and he enrolled in a T cell clinical trial that would begin in January 2015. When the trial failed he was shifted to a portable med pump that he wore on his body, which also failed, leading doctors to move aggressively forward with the transplant. In April 2015 he achieved remission only to develop a liver disorder that kept him in the hospital until early July, after which he lived four months in remission before routine bloodwork in November alerted him that the cancer had returned. So, then, another T cell trial, but this time with his sister's cells. This lasted from January through April 2016 and was successful. Having achieved remission again he was able finally to go home at the end of May. A little more than four months later he developed the infection that would quickly take his life in October, while still in remission.

This summary leaves out everything that matters, including the suffering, the fear, the unlikely smiles and deep cadre of friends who gathered bedside to surround Dylan and create the shield that would maintain his privacy from those who would imagine it was their right to know such details of where and when and how. In the end, there's nothing to be learned from cancer, no lesson to Dylan's or any other too-early death. Except how the person is loved.

The public account of Dylan Rieder begins in Westminster, California, near Huntington Beach. A childhood of ample resources and easy access to skate parks accelerates around age twelve, when he began going on trips with the shoe and clothing brands Osiris and Quiksilver. He was a handrail chomper who turned to transition, and eventually joined the legendary board company Alien Workshop at eighteen and began filming for *Mind Field*, their long-awaited follow-up to the seminal *Photosynthesis* (2000). Under these new expectations, Dylan fell into pills and his *Mind Field* part showed it. So, he set to work on a follow-up video with cinematographer, friend, and neighbor Greg Hunt.

Because it is baffling, mankind has conceived of a number of models and metaphors for time. The everyday, conventional, secular concept of linear time that proceeds moment-by-moment, we call *chronos*. The generational notion of time as a series of periods or ages, we call *aeon*. Then there is a more sacred approach that separates time into periods of before and after—as in the liturgical calendar of Advent, Christmas, Lent, and Easter. This is time as *kairos*, and the film that Hunt and Dylan would release in 2010, just one year after *Mind Field*, is a seven-and-a-half-minute masterpiece that would mark a before-after moment in skateboarding's history. Done, now, was all the hypertechnical ledge wizardry of the late aughts. This would be the decade of renaissance, of simpler tricks executed elegantly. After *Dylan.* was released, Dylan shot to the top of the skateboarding world and into the pages of *Vogue*. He refined his image and birthed a thousand imitators, created the smokiest and most artful skateboard clip of all time for his HUF[1] shoe, and played no small part in the ascendance of two of street culture's preeminent contemporary brands, Fucking Awesome and Supreme. And then leukemia,

---

1   HUF's namesake, the great and quick-of-foot Keith Hufnagel, did himself pass in 2020 of brain cancer, which, like Dylan, Hufnagel chose to keep private. Huf's style was nothing, not a whit like Dylan's—he had heavy arms, and his movements were compact and efficient in all ways but his push, which saw his left hand swing behind his body and open upward as if waiting for another hand to reach for it and take hold.

death at twenty-eight, and now regular annual remembrances of his legacy. He is loved, now, by all.

There is, however, a very big piece that this version, and many versions, of Dylan's story leaves out. Which is just how reviled and ridiculed Dylan was by large swaths of the skateboard community. Somewhere between 2006's *A Time to Shine* and *Mind Field*, he'd gone from kid wonder to kid pretense. The hair, OK, we were used to hair. But the slim pants cuffed to the shins, the blousey shirts with huge necklines, the nail polish and jewels—Dylan was not what we believed a skateboarder should look like, and our opposition to his look was not gentle. We laughed at his photo shoots. We had great fun at the expense of his Gravis shoe with its barely there rumor of a sole and oxblood leather pinched into an elvish point.

How *vain*, I personally thought. Every move seemed to have been rehearsed before a mirror. How easy to imagine beautiful Dylan sleeping each night inside a custom-built chambered and reflective bed, rising each morning to a great hall of taxidermy and mirrors and secondhand animal skulls. There was nothing easier than to mock and ridicule his beauty and his obvious awareness of his beauty, which struck me and others as an insult to…well, by this point, it's difficult to say. In 2010 skateboarders were all still mostly men and either heterosexual or closeted, so we made jokes about gender. We behaved like terrible, small-minded children because in large part we were exactly that. Until, that is, the short film whose title's punctuation made for full sentence, with subject, predicate, and object all contained in that one word: *Dylan.*

After that, we quieted down, backed away scuffing dirt with our hands in pockets. Soon enough the objections grew quieter and faded. Soon, in a reversal, the objections to Dylan seemed petty, vain, and clownish. And the importance of this shift, the lasting significance of Dylan Rieder, is not just that he changed minds, but the way he went about achieving this change with the selfsame tools that had shaped those minds in the first place.

Dylan was both product of and challenger to the collective

norms and beliefs and practices that adhere skateboarding into a community. He embodied the traditions, attitudes, and a host of qualities that we might call *the spirit* of skateboarding. By embodying this spirit so fully, and so uniquely, he forced all of us to step back and reconsider almost everything we'd assumed about what was rad, what was important, and the very activity of our looking. Orson Welles had it that, "If the camera doesn't like an actor, it just stares at him." Cameras loved Dylan, but skateboarders loved him better. Eventually.

TWO:

The camera is a tool to capture light, shapes, and distance—it does not see style. Language, historically, hasn't done much better. E. B. White wrote that trying to find a satisfactory explanation of style was like "steering by stars that are disturbingly in motion." We might start by saying that, were Dylan a language, it was one written in cursive. He was long and looping, with legs that could as easily compress as explode, though both steps, the sink and the rise, seemed to happen inside of liquid. There was always something auspicious in his skating, something in that slender shadow of his that felt as if it was all premised on rumor. You knew him immediately: a handful of frames, a fraction of a second and it was him. He had a driving force that far exceeded his body's mass, and a flick that hefted his board into rotations that felt, at times, to be his body's own.

Every icon needs a signature—Bond's martini, Malcolm's eyeglasses, James Dean's jacket—and nowhere was Dylan's physical grace clearer than when he performed an impossible. The challenge of the impossible is what physicists call the intermediate axis theorem. If you, say, try to toss a tennis racket, book, or cell phone into the air in a way that it rotates flatly, end over end, it will be difficult. The object wants to flip as it rotates. Objects longer than they are wide or thick create different moments of inertia, which makes rotation along the intermediate axis unstable, and leads to this seeming desire to flip along another axis. Dylan's signature impossible, like a lot of now-standard tricks, was pioneered by Rodney Mullen in the 1980s only after rotations along the other two axes—kickflips and shove-its—had already been "solved." The only way to do the "impossible" rotation along the intermediate axis would be to, as Mullen describes it, "somewhat vertify" the 360 shove-it and use the back foot to guide the board and stop it from flipping over. The more vertical, the more proper, the more effective the impossible. Because the rotation takes so long, learning it takes commitment—people either have them or do not. What's more, many skaters who have the trick in their arsenal cheat them by not fully vertifying the spin. So, while there's a blurry line between a 360 shove and a cheated impossible, a proper impossible is both rare and unmistakable.

Nobody's, but nobody's, was better than Dylan's. There are five (or six) in *Dylan.*, and each is as cohesive and singular a motion as someone else's snap of fingers or curve of lips—he crouches and lifts and seems to heft the rotating board up and over the obstacle, or into a nose wheelie, or grind, or any number of variations. So, I was not surprised to learn that the most memorable impossible of his career, the one over the bench, the one that ridiculed gravity and is seared into the brain matter of all who have seen it, was one he did easily.

In July 2020, ten years later, Nike SB released a short clip of Norwegian skater Didrik Galasso, aka Deedz, during his first ever visit to New York City. Deedz and his guides move among familiar spots, go surfing in Rockaway, and then, late in the video, there's a shot of Deedz in full tourist mode, his face radiant. "That's the bench," he says, and you would think he's just rounded a corner in Rome and come upon the Vatican. Even as he says it his body moves a step or two forward, as if by magnets. "The golden bench," he says, as the shot cuts to a standard issue seaport bench under FDR Drive, across which a body is sprawled, asleep.

Dylan did it twice, in fact. They were there for twenty minutes and he impossibled over the bench twice. Which explains how we've got two angles of the trick in *Dylan*. First, from the front in slow motion, and later, in the credits, in full speed. I've pulled them up on the monitor to compare them side by side. The second finds him landing slightly more on his heels, just a bit less prone to swerving across the bike lane. But in both there's a swing to his arms that I only notice now. His hands go from very low on crouch to very high as he leaps, then forward briefly as his torso pulls back and knees come up, then follow a looping, widening circle back, down, and then swinging forward and up they rise up again in front of his waist as he lands, *olé*. It is a wild thing to behold, these details, leaning into my monitor and watching so unnaturally. And the motions of the two are identical—and, well, identifying. As we expect from a signature.

THREE:

It is telling that the fiercest and cruelest barbs of our opposition to Dylan pointed to his style. Whatever he had, whatever we saw, "style" implied a safe distance between him and substance. Here Susan Sontag proves useful. "Merely by employing the notion" of style, she wrote, "one is almost bound to invoke, albeit implicitly, an antithesis between style and something else."

Skateboarding's something else is a notion we have fetishized and leaned upon for any number of otherwise vague valuations. We can call it, boringly, "authenticity." This year, 2021, will mark the thirtieth anniversary of one of skateboarding's longest-running companies, REAL,[2] capitalized as such. We have elsewhere discussed heritage and the way skateboarding values longevity, but for many skaters authenticity is synonymous with a kind of affectless

---

2   A company that has, however ironically, remained relatively innocent of the standard industry practice of dolling up and trotting out legacy every five years as a reminder.

core, or stripped essence. It calls to another Strunk and Whiteism, that advice to turn away from "mannerisms, tricks, adornments" and find style by "simplicity, orderliness, sincerity."

The allure of this rather circular argument is the sheer variety of ways it can be weaponized. Anything you don't like, for any reason whatsoever? Insincere. Fake. Done for the wrong reasons. I have, for example, caught myself more recently levying this charge against the fashionable Parisian crew, Les Blobys. When I first encountered them, I could not but think of that scene in Jean-Luc Godard's *Breathless* when the scoundrel and performer Michel famously stands before a cinema poster, studying Humphrey Bogart. This fantasy, which ultimately brings doom to Michel, is Hollywood's fantasy, one that Godard stood essentially against. To my eyes, the vanity of Les Blobys rang of deliberation and labor. They were Michel standing before the images of US skateboarding, modeling the movements into their own affectations.

To be clear: there would be no Les Blobys were there no Dylan, and the blowback he suffered was similar but even more barbed and personal. The opposition to Dylan began with beauty. The hair, the clothing, the jewels and too-pleasant smile. There was also the matter of his body, which was not only lithe and tailored but would assume shapes and forms misaligned with the skateboarding activity, unnatural and therefore criminal postures. I am speaking, mainly, of what some of us called "vampiring." He had a way of bending his front, right elbow and raising his forearm up around his face like a vampire lifting its cape to shield its face from the sun.

See for example at about 2:40 of *Dylan*. He executes an alley oop wallride that seems to climb for too long, and when he finally comes down he lands crouched and vampired. Or, better, the following clip, a quick backside tailslide on an out-ledge that he kickflips off of and clears the protrusive bottom step easily. As he lands, his front, right arm hangs limp and natural across his body. Then, seeming to recall who is he, he lifts that arm up and *into* a vampire, crooking his right elbow as his left arm rises behind him. It's the most excessive vampire of Dylan's career's output, a forced pose, like a gymnast raising their arms overhead for the judges.

In other words, the alarm of vampiring was a matter of conspicuous control. And it may have been that we were particularly sensitive to matters of control, given the historical conditions in 2010. There was Nike, remember, and more broadly the contraction of the industry in the wake of a global recession. Classic legacy brands were struggling and shuttering sub-brands and selling themselves to non-native buyers. Alien Workshop was bought by the snowboard and apparel company Burton, and Jake Burton is credited as *Dylan*.'s executive producer. So, we were uneasy regarding the authentic and wary of change. Really, we were afraid. And Dylan suffered as much of this communal fear as anyone.

As Sontag put it, we found in Dylan "evidence of the artist's intrusion upon his materials, which should be allowed to deliver themselves in a pure state." Of course, in skateboarding as in literature there is no "pure state," no way to do the thing without doing it some*how*. Purity is a facet of nostalgia. Every skateboarding body has always been an intrusion, and its style an expression thereof, a force inseparable from the materials themselves.

But the one person who would know better than anyone disagrees. "That video part is all him," said Greg Hunt, who is modest, I learned, and also generous and open to talking shop for two hours. But you should have heard how much he stressed this point: "Some filmers are crazy motivators and coaches. I was just there trying to capture it as best as I could, then put it together in a way that I felt represented him in the most honest way. But it all comes from him, because that's what I wanted to see."

FOUR:

Go watch *Dylan*. Whether it's the first time or the thirtieth, look at it again. A decade later and I cannot watch without recalling the experience of my first time, how fiercely I was prepared to reject and dismiss it. Its first section of three serves as a kind of showcase: a couple smith grinds, kickflip, and a nose blunt and a tall handrail into a few transition reminders followed by some high-speed lines. Nothing exceptional. Even as it begins to work against your resistance—it really is a *high* kickflip, a *lengthy* nose blunt, and boy he's going *pretty fast* at that kind of massive rail . . .—the opening lulls you a bit.

When the title cards come they're in Helvetica, ha ha, and proclaiming it a "short film," and any eye-rolling at these might last until about halfway into the next clip, the film's first slow motion of an alley oop frontside flip to the opening piano notes of Graham Nash's "Better Days."[3] Some portent here, even before the song has a chance to get moving. A second slow-motion clip confirms it—a floating impossible shot with gradual cinematic pan. This is an escalation. This, for the Dylan-opposed, presented a bit of a problem. Suddenly we're moving full speed ahead and it's difficult to hold on to whatever we thought just a couple minutes prior.

Even now, it is very difficult for me to watch what follows without making some kind of sound. On that first watch a decade ago, this effect would have had to include the real-time disintegration of that part of me, the reluctance and judgment from which I was shocked into a kind of stuporous disbelief. That any surprise remains ten years later is at least a small miracle. Sometimes that surprise arrives in the midst of a trick, like the early lipslide that just keeps going. Or the front tailslide that anyone watching closely knows is going to end with a kickflip dismount: you believe you're prepared for what's ahead but when it comes the kickflip is so meticulous with such lift from the slide and rise to meet his oxblood elf shoes—please go ahead and laugh, he dares you, have yourself a nice chuckle—and there is such cool composure on the stomp that comprehension starts cracking.

---

3   A sad song, it took me a long time to realize.

I remember thinking, this cannot continue at this pace. But it does. Everything is about 20 percent bigger or longer than you'd expect. He just straight up ollies off of a Montclair roof, which I do not think anyone saw coming. And like all great physical performances, this one involves moments of total control and the outer border of mayhem. His arms flail about during a two-trick line in a ditch, a kickflip, and a wallride back 180 out. He lands the impossible nose wheelie down the long hubba thing by the water and is wild and loose. And then the back tail up on the blue bars is clean, composed, his right arm bent at the elbow and raised before his face. Framed just so.

This bothness, the natural struggle for balance mixed with Dylan's deliberate modeling of "Dylan" as form, brings us back to Greg Hunt. Recall that Hunt's goal was to edit this short film "in a way that I felt really represented him in the most honest way." And like other people who knew Dylan well, Hunt won't say much about him personally. He opens up, though, when describing their work:

> The main thing was, I wanted it to breathe. Up until that time, the norm was to let people ride out of frame. But I really wanted to see Dylan riding up, riding away. I wanted to really see everything, like the board going under the bus, you know? When you watch Dylan skate, everything around him was so interesting too.

Hunt calls himself an emotional editor driven by feeling over anything planned or analytic. He starts with music, moves things around to see where they fit in, emotionally. Then he builds outward from that.

But not only builds. Hunt's role in *Dylan.* is at once heavier and lighter than he'll let on. Like consider the sequence that starts at 3:35 as the drums recede and the song settles into a break, with the slowed and very high frontside flip on a natural pyramid. Hunt gives us a brief, over-the-shoulder shot on the approach, seeing Dylan from behind and then cutting to the pyramid's far side so we see him coming at us. Next is a single, low angle for an impossible 50-50 down a hubba, also slowed. Then Hunt returns to the multishot pattern for another frontside kickflip, but complicates it with a third step—first we're behind on the approach, then in profile for the trick, both at full speed. The third angle is shot from directly ahead, slowed in motion and paired with the return of Nash's drums and the (emotional) arrival of backing vocals.

So, there is feeling here, but also disorientation. The next clip seems by all measures to *begin* in slow motion on Dylan's approach and then ramp into full speed as he backside flips over a hefty LA handrail. Until you see his shirt blowing in the wind, it's impossible to know how fast he's going. These shifts between normal and slowed motion create a sort of temporal lean, or imbalance. We stay full speed until the second angle of the impossible tail grab up out of the arroyo and over the fence, a slowed, second angle that reveals the drop's full stature. Then another approach shot, another rail we see from behind Dylan followed by a partially slowed fakie flip over the rail and into the bank as the footage ramps back to natural speed on the roll away.

After five minutes, the film transitions to credits and B-roll and lifestyle clips that serve to round out the portrait of Hunt's film. But by then, the effect of Hunt's paired techniques—the sympathetic approach shots that give us something like Dylan's view of the obstacle and the disorientation created by slowed motion—has already done the bulk of this work. Again, it's both heavy and light on Hunt's part. It's the artificial used in the service of reality. But if you ask Hunt, he'll stress that none of it feels conceptual to him.

He set about his work with two goals: to create an honest representation of Dylan himself, and to create a feeling.

More than anything, what I feel as I watch Hunt's film is: present. Gravity has me, this chair contains me, these images and sounds from my monitor locate me on the big cosmic map. But that is not so strange, really. This is what knowing a person does. "Why are certain people so loved?" said Hunt. "The way they do what they do, and the way it makes people feel." Sontag would have agreed. At one point in "On Style" she quotes Jean Cocteau, who goes further: "Decorative style has never existed. Style is the soul, and unfortunately with us the soul assumes the form of the body." Unfortunately? Maybe. Soul, though—yes. I believe yes. In picking up this transmission from Dylan across the void I end up knowing myself just that much better. I am affected by *Dylan.* because I am affected by Dylan.

FIVE:

There is also, however, the unlikely fact of Dylan's Street League tenure to consider. To begin to know someone, to shed your prior resistance and come around to a more intimate relationship, and then to be surprised like this? Violation! As far as I can tell, Dylan competed in three years of the contests, and generally finished solidly down near the bottom of the rankings—twentieth, fourteenth, twenty-first, twelfth. But in June 2013, something clicked, and the footage of that weekend's finals makes for one of two Dylan Rieder SLS clips that counteract any sense of personal violation.

After ten events, it's his first time making it to the finals, and speaking in terms of visuals, he's clearly out of place. He is the only one without any brand identifiers on his person—Paul Rodriquez is wearing a Nike SB tee and hat, Luan Oliveira a Nike tee; Chris Cole is in a DC shirt and Monster wristband, Nyjah a DC shirt and Monster hat. Anyway, they all look stupid except for Dylan, who looks like Dylan in his plain white tee with a blown-out neckline, less a deep *v* than garage door opened onto his chest, and it's peppered by holes down by the beltline.

Of Nyjah, Felix the announcer says, "So solid, so confident. No expression on his face whatsoever."

Also in these finals is one Mikey Taylor, former Alien Workshop teammate of Dylan's who since 2013 has retired and turned into a venture capitalist, antiscience motivational real-estate crank.[4] And the more you dislike Mikey Taylor, which I do a fair but not debilitating amount, the more enjoyment the following moments provide.

In 2013, Mikey Taylor's physical presentation had turned, like much of skateboarding's, unabashedly derivative of Dylan's. His pants got suddenly shorter and his hair took on sheen and length. So, here we are before the control section of the contest, dropping into live action with a shot of them side by side, Mikey and Dylan up against the black wall of the course's edge. It's a bit like *The Truman Show*; the world seems to just suddenly end at this wall. Though he is not trying to, I don't imagine, Dylan by just being Dylan manages to make Mikey look like the most awkward creature to ever stand on two feet.

And what is Mikey doing, standing there? Why, he's using both hands to pull at and loosen the crewneck of his DC shirt! As if suddenly, by proximity to Dylan, Mikey feels the pinch of his NASCARed contracts, the firm limit of his attempts to mimic his way into another way of being. And then it turns out they're on the jumbotron, so that is maybe a little awkward. You cannot look good on the jumbotron if you're watching yourself on the jumbotron, so Mikey puts his hands on his hips, and sneaks a glance up to the jumbotron. Then he turns to Dylan and asks, "Is it me or you right now?" as if turning and asking might shift the camera's focus to its rightful subject.

Dylan, meanwhile, is also looking at the jumbotron, but without any awkwardness. And here is what he does, seeing himself up there: he gives it the finger. Not for the cameraman, this finger, and not for Mikey. Not for us, who are watching it seven years later, five

---

4   And podcaster, in case that's not implied by the rest.

after he died. Mikey's hands are on his hips and his shirt's neckline is sagging weirdly, like wet paper. His grin goes very wide.

Dylan, collarbone exposed, watches and then drops his hand and smirks at what he's done on live television. The announcers pretend it didn't happen. Soon Mikey has left the contest with a groin pull. Dylan meanwhile takes two long pushes and smith grinds up and down the A-frame. He pushes along the top of the quarter-pipe, drops in, and tries to kickflip *up* the giantly long set of four stairs, something of which none of the contest technicians had even conceived. In fact, aside from Luan Oliveira, the rest of the contest seems by comparison to be taking place in the shallow end of the pool. Suddenly what they're doing doesn't look quite like skateboarding, even. It's strategizing, calculating, executing. Dylan is skating the course like he might have discovered it accidentally while out for a drive.

The final section of this event is almost too much to bear. Suddenly everyone onstage is landing their tricks, Dylan included. He gaps to the bottom kink of the long rail, locking in to just beautiful smiths and lipslides. But everyone is elevating, it's bananas and hard not to think that everyone else's success has something to do with him, the threat of Dylan, a sense that Jesus, what is he, coming for this world, now, too? "Anyone's game right now," goes the announcer, and Dylan is there, implausibly, just off the lead.

A brief pause here for the work of Brian Glenney and Steve Mull, whose revelatory article, "Skateboarding and the Ecology of Urban Space," argues for the pluralism of the activity. Skateboarding, they say, "*vacillates between* achievement and disruption of rule-bound competitive success," challenging rules even as it participates in them. To support this claim the authors draw on the transcendental ecology of Thoreau and Emerson, pointing to skateboarding's "wild" qualities, calling it "an activity that rewilds its environment." Thoreau believed that the wild was less about outdoor activity per se as the attitude of one's doing it: "merely walking can be a wild activity if one walks in a way that participates with the ecological order as opposed to, for instance, social or political orders." I find these arguments convincing and recuperative. "Skateboarding," they agree, "remains a mystery."

Unlike with, say, Olympic diving or figure skating, in skateboarding contests, "innovative rule-breaking play is not only encouraged but anticipated." This is true. But what Glenney and Mull don't accommodate for is the activity of watching skateboarding, either as a skater-viewer or, more importantly, as a judge. I may revel at the fractional moment of Dylan's final trick of this 2013 Kansas City Street League, as he comes down from the back smith off of the kinked rail and his wheels skid out and his arms flail and he carries all of style-driven skateboarding upon his nearly exposed shoulders, but my values are not this event's values. No matter how close he came, this was never a format Dylan was ever going to win. Even here, on Dylan's best possible day when all was falling just perfectly into place, he was literally out of his league. Dylan knew as much, of course. "It's kind of the same outcome every time," he said to Chris Nieratko. "All those dudes train for that shit, they take Street League season off from real skating to, like, practice."

Like a camera, the scoring algorithm does not, cannot account for style. Style is analog. Style is a matter of perception. By comparison, Nyjah is too good for perception. Too successful for style or facial expressions. By the time of the postcontest interview with Nyjah, Dylan is already somewhere out back, probably smoking, amused.

The second Street League clip worth watching is much shorter. It was recorded by journalist and current director of marketing for USA Skateboarding, Rob Brink, from the stands before the 2010 Arizona event. It's practice, so nothing counts, nothing matters, and Dylan is rolling around the course with a cigarette in his hand. Eventually he decides to take a break and smoke it. To leave, he sort of casually hefts one of his impossibles over the barrier that separates the stands from the course. He misses it and starts to walk off when the small crowd of industry folks who sometimes hang about during practice urge him to try again. So, he goes back onto the course, cigarette still in hand, and this time he does it. The barrier is waist high, stupid high, and the sparse crowd completely loses their shit as he rolls away, glancing back to smirk just before disappearing.

SIX:

"God," goes the message of Octavia Butler's *Parable of the Sower*, "Is Change." Something improbable has occurred—the most maligned became the most beloved. The more unlikely, the less possible this change, the more godly. That he did not set out to change a community, or that the community is skateboarding, which is meaningless, these details do not matter.

What matters is that the change began with Dylan Rieder himself—the bothnesses, I mean, the contradictions that make a human human. The wild arms and the framed, deliberate landings. The bothness to deride Street League as less real while also participating in it—basking in the jumbotron's glow while giving it the finger. The beautiful man in tailored, nonskate apparel made filthy by impact and abrasions and commitment to the activity he loved.

So from the bothness emerges the love, which cannot but be felt in *Dylan.*, knowing what's required to film a full part in only a year. And the spirit, the gall, the absolute fuck-off pride it takes to commit to that path of ridicule, to cultivate and maintain a personal style so maligned that one *cannot but* see in Dylan the very spirit of the community that maligned him. Skateboarding as style, I mean. And style as spirit. Even as he embodied and performed a selfhood detached from and disinterested in skate's status quo, Dylan affirmed the community of skateboarding and the cultural, physical, and spiritual values that stitch its borders.

Suppose it was not just improbable but impossible. What if, I mean to say, Greg Hunt had succeeded? This is going to sound naive, and I am OK with that. Suppose Hunt managed to make a movie that conveyed Dylan Rieder as he was. Suppose that, by knowing his friend so well, and going out shooting with him and editing that footage and presenting it as he did, Hunt achieved that most impossible thing—gave us a way of knowing another person without ever meeting him. Suppose he successfully captured style, and suppose that style was, as Cocteau had it, his soul.

Style, spirit, soul. Whatever the change he caused, it was not language that did it. Dylan Rieder was no rhetorician, was not inspired to speak a movement into existence. When he spoke on record about skate aesthetics he did so in the blunt terms of cool, looking good, and not caring that "little Billy can fucking big spin heelflip down twenty stairs." His values were those that are familiar to much of skate culture: antiachievement, antiquantity, antirank. No, the revolution of Dylan was not linguistic. It was formal, visual, and spiritual.

Forgive me, but I am inclined to say that a miracle has occurred. The impossible made possible—to know the unknowable, and to do it by way of performance and form, on one side, and perception on the other. To see a self performed and *know* that self, and through it, know your own self more fully. But only among those of us who have been trained by the community to recognize the nuance of that performance. To perceive and give value, for instance, to a proper impossible as opposed to a cheated 360 shove.

Once more, we find ourselves leaning on a phenomenological approach to understand this miracle. The French phenomenologist Jean-Luc Marion speaks of real, lived events that transcend values, resist clear meanings one way or the other, and can only be experienced as "the impossible." He means birth, death, but also love and god. Or, as Richard Kearney puts it, "God becomes the impossible possible, the possible beyond the impossible, the impossibility of impossibility."

One needn't believe in any specific God, or even god at all, in order for this to resonate. Faith can be very simple, says Simon Critchley. "As when I speak of faith in another person, the other person"—the meaning of transcendence can be "found in the human relation." By being himself, and by conveying himself, Dylan Rieder changed skateboarding. By having been trained in the ways of skateboarding, that baffling set of values and contradictions, we were able to perceive Dylan as a self expressed. Between his body and ours something was conveyed. In participating in this conveyance, we became the change that Dylan caused. Skateboarding, then, the community, becomes the medium through which the soul passes: the shared values, the common language, and practices that allow a person's performance to be seen in this strange, miraculous way.

It is all quite impossible. And quite the stretch, I know, to connect the miracles of faith to a beautiful skateboarder by a coincidence of language. I suppose this is my own small act of faith, a sacredness that I have long encircled, poked at, have essayed over these years but never confronted completely. The question has always been: What is it that we are doing when we're skateboarding? The nature of my asking has long since eclipsed the board and wheels where it began and has spread to the activities of watching and communicating. The Bulgarian-French philosopher Julia Kristeva calls her field of study, "post-Christian humanism." To her, a humanist interpretation of god is "a thinking through the body" but without a space between thinking and the body—rather, a "thinking with the body."

I mean to say that much of what we call contemporary theology and phenomenology—the studies of what it means to be human— overlap with the activity, perception, and discussion that we call "skateboarding." We move, we express, we convey, we perceive, we process, we replicate, we tweak. We are and are seen and are known. We contradict, we baffle, we change, and are changed. There is only one true gift, and that is the gift that lays bare the many other gifts already in existence.

SEVEN:

On March 3, 2020, Fucking Awesome released a two-minute clip of previously unseen footage that they called "Time Does Not Heal All Wounds." *Thrasher* called it "a gift from beyond," and that feels accurate. It is no small feat to manage a dead man's memory; FA and HUF have been tasteful in their use of his image and name, donating proceeds of his product—each new pressing of his pro board sells out quickly—to the Dylan Rieder Foundation to benefit City of Hope Cancer Center. Given the towering differential between hours shot to capture the seconds that make it into a video, there are surely troves of Dylan Rieder footage sitting on a few select hard drives. But the people who have this footage are also they who knew him best, who formed that shell to preserve his privacy as he suffered his body's decline. So far, people have kept his legacy sacred.

The video opens in the back seat of a car passing by some kind of police action. Like most of FA's stuff, it has the air of the political without saying anything. The draw, of course, is "previously unseen," and the big glory is Dylan's kickflip from a sidewalk bump over a shopping cart, presumably shot the same day as the 360 flip we see in *Cherry*. It's a reminder of what was lost and what was achieved before that loss. And time, too. It's time all the way down.

But the clip I go back to see is the five-second shot of Dylan walking away from the camera in slow motion. He's in a tank top and passes a family of Orthodox Jews who are moving toward us widely, seven of them, three generations, the men with payots dangling and all of them in formal dress, only their hands and necks and faces exposed. The smallest child, a girl, rides in the carriage of the eldest son's arms, and two more girls walk holding hands that link to their father's. Dylan passes between this family and a Coca-Cola vending machine and then disappears behind them.

Of the seven, it's the two youngest who turn to watch him go.

The child in her brother's arms has the best view. At the far side of their group, the second-youngest daughter cranes her neck, ponytail swinging, to see. He's dressed differently. His body is a visible and striking sight. But it is not a spectacle, not something abject or terrible they cannot help but watch, no carnival of color or light. It is only a human body engaged in the commonest of motions. And theirs is the curiosity that comes prior to meaning or understanding. Who is that? What is he doing? Why? No answers. All they can see is how.

PON, DANIEL NICOLAS

PON, DANIEL NICOLAS

Hold Slip

Kensington Branch Library
08/18/ :36PM

PON, DANIEL NICOLAS

Item: 31383122352183
Call No.: FIC
Dead collections /

Hold for 8 days.

This receipt helps plant a forest...underwater.

(scan to learn more)

BPA/BPS Free   Recyclable   Sustainably Sourced

CHAPTER THIRTY-SIX

Still

Failure, too, can fail. That's a pithy wording for the much messier and cumulative truth of the matter. This morning I am once again up early and on the terrace with another book and another of these pens that I favor above any other. A cup of tea. It has been raining and there's a chill today that's odd after these last weeks and the forecast ahead. Across the street a woman walks what I think is a puppy, but I'm not wearing my glasses. Brindled and small. I see her stop, turn back, and give a jerk to the leash. Bless this dog and every other—I watch it set its legs and dig in with its weight, staring up at the woman, rigid in defiance until she relents and follows it down the block.

Inside, K is sleeping. Sometime in the night I believe I heard Mimsy fall off of the bed, but that is OK. We keep a pile of pillows on that side's floor as protection against just this situation. There was a time, soon after she first moved in, as K and I were preparing to host a Fourth of July barbecue and going about our work in the kitchen, that Mimsy slipped without notice through the back door and down the short flight of steps to the common deck that's on top of our garage. She is silent, Mimsy. A sneak. Soon enough, K's phone rang. The neighbors across the alley had found her and called the number on her collar. She must have walked off the garage and fallen the twelve or so feet to the pavement.

But was fine, mostly. This was the day we learned that she was indeed quite blind, as the emergency room vet snapped fingers in front of Mimsy's face with no response. "A little bit of dementia, too, looks like?" Well, OK, but also get a load of that floppiness, will you? To fall from the roof like that and be fine! An unwritten essay: Who might we call the world's floppiest skater?

I can explain why we are still sleeping together. When the time came, K and I found that we couldn't do it. There is more to say about our decision, of course, but I don't think those are words I want to share with anyone but her. I'll say that, on a practical level, the reality of separating felt to us both just terribly wrong. One way to put this is: the quarantine saved our marriage. And if that is the case? I'm not sure. Perhaps we're doomed. But, well, so we are. I believe that what saved our marriage is the thing that emerged the second—and this is accurate, this is as true as anything I've written—the very moment we decided to separate. I have heard of switches being flipped, of the clouds parting, fog clearing, a complete change of conditions. Suddenly and again K and I were friends.

Suddenly the house was different, open, providing. Suddenly everything was funnier. Suddenly the sex—"Can we have sex?" "We had better, yes."—was fiercer and fuller, the hesitations and caution of…god, *forever* it seems, gone. When exactly had caution so poisoned our world? Now we were friends again, laughing and speaking freely. We were what we were before marriage came around and fucked it all up. All those undue demands and cruel withholdings. I wanted to be adored. She wanted to be known. Both of us, of course, already had what we wanted. We just weren't seeing it. Something was getting lost between performer and audience. But there are different ways of being, different ways to be married. We are that, still. Differently.

I go inside now for a second cup of tea. She makes a noise as

I'm walking past the bedroom, and when I open the door she raises an arm, so I set the mug down and crawl behind her and put my lips to her shoulder, which is covered by a tattoo given to her by an ex-boyfriend. "I hate it when Mimsy falls," she says. There was a period when it felt as if we were only staying together for the sake of our dogs, the two elderly ladies. Well, one of them is gone and this one won't be long, and the devastation is everywhere you look. But the floppiness!

The other night I put on my mask and pushed to the liquor store just before the 9:00 p.m. cap on sales that has been in place for months. I pushed down Milwaukee Avenue holding a six-pack and cut into an open lot where people will come and pose before the big Chicago mural next to the "L" tracks. Just on the other side, in an alley, my friend Jesse sits outside the apartment he's shared with a rotating few skaters for the last X years. I'm here because Jesse has skated the Picasso in more and more interesting ways than anyone else I know. This week has been full with DMed clips, long phone calls, and message threads, all amounting to a deep, thick history of the Picasso statue that won't make it anywhere into my writing about the thing.

Jesse is thirty-three, the age I was when I began writing this accidental book, and in my eyes just a far more talented and interesting skateboarder than I am or was or even might have been. He's got a vision that I do not, a creativity I lack. Right now Jesse is coming off of back-to-back injuries, a broken leg and then a broken hand, and having to find new ways to relate to skating. Earlier this afternoon he went to Clemente and worked on his, as he put it, patience. He understands healing and knows that patience is not one of his strong points. A question: What kind of love is this, what kind has it been? For it is love, that is certain. The cruelty and pain of it, the joys and sheer fortitude and stacked years, the love's endurance or let's put it *survival* as the rest of a life has issued its demands.

Jesse and I speak of caution and he says kind things about my skating at this age, and of course it is not adoration that I want, has never been adoration. I want what K wants, to be known. We speak ourselves into being, which is to say *being seen*. See, learn to see, and one day know. Isn't it funny that healing is like aging? Nonlinear, I mean. Isn't it funny that the only way any relationship survives is by constantly becoming something new? Obvious, obvious, obvious. But the other option is to quit, which of course almost everyone does, because the things that we love cannot keep being what they have always been. The joy to this work is, of course, the discovery of new ways for skateboarding to be. New ways to be a skateboarder. And, presumably, new ways to not.

How to convey a learned truth? Three years ago, I called K during an afternoon walk downtown to tell her what I would like her to give me as a gift. This, I understand now, was not failure. It was only my half of the gift. Maybe this was obvious to you at the book's outset; to me it was not. I spent years trying to write a fictional path into certain hidden truths only to discover, accidentally, that I could write truthfully about these same truths. Both of these discoveries required great and sustained bouts with failure, the sort for which I was profoundly unequipped. Currently that novel is here on my desk and I will tell you: I love its flawed and unbalanced shapes, its difficult and hideous little beauties. So, is this failure, even? How to give any of it a name!

Well, this book could go on forever. Loves, I might have told Jesse that night, between the trains passing overhead, will merge. He and I spoke that night for hours and my memory is shit. Maybe I did try and explain how, over time, the only loves that survive are the loves maintained, and that the recipients or causes of these loves have a way of merging with us, the lovers. The object seeps into the body. And by such seepage, one love will affect that body's others, one way of being will change the being self. Marriage and skateboarding, being and time, space and movement. How terrifically complex and unknowable this all is. How impossible, I suppose. How sacred this obviousness.

Loveletters

How can a man improve? I am asking on behalf of a generation or several. I do not mean redemption—whatever interest I may have once had in redemption is gone. Redemption is narrative's game, a fantasy that conceals its primary tool, which is erasure. Narrative is change, of course, and story's habit of backloading change, saving the great epiphanies for act three, has given form to our popular notions of life's meaning. But the harms a man has caused remain. Joys less so. Redemption, I mean to say, has commercial value but what I am looking for is the less celebrated phenomenon. An opening, I suppose. A crack in a man's protective shell of inertia and habit. Evidence of a seam that can be wedged into and widened.

The first of what would become ten seasons of *Jeff Grosso's Loveletters to Skateboarding* is dated January 24, 2011. It's a teaser episode called "Who is Jeff Grosso." I now believe the best answer to this question is the one I heard during the memorial that Vans footwear aired on April 28, 2020, four weeks after Jeff Grosso's death. He was skateboarding's biggest fan.

Here is some of how Grosso described the situation during an appearance on *The Nine Club* podcast in February 2018:

The only thing that's ever fucking saved me. The only thing that's ever made it okay. The only coping skill I have…and I've tried to talk about it in *Loveletters*. I've tried to be honest about it in things like this, or whatever, it's like, I'm a skateboarder. I can't stop that, and like…I am fucked, I am like truly fucked the day I can't roll anymore. Because I've had to go through periods, you know I went two years I couldn't skate, and I lost my marriage. You know, if I can't roll I am fucked, like that's just how it is, like things just don't work right in my world if I can't go and roll it away…I don't even want to fucking hear it, like "go and get another outlet," fuck you. I don't want one. I have my outlet, I've had it since I was fucking five.

Grosso knew what it felt like to be the hottest up-and-comer at the peak of skateboarding's half-pipe boom. As a teen he went from Variflex to Santa Cruz to a prime slot as Powell's next-in-line for the Bones Brigade, if only he'd had the patience to see it through. Instead he bounced to Schmitt Stix for a time and then back to Santa Cruz for four years of rock star myth-making by way of high monthly pay and steady cocaine use, and then quit just as they were preparing to drop him from the team. He knew indulgence, addiction, and their damages. He knew that Narcan felt like being lit on fire from the inside because he'd been pronounced dead three times during his long battles with heroin. Late in life, he came to know fatherhood. Through it all he knew skateboarding as well as anyone.

I did not expect to be as moved as I was by Jeff Grosso's death. Did not expect to weep upon hearing the news, weep at seeing old cell phone footage of a hefty Grosso joining the fifteen or so to have ever done the full loop in 2008 and dancing in celebration. I might have expected to weep at revisiting the short clip of him dancing with his son, Oliver, posted to his Instagram only hours before he passed of heart failure. But there are many reasons for weeping, and wildly enough, none of them are exclusive to any other.

At noon on April 1, 2020, the day of the news, I sat down with my coffee to start from the beginning and watch all of the *Loveletters*. Barring a sun flare it is certain that the series, which was entirely shot and edited by Buddy Nichols and Rick Charnoski, will endure as one of skateboarding's most important documents. Its value is historical, of course, but it's impossible to imagine it being a success in anyone else's hands. Grosso's love for skateboarding is apparent in every second he is on screen. He's laughing, he's gazing up at the ceiling and remembering. You see lines around his eyes that betray the hard fifty-one years he clocked, especially when he smiles or laughs, which is often. In fact, whatever Grosso's demeanor when he begins one of the monologues that balance fact and shit talk and many other rhetorical modes, he almost always ends up delivering the final words through a smile.

As host, Grosso is as fallible as he is knowledgeable. Take this typical sequence from the finale of season two, "Curbs." We open with Grosso alone on camera explaining why curbs deserve their own love letter. "Give a kid a skateboard, there's the front door of your house, what's right outside the door of your house? Fucking curbs. Curbs and chaos."

Then we hear voices over archival footage of classic curb skating, followed by a cut of Grosso's friends and industry legends discussing what makes curbs special. Here's John Lucero sitting before a wall of storage bins of old, hoarded skateboard product. Then it's Julien Stranger and Eric Dressen and Barker Barrett, one after the next and they're speaking of each other, Brian Lotti describing John Lucero, Lance Mountain walking through a parking lot and telling a Lucero story. And it's all stories, this show. This one is about how they started skating curbs because Lucero got kicked out of the Whittier Skate Park.

The best *Loveletters* include some kind of disagreement. Now Grosso is sitting on what I think is a storage cabinet for a garden hose. Lance is sitting in an inversion chair. Because we're talking curbs, a voice off camera, probably Buddy's, asks who invented the

slappy. Both Lance and Grosso say "Lucero," but only Grosso looks
certain of it. Lance, who has leaned the inversion chair back so his
body is sort of halfway extended, says "Lucero" very quietly and
then casts a super-quick sideways glance to Grosso.

We cut to Grosso sitting with Lucero again, now with an archaic
old board that seems to be made from a two-by-four across his
lap (along with, I think, a taser?). Answering the same question,
Lucero says, "I'm gonna go ahead and say Lance." To which Grosso
starts absolutely cackling.

After a quick clip of Brian Lotti affirming that "supposedly"
Lucero invented slappies, we're back again with Grosso and Lance
looking at each other. It might be only seconds after the cut that
took us away from here and into Lucero's storage garage or wherever. By now the disagreement has registered. Grosso, to a humble
and still quiet Lance, says, "It had to have been [Lucero who
invented the slappy] because I remember you were…not good at
slappies at first."

To which Lance's face contorts, looks into the camera, and
becomes a bewildered rictus of pure shock, his mouth agape and
brows lined by something that is not age (and also age). He points
around the inversion chair at Grosso, like *This motherfucker right
here, can you believe him?* He is smiling and also not. "Oh you got
to be out of his mind—I was good at slappies before you were
even skating Whittier." Note please, *you* out of *his* mind, speaking
both to Grosso and about Grosso, because that's how this works—
Loveletters is a show hosted by Jeff Grosso that is sometimes also
about Jeff Grosso. But mostly it is a show about memory. Which
can be, as Grosso's was here, wrong.

He could also be uncomfortable. In season ten's "China" episode, the locals he meets on location share with him how the 1989
Christian Slater film *Gleaming the Cube* had an unlikely, outsize in-
fluence on nascent Chinese skateboard culture. It was "like a bible"
says Yuan Fei, credentialed on screen as "OG Chinese Skater." It's
classic *Loveletters*: deep research and casual conversation.

Except then, and weirdly, we're watching Grosso settling into what from the outset is an awkward interview with Christian Slater.

Slater sits, looks at Grosso, and says he feels like his chair is lower than his, but whatever. It's like a planned comedic bit minus all the planning and half of the comedy.

"Do you want to switch?" jokes Grosso.

"No, no, no, it's fine," says Slater, lying.

They switch chairs. It goes on like this but not for long. At some point Grosso's jacket comes off, presumably because he's sweating. Slater, meanwhile, has nothing at all to say about *Gleaming the Cube*'s importance to Chinese skateboarding because Slater, it's clear, does not care even remotely about skateboarding. Grosso, who lives and breathes skateboarding, believes in it more than he believes in himself if the two can even be separated, can obviously tell Slater's disinterest, and his face reveals what sure seems to me like a creeping but bashful rage.

"I am certainly thrilled to hear that it is playing a very positive role in other people's lives. That's fantastic."

"Yeah. Sweet," says Grosso. By the end, they're not even looking at each other, triangulating their interview through whoever's standing behind the camera. It's not sweet. Grosso ends up with the last word, and it is perfectly weird. "Art for art's sake," he says, and raises a fist.

The final *Loveletter* goes directly at the question of a man's improvement, and skateboarding's potential role in that process. Recorded in late 2019 and released two months after Grosso's death, the "LGBTQ+" episode is devoted to marginalized people who have discovered or, more significantly, built their own communities in skateboarding. And in finding comfort through skateboarding have found, many of them, new comfort in themselves. It is a beautiful and thorough thirty-five minutes that features a broad swath of queer and nonconforming skaters—Leo Baker, Stephen Ostrowski, Kora Colasuonno, Chandler Burton, Breana Geering,

Victor Valdez, and more. A perfect coda and testament to Grosso's project and the endless behind-the-scenes work of Nichols and Charnoski. Not least of all because the Grosso we see on screen this time is a totally different person than any other episode. Throughout these interviews he is mostly silent, mostly listening, with a body that speaks raw, uncut dis-ease. His hands are between his thighs and his shoulders are hunched, knees touching. His arms are crossed and his eyebrows raised.

Clear immediately is that Grosso is out of his depth—this, in a way, is the point. As Cher Strauberry speaks while setting up a new board, he reaches to take it from her hands: "Gimme that, and you can talk, because *this* I can do."

As the stories mount they grow more and more moving. Skylar Jones says, "When I started to figure out gender and stuff, it just really opened up a whole new world and possibilities and freedom, I guess?" We are all skaters, after all, and Grosso's red, withdrawn eyes see what they have in common: "Fuck man, like, we were all fucking freaks." Here, Buddy cuts to a clip from season six's "Freaks" episode, when a natural and easy Grosso recalls the 1980s and what drew him to skateboarding. "We were the fucking people that nobody wanted to be, doing things that nobody wanted to do and that nobody understood—listening to music, dressing, hairstyles, eventing, nobody got it. We were fucking weirdos, we were the freaks."

Grosso pushes up his sleeves, fidgets as he sits there. And now the more serious distress starts to emerge. Grosso understands. He knows he's on the hook for much of what he's hearing. He stutters and pauses, and it all feels palpable. Chandler Burton tells his story of coming out, and Grosso's hands are visible inside his hoodie's pocket, fingers clutched tightly around themselves. There's an intensity to his eyes and mouth; he's looking hard, listening hard. His eyes shift groundward and it's as if he departs for a moment, then he comes back and nods hard.

His brow is folded as he listens to his friend Elissa Steamer speak of being out, being who you are, freedom. "To not have to live in secrecy." There is no laughing, no tacking his own opinion onto the stories, no rocking back and forth with excitement. Just nodding, quiet listening, because Grosso is implicated in this.

"I've been guilty of it," he says, eyes very red. "I grew up in a time, I don't know how many times, you know, 'Don't be a pussy,' or 'You're just being a fag. You're just being a fag because you didn't make it, you bailed that lien air again.'"

They are not easy on him, his guests. When he says he can't even imagine what it must feel like to someone overhearing the way he used to talk, Steamer says, "No, you can imagine it," in fact he has to. And you can see in Grosso's face, in his hands, in the way that his body pulls toward the water behind them—he is trying to imagine it. And yes, he can imagine, and it feels fucking awful.

When I reach out to Buddy Nichols, the first thing he says is that he doesn't like my writing. I pass more judgment than I offer insight, and he finds it pedantic and sanctimonious. My treatment of Craig Stecyk is completely misinformed and wrong—without those foundational myths, what would skating have become? Buddy is a pool skater. Having over the years known some pool skaters, having moved among their spiritual descendants, I understand. So, I say all right, you are not the first to find my work pedantic, but also you are wrong about knowing; I do not know shit, I tell him, and that is why I've been doing all this. Then we have ourselves a real solid phone call loaded with stories and arguments. Buddy knows a lot and believes even more. We argue a bit, agree a bit, then talk about what's happening to Jeff Grosso in this last love letter.

"What you see in that episode is Jeff's brain crack in half," Buddy said. "He cried in all three of those interviews."

Do you know how, when a tree falls or a large branch breaks off in a storm, or from rotting, the sound of the crack lasts longer than you expect? It is not a single crack but a process. Long enough to be happening.

"I been beat up on and stuff for who I am," says Grosso. He didn't like it. And the last thing he wants to do is beat up on somebody else and make them feel not safe. Especially inside the world of skateboarding. "You know, and it sucks, it sucks to admit that I'm part of the fucking problem. But..." and now his back straightens and he looks directly into the camera, and you can see it, you can see him looking into his past. He's looking into his memories of addiction. Into his memory of giving himself away to a Narcotics Anonymous plan that insists only that each day he wakes up and tries. "But I'm trying." He nods once.

I am tempted to draw a connection. If Dylan Rieder, embodying the spirit of skateboarding, successfully leveraged style against skateboarding's prevailing norms and in so doing changed those norms, shaped a decade of skateboarding to come, then mightn't one say that the case of Jeff Grosso represents the opposite of this process? Isn't it clear just by watching that Grosso—addict, one-time freak, speaker and thinker of "pussy" and "fag" and whatever else—was changed by skateboarding's spirt? Not saved, by the end. I do not mean redeemed. But improved.

"I think that's a bit of a stretch," said Chris Nieratko, who would know. Chris, like Buddy, spent a great deal of time around Grosso toward the end. He hosted the Vans memorial. The improvement, he agreed, was real. But the cause for this improvement was even simpler—fatherhood. And as with Buddy, I have the great, private joy of sitting at home and hearing Chris unspool his thread of Grosso stories. Like Buddy's, they are a wonder to hear, and I am outrageously fortunate to have found myself on the phone with these two people talking in the rhythms and terms of the strange object we all share. And this is it: at a certain point skateboarding becomes a gratitude factory. I'm not sure I've made this clear, yet, the warm and abiding thankfulness I feel for my body's undue labor, for permanent friendships that require zero maintenance, the countless run-ins with strangers and half-known acquaintances, for all the unspeakable rewards—emotional, conceptual, professional—that I never imagined might come of my years with this most fun and useless thing.

Anyway, regarding Grosso's late-life shift toward openness, toward difficult and self-implicating conversations that may just help nudge skateboarding's movement toward its next and better form, Chris is pretty clear: "Skateboarding has Oliver to thank for that. Oliver doesn't have skateboarding to thank for that."

In the end, it is so difficult to avoid stories. It is difficult to avoid story. But we do well to cultivate our resistance to them. Better to turn from story and create our own time. Better to occupy moments and see what they yield. Like a spot, like Daley Plaza. Like Grosso and Cher Straubery sitting against the scuffed and used-up wall of a parking garage, when she's talking about the origin of Unity, which is not a company or a brand but a collective, horizontal and open and inclusive and safe and new to skateboarding, a strange new thing that arose from inside this strange and big and increasingly old thing. And Grosso, not new, no longer strange, is, all things considered, pretty comfortable. It is the easiest we see him in this uneasy episode because here he has devoted himself to screwing her trucks onto the board he'd earlier taken so she could talk. His fingers move naturally, with an expert's grace. It was in this parking garage, says Cher, that Unity really started, she was down here relearning heelflips and kickflips. And Grosso, without looking up from what he's doing, goes, "Oh, that rules."

It does.

ACKNOWLEDGMENTS

Thanks to skateboarders, all of them, and especially the ones in St. Louis and Chicago. To Rob Fulstone, Joe Herbert, Ted Barrow, Kristin Ebeling, Ryan Lay, Ted Schmitz, Alex White, Jim Thiebaud, Chris Nieratko, Rob Brink, Greg Hunt, Randy Ploesser, David Uthus, Michael Worful, Jack Donze, Brian Panebianco, Josh Kalis, Mark Suciu, Sam Maguire, Tim Pigott, Thomas Callan and the Pushing Boarders team, Claire Alleaume, Paul O'Connor, Dani Abulhawa, Noah Shannon, and #skatetwitter. To the Ruta brothers, Andrew Smith, and the whole crew at Uprise. To the editors who gave homes to these chapters, especially Ian Michna, Will Harms, Arthur Derrien, David Roth, and Mike Schuh. To Iain Borden, Ocean Howell, and Becky Beal for taking skateboarding seriously, and to Pilot Light at Boil the Ocean, the MF don of all this.

Thank you to my editor, Wes Miller, who skates, for his vision and trust. To my agent, Emily Forland, who does not skate but has always believed in its promise. For inspiration and support, thanks to Christian TeBordo, Odie Lindsey, Margaret Patton Chapman, Chris Bower, and Serengeti. To Jorah Dannenberg, John Matson, Dylan Nachand, Jake Cosden, and Tom DuHamel. To my colleagues and students at Roosevelt University. Might I thank poets? Thank you, poets, and all the writers I've quoted herein, especially Matthew Goulish and Dan Beachy-Quick.

Finally, thank you to my family, Roger and Terry and KC, and above all, beneath all, to Kristin Lueke.

ABOUT THE AUTHOR

Photo credit: Michael Worful

Kyle Beachy's first novel, *The Slide* (Dial Press, 2009), won The *Chicago Reader*'s Best Book by a Chicago Author reader's choice award for the year. His short fiction has appeared in journals including *Fanzine, Pank, Hobart, Juked, The Collagist, 5 Chapters*, and others. His writing on skateboarding has appeared in *The Point, The American Reader, The Chicagoan, Free Skateboard Magazine* (UK and Europe), *The Skateboard Mag* (US), *Jenkem, Deadspin*, and *The Classical*. He teaches at Roosevelt University in Chicago and is a cohost on the skateboarding podcast *Vent City* with pro skater Ryan Lay and others.